# CIVILISATION

### WINNER, 2013 NEW ZEALAND POST BOOK AWARD FOR NON-FICTION

'An exceptional New Zealand book, beloved by us all … In print,
as in person, Braunias gives the impression of casual ease, but there
is nothing casual or easy about writing this good'
*Judges' Report, 2013 New Zealand Post Book Awards*

'The secret to the success of *Civilisation* is that the author didn't
set out to celebrate anything. He chose simply to listen and to observe. …
It's a kind of rough music and he plays it by ear, note-perfect'
John McCrystal, *Canvas: The New Zealand Herald*

'Like a superior form of travel writing, Braunias's 20 essays
take us to mostly overlooked New Zealand places … Grim
comedy mixes with genuine human warmth'
Philip Matthews, *Your Weekend: The Dominion Post* & *The Press*

'Sharp, brimming with wit, and thoroughly entertaining'
Ben Sanders, author of *Only the Dead,* in *Herald On Sunday*

'This is one of those books that, as you read it, you keep thinking
how much you love it. … Buy it for (almost) everyone you know'
Linda Burgess, *New Zealand Books*

'A keenly attuned sense of self-awareness and acerbic wit
underlie the gravity of Braunias's largely empathetic
(and brutally honest) reflections on New Zealand'
Gillian Terzis, *The A*

'Steve Braunias is back with his inimital
unexpected, funny and warm, this deli
Braunias's particular eye for
*Time Out Books*

'Steve Braunias is an entertaining
offers plenty of insight and …
Caroline Harker, *Wanaka Sun*

'A read that is in equal parts challenging, funny and provocative. …
Along with the laughs there is a good dose of social commentary
that is at times uncomfortable but always entertaining'
Jillian Allison-Aitken, *The Southland Times*

'Once I started reading this extraordinary book,
I found it hard to put it down'
Christine Frayling, *We Love Books,* Booksellers New Zealand Blog

## ALSO BY STEVE BRAUNIAS

*Fool's Paradise*
*How to Watch a Bird*
*Roosters I Have Known*
*Fish of the Week*
*Smoking in Antarctica*

# CIVILISATION

## TWENTY PLACES ON THE EDGE OF THE WORLD

## STEVE BRAUNIAS

AWA PRESS

First edition published in 2012 by Awa Press, Level Three,
11 Vivian Street, Wellington 6011, New Zealand.
Reprinted 2013 (twice).

ISBN: 978-1-877551-35-2

ebook formats
epub 978-1-877551-78-9
mobi 978-1-877551-79-6

National Library of New Zealand Cataloguing-in-Publication Data
Braunias, Steve.
Civilisation : twenty places on the edge of the world / Steve Braunias.
1. Braunias, Steve—Travel—New Zealand. 2. Small cities—New Zealand.
3. New Zealand—Description and travel. 4. New Zealand—Social life and
customs. I. Title.
919.304—dc 23

Cover photograph by Sandii McDonald, Photonewzealand
Cover design by Keely O'Shannessy
Author photograph by Jane Ussher
Typesetting by Tina Delceg
This book is typeset in Veneer and Minion Pro.
Printed by Midas Printing International Ltd, China.

Written with the assistance of a
Copyright Licensing New Zealand Writers' Award.

STEVE BRAUNIAS has won nearly 30 journalism awards, the New Zealand Post Book Award for Non-fiction, the New Zealand Society of Authors' E. H. McCormick Best First Book Award, the Buddle Findlay Sargeson Fellowship, the Copyright Licensing Limited New Zealand Writers' Award, and fellowships to Oxford and Cambridge Universities. A senior journalist at *Metro* and columnist for *The Sunday Star-Times*, he is also editor-in-residence at Wintec School of Media Arts, Hamilton, and a writer for primetime television series.

*To Emily and Minka*

# CONTENTS

# 01 HICKS BAY
## A BRIEF HISTORY OF MEAT

There was an old man who lived at the edge of the world. 'When I look back on my life,' Lance Roberts said, 'I've done a lot of killing.' I met him at his monstrous house. Someone had once written that they heard screams and bleats there on still nights. Outside, the long horizontal line of the blue Pacific looked sharp as a knife. The blade flashed in the bright sun. It cut the sky in half.

'Good on you, boy,' Lance said with real enthusiasm whenever I did something as incredible as pass the sugar. There were bones in the ashes of his woodstove. He lit the stove with chainsaw shavings and put on the kettle. It was late summer.

Small, nimble, in gumboots and an oily jersey, he had approximately one yellow tooth left in his old bristled head, and his voice croaked from a swamp inside his throat. He was about to turn 85. When I first saw him he was sitting outside at the top of his wooden staircase and something like ten or eleven cats had formed an orderly queue to take food from his mouth. His hands were black. So was his neck. It was moot when he had last changed his clothes or showered, but Lance didn't live in civilisation. The deserted shoreline, driftwood tipping out of the surf – you could buy a car for an ounce of dope in the East Coast village of Hicks Bay, where Lance lived in a kind of converted loft.

Hicks Bay was a long line of sand beneath high green hills. It had a shop. Across the road there was a bus shelter and a stack of firewood. It had a road. There was a sign in front of a house that read NO TURNING ON THE FUCKING LAWN. Two other words had been painted over. 'They were a lot worse,' said the woman who lived next door. There was a two-litre plastic bottle filled with water on top of a fence post at the cemetery for visitors to wash their hands.

A river beat a path through gorse and shingle; Lance's peculiar home was on the other side of the riverbank. He boiled the kettle and recited terrible verse. 'The clock of life is wound but once,' he said. He'd committed the poem to memory. 'And no man has the power to say just when the hands will stop.'

The old and almost toothless head, the cup of tea and plate of Cameo Cremes – he wept when he talked about how his father had found relief work building a railroad in the Great Depression and secretly opened up a Post Office savings bank account in Lance's name. 'I always think of the past,' he said. 'As far back as I can remember my mother used to carry me on her back in her shawl. She'd go out looking for pūhā and watercress, and when she'd bend over to pick up this stuff I was that fearful of falling out of the shawl I used to cry me bloody head off.'

And then he said, 'I was about six when she died. I'm not too sure what happened. I think she ended up with pleurisy or something. She was always looking for mussels in cold bloody weather: that's probably what done for her. Yeah.'

The warmth of the fire, the gummy voice – he had a high yapping laugh and a big cut on the back of his head. He didn't know how it'd got there. He searched a drawer for one of his most prized possessions, his knife. It had a wooden handle. The blade was sharp and clean. It looked good in his grip, the way it rested in his palm. I tried to imagine him using it. Later that afternoon, a man in a caravan would give him the opportunity.

I went to Hicks Bay because no one went there. For three years, whenever I could, I went to places no one went to, drawn to their averageness, their nothingness, their banal and exhilarating New Zealandness. I went to the damp Wellington town of Wainuiomata, to the vigilant Otago town of Mosgiel, to Mercer, Greymouth, Collingwood and Tangimoana, to 20 places: small towns, unremarkable suburbs, frozen bases and equatorial outposts, in the country, in the cities, out of the country altogether, wherever there was any sign of New Zealand civilisation.

I chose them at random. I'd look at a map and say out loud, 'There.' People said, 'Where?' The next question they asked was, 'Why?' They especially asked that in the places themselves. They couldn't believe anyone would find where they lived of any interest.

But I wanted to go and live in just about every one. I adored the qualities of silence, the sunlight on fence posts, the sound of river water on rock. I wanted to belong, to be part of the established order of the town clock and the menswear store, the main street deserted by six p.m., the cat curled up on the windowsill.

I arrived without any exact purpose. I spoke to anyone who had the time. I asked about their everyday life and took note of everyday objects. I craved the normal but I seemed to spend a lot of time visiting people living in abodes as weird as caves. They were sometimes damaged people, often solitary, always resourceful. They hung on in there.

New Zealand did the same. The country was broke. It drank at home and read Dan Brown. Its bum looked big: McDonald's registered record sales. It filled the supermarket trolley with Home Brand and Pam's. It bought Christmas presents at the $2 Shop, and put up the same signs over and over: SPACE TO LEASE; EVERYTHING MUST GO; WINZ QUOTES. There was a change of government and nothing changed. Ordinary people living in ordinary homes, bringing up the kids and bringing in the washing, getting on with the uncelebrated business of being New Zealanders in an economic slump.

The recession haunted every place I went, even the end of the world – Scott Base, Antarctica. One day I saw a week-old copy of *The Press* lying on a table in the games room. The front-page headline read MORE JOBS TO GO.

More jobs did go. That was very often decided in a head office across the Tasman; it was as though Australia had foreclosed on New Zealand. Australia, always Australia, constant and flush with confidence, wealth, warmer temperatures. New Zealanders left in their droves for an apparently better life – higher wages, less self-loathing. The two most important statistics in New Zealand life became the number of people who left for Australia every month, and the holiday road toll.

For three years New Zealand toughed it out, switching off the lights to save power, waiting for better times. It sometimes felt as though it had gone missing. In limbo, it stuck its head in, passed the Home Brand salt and watched *Fair Go*. It said, 'Whatevs.'

The age of austerity suited the country, with its cherished notions of modesty and endurance. Author Jonathan Raban has written of his homeland: 'Like all small islands, England has got into the singular habit of thinking itself enormous, continental.' Not all small islands: New Zealand thinks itself smaller than it is, a buried treasure, X marks the spot. It constantly talks of being put on the map, as though waiting to be discovered and rediscovered.

It constantly talks about itself. Oliver Duff, in his 1941 book *New Zealand Now*: 'A land lying so far from the controlling centres of the world that no one but its own people take it seriously.' Austin Mitchell, in his 1972 book *The Half-Gallon Quarter-Acre Pavlova Paradise*: 'As a country, New Zealand has one major preoccupation: New Zealand.'

The ancient studies have set the tone, created the foundation myth of New Zealanders as conformist, afraid of something, defensive and belligerent. 'A queer, lost, eccentric people,' John Mulgan wrote in his 1947 essay 'Report on Experience'. Bill Pearson in his 1952 essay 'Fretful Sleepers' wondered 'if it isn't death the New Zealander waits for'. And: 'Who is he trying to fool, to reassure,' American visitor Robin Winks asked in his 1954 book *These New Zealanders*, 'with his band-beating and horn-tooting?'

Civic pride is easily offended. National pride is at stake every minute of the day. Personal reputations can be destroyed in a trice. In 2011 prime minister John Key gave this chilling assessment: 'Everyone is accountable for everything they say.' Someone is always listening, waiting for the chance to purse their lips in disapproval.

Anything else? Yes. We drink too much, drive too fast, and let mad dogs off the leash. Our national pastimes are golf, drowning, and child abuse. Also, we moan and bitch and complain about everything. Poor old New Zealand, driven mad by the voices in its head.

I hit the road for those three years to get away from it all. I kept finding deep signs of happiness. Everyday life rose above the recession and the claims made for New Zealand's apparent despair. As I wandered from no place special to no other place special I kept seeing an explicit New Zealand contentment, at lakeside and riverside, in the middle of arid plains, in the middle of polluted suburbs, in an ingeniously converted slaughterhouse loft.

Lance used to work as a slaughterman at the freezing works along the coast at Tokomaru Bay. They issued him with three knives. One he later gave to a mate and never got back. Another he lost in a river. The knife he kept was as valuable as a historical document.

A brief history of meat: One of the most profound dates in New Zealand civilisation is February 15, 1882, when a maiden voyage of frozen meat left Port Chalmers in Dunedin for England. The inventory included 2,226 sheep tongues – if only those tongues could talk. England soon clamoured for the various cuts of chop, brisket, rib and liver, leading to an industrial revolution in the new colony. By the time the freezing works at Hicks Bay opened in 1921, there were already four other massive slaughterhouses operating in Poverty Bay. Meat was red gold, a recipe for success, a major new export commodity in addition to wool and grain.

'The new option radically changed the nature of farming in New Zealand,' wrote historian Michael King. 'Previously sheep farmers had been forced to slaughter animals – sometimes by simply driving them over cliffs. Now they could raise sheep for meat and wool … [It] would deliver to New Zealanders one of the highest living standards in the world.'

Lance Roberts, 85 and fangy, survived as one of the architects of New Zealand. He was fifteen in 1941 when Oliver Duff wrote, 'Have we a New Zealander? Is there one among us so typical of all that New Zealand comes and goes with him?' Lance worked as a cowboy, station hand, fencer, farmer, shearer, killer. 'I enjoyed it all. I was a fit bugger. I used to say to the young guys, "If I put my heart in your frame, it'd rattle it to pieces."' At Tokomaru Bay, slaughtermen had to account for 84 big sheep or 96 lambs in under seven and a half hours. What you needed to do, Lance explained, was kill with both hands.

He looked back with pride on his 85 years. He'd broken the land, married three times, mastered the art of walking upright in New Zealand. He was its two races, its mixed blood. He said, 'I'm not a full Pākehā, not a full Māori either. I'm a bit of each. That's the best way to be.'

His first horse was a chestnut pacer called Socks. He saw the great Australian aviator Charles Kingsford-Smith land his *Southern Cross* on the beach at Gisborne on a summer's day in 1933 – he was across the road in a kind of orphanage, where he'd been placed after his mother died. His family of two sisters and two brothers were split up. His father taught him how to use explosives. Other men taught him plumbing, killing, shearing. 'They were real good men. They looked after me.' He wept at the memory, and said he thought about them in his bed every night.

The past, mobilising in the dark, tapping his shoulder as he lay in bed – what was that about three wives? 'I played up,' he said. 'If I couldn't jump over the fence I'd crawl under it.' There were dusty old black and white photos of him on the walls; he'd been a strapping young guy, with a barrel chest and a wide face. One big paw usually held an axe while the other curled around the shoulders of various lascivious broad-hipped women. I asked how many children he had. 'I haven't chased them through the gate to tally them,' he said. 'Oh hell, let me think. One, two, three ... oooh hell ... eight, nine...' He wasn't sure, but he thought there were fourteen.

Memories of pūhā and watercress, women and children – his life was passing before him. It was a good life. He knew the East Coast like a room, knew its valleys and skies, knew how many miles of fence lines he'd dug with his bulldozer, how many sheep he'd sheared on the board. He knew who he was. He knew his facts. But it was news to him when I told him he occupied a unique place in New Zealand fiction. He lived in the ruins of the Hicks Bay freezing works, the setting of David Ballantyne's 1968 novel *Sydney Bridge Upside Down*, a masterpiece right from its opening sentence: 'There was an old man who lived on the edge of the world...'

Travelling south on State Highway 35 on a Friday in late summer was lovely and empty, full of sea and sun. There was a chestnut mare in the playground of an abandoned school, a black bull in the shade of the only tree for miles, road signs advising WANDERING STOCK PHONE 0800 444449. A tattooed Māori man and his blonde 17-year-old girlfriend, who wore cut-off shorts and red nail polish, prepared to head for the hills, where they cultivated a dope plantation. Yellow cornfields peeled in the heat. Washing hung over fences.

In Hicks Bay no one was around, except for a girl smoking in the doorway of the store. Pears from an overhanging tree lay scattered in long grass and wasps crawled inside the white mushy flesh. 'I haven't been there since 1978, when Dad & Mum & my little son drove down to Wgtn via Dad's landmarks in my car,' Stephen Ballantyne wrote to me. 'Dad showed us the shack where he lived. Looked like a big chicken coop.'

His dad David spent five years of his childhood in Hicks Bay, which he renamed and reimagined in *Sydney Bridge Upside Down* as Calliope Bay. It's the only place name in the book: one of the small, crucial achievements of the novel is that there's absolutely no reference to New Zealand. His book is set free, rids itself of New Zealand, and travels only in the mind of its protagonist, schoolboy Harry Baird, who tells of what happened at Calliope Bay one particular summer.

Another narrative of Hicks Bay is played out in the *Papers Past* archive, which records that the two most important subjects in the town's history are death and meat. Newspaper report, August 12, 1897: 'A Māori woman named Kamiera committed suicide at Hicks Bay by hanging herself to a tree.' July 23, 1921: 'J Lamb, aged 60, whilst working at Hicks Bay, met with a fatal accident, a large boulder rolling on him.' Headline, December 16, 1919: PROPOSED FREEZING WORKS AT HICKS BAY. August 27, 1920: 'Considerable damage was caused to the construction of the Hicks Bay freezing works when a fierce hurricane lasting over an hour was experienced at midnight.' October 14, 1921: 'The first shipment of meat from the new freezing works at Hicks Bay is being made by the steamer *Kumara*.'

All that red gold shining in the refrigerated holds, five slaughterhouses, an industrial revolution on the shores of the Pacific – all that promise and wealth to be delivered by meat. But the golden age was brief. Sheridan Gundry chronicles the rise and fall in *Making a Killing: A history of the Gisborne–East Coast freezing works industry*. She writes of the excitement and optimism as money was raised for the Hicks Bay meatworks; the problems with building a suitable wharf – the first attempt was battered by heavy seas and the pilings collapsed; the great Māori leader Āpirana Ngata naming the new wharf Hinemaurea after a great ancestress. The wharf had tram tracks, a locomotive. In the spirit of the times when New Zealanders gathered to celebrate the opening of an eyelid, it was opened 'amid fanfare' on April 14, 1925.

The meatworks closed down the next year. The business was no longer feasible and perhaps never really had been. Access to Hicks Bay was difficult, and the price for New Zealand meat had begun to plummet in 1921, the year the works opened. As Lance put it, 'The guts fell out of it.'

The building was stripped of machinery, fittings, even the roof. It was already a ruin when David Ballantyne came to live in its shadow. The long summers of childhood, the crash of the ocean, the secret caves, the thrill and menace of the roofless crumbling meatworks – something took hold in his imagination, and was still there when he set to work on *Sydney Bridge Upside Down*, which he began writing in 1966 when he returned to New Zealand after working as a journalist in London.

Ballantyne was a drunk – the first thing he did when he got back to New Zealand was go on the piss – but he was also, for a time, in possession of genius. His friend Bryan Reid writes in his sympathetic biography *After the Fireworks*: 'He was not yet so gripped by alcohol that his talent was impaired. … As he banged away on the typewriter, [his wife] Vivien could actually hear her husband singing at his work. He would have known he was producing something special.'

Singing! Ballantyne himself said of *Sydney Bridge Upside Down*: 'It was meant as a Gothic joke.' Whatever that means. It's a creepy, brooding, harrowing book, full of screams and scones, threat and sex. 'Not a single thing in the novel is original,' Patrick Evans marvels in *The Penguin History of New Zealand Literature*. 'Least original of all is the novel's sad, last-childhood-of-summer feeling, whose lamenting note sounds through so much New Zealand writing – but in Ballantyne's hands everything is new and intense, made over as if being explored for the very first time.'

It's a summer of sensual childish delight – the passionfruit vines choking everything in their path, the pots of rich sticky plum jam, the precious bottles of home-made ginger beer. Harry and his friends play in caves and on the wharf. Things only appear innocent. Things are not right. Harry's neighbour makes one of the most dazzling speeches in New Zealand literature:

> When people first came to Calliope Bay, what troubled them most was loneliness. I don't mean the people in the very old days, the first one or two who farmed in the district before there was any sort of settlement. I mean those who came to build the works, then those who came because there were jobs for them at the works, then those … who came to help pull down the works. All these people were very lonely for a time. They seemed so far, far away from everything. No part of the country, of the world even, seems so far away as this. And when people are faraway and lonely they often behave curiously, this is well-known.

The speech is a warning. Calliope Bay is falling apart. There is a mysterious house without windows, also a broken-down windmill. Most potently and savagely, there are the ruins of the meatworks. Ballantyne sent the book in drafts to Frank Sargeson, who loved it, noting, 'It's a very brilliant idea using the meatworks ruin as a kind of Mrs Radcliffe's castle.'

The meatworks is the star of the book, its metaphor of death. Harry plays in it and says, 'You can imagine all the big killers busy with their knives. … Even now, when you walk across those concrete floors, you can imagine stains, and some days I've heard squeals and groans below me and I've thought this is not the wind I can hear.'

Death and sex and loneliness, distance, madness, cruelty, the slowly drained cargo of ginger beer – the whole book is an electrifying New Zealand classic, timeless. It doesn't matter when it was written. When it was published in 1968, it sank like a rock. It was reissued in 2010 and sank like a rock all over again.

'First I've heard of it,' said Lance, the tenant of a metaphor. I wandered inside the ruins for those three days, happy and delighted to be there, a pilgrim on a literary pilgrimage. I wasn't the first. Stephen Ballantyne told me, 'James Ashcroft, artistic director of Taki Rua, went to Hicks Bay for his honeymoon last year for the same reason.'

Calliope Bay, Hicks Bay – it was all the same. There was the wharf, which appeared to have bullet holes in a sign reading HAZARDOUS AREA. WHARF COLLAPSE COULD ENDANGER USERS. VISITORS USE AT THEIR OWN RISK. The pilings looked as weak as twigs. I walked out to the edge, over the deep water where boats had once been filled with meat bound for England. Shags roosted in a tree hanging on to a cliff, and dived in the sea. A thunderstorm was approaching; violent waves pushed and jostled each other as they attacked the shore.

There were the remains of the tram tracks, and a long dark cave, possibly the one Ballantyne had Harry Baird play in. I crawled inside the dank cobwebby hole, touched the ferns that grew on the floor, and listened to the sea boom low and deep.

There was the bridge stained with blackberries, and the Wharekāhika River, which ran past the meatworks, took its blood out to sea.

And there, more than anything, looming over everything, were the ruins of the meatworks. They were immense. It was impossible to know what you were even looking at because there was so much going on – big fat black pigs snorting at your feet, chickens and roosters scratching in the dirt, a trailer full of pumpkins, and the sheer size of the ruins. Timber and machinery took up the ground floor. Lance had fashioned a kind of apartment on the first floor. It used to be the sorting room: he slept where the offal was stacked, bathed where the livers were separated, cooked where the lungs had stopped breathing.

There were rough strips of carpet on the concrete floor in the kitchen. The rooms went on and on – there were a couple of empty fridges and one with a flounder in it. Everywhere there were thick columns of reinforced concrete. The pillars and arches and high roof made the place feel like a castle, or some kind of demonic cathedral. But it was just Lance's home.

He bought it in 1984 for $25,000. He'd been farming nearby on a 21-year lease from Māori Affairs. 'I had to go somewhere when the lease ran out. I certainly wasn't going into town. Luckily I heard about this place. I had a mate tell me about it. I thought, this'll do me.

'There's 69 acres. I own the lot, right down to the beach. I cut it all up into seven paddocks, planted all the trees you can see. It was a total bloody shambles when I come here, but it didn't worry me. I had all the know-how and gear to bloody knock it into shape. The other buggers that had it before me, they never done a thing to it. Hopeless bloody cases. Lawyers. There was blackberry and woolly nightshade and every bloody thing you can put a name to.'

We were drinking tea in the kitchen. Lance said, 'I bet you'd like to go up on the roof, wouldn't you, boy.' Boy, 51, followed him to a wall where he'd stacked chairs, cupboards and various other pieces of furniture to form a ladder. At the top a manhole led to the top floor of the meatworks; just the walls were left, and gaping holes where the windows had been.

'There was so much bloody rubbish growing up here,' he said. 'Trees growing out of the bloody roof! And bloody cannabis. It took me a bloody week to clear all this bloody stuff off. I brought a wheelbarrow and a shovel up here, filled it with load after load, and then I dug a big hole with the excavator and buried the lot.'

There were lids on the chutes where the big killers with knives used to dispose of offal. There were runnels for blood. Lance had put in a chimney, and a tank for his spring water. 'Here,' he said, and passed the hose over. It was possibly the best water in New Zealand. 'You might be right about that, boy,' he said, 'and it's been flowing like that since the day I put it in. Seven hundred and fifty bloody gallons in 24 hours, just from that constant trickle.' He pointed to the spur of rock across the road. 'That's where the spring is. I dug the pipe two feet deep. Did it all with a bloody pick and spade.'

There was the river, the beach, the wharf. We looked out over the paddocks. 'All that was bloody swamp and bog. The bloody mosquitoes would carry you out of bed, that's how bad it was. But I'll tell you something, boy. I'm not frightened of work. I worked like a dog on every place. I worked like a dog on the shearing boards. I worked like a dog in the freezing works.'

The sun was high and warm as we stood together in the open air. Lance pointed to the ground we were standing on and said, 'Here's where the killing was done.'

Lance asked if I'd ever gone inside a meatworks. I told him about the time I went to the grassy Taranaki town of Eltham. The great warrior Tītokowaru passed through Eltham in 1869 and boasted, 'I have begun to eat the flesh of the white man. I have eaten him like the flesh of the cow.' It wouldn't have tasted half as good as the flesh of the cattle slaughtered at the Riverlands freezing works, which produces top-quality export beef.

I arrived on a morning in autumn. There were stretched cowhides on the walls in reception. Trucks and trailers pulled up in the yard; cattle were led out and hosed down. Inside the works, among the staff of 540 in white overalls and gumboots that had begun the day spotless but were now more red than white, I watched a cattle beast released into a narrow pen. A metal clamp seized its head. An electric plate rose up and delivered a short sharp volt. The beast collapsed; a door opened; the beast rolled through on its side and a halal slaughterman from Morocco slit its throat.

First to go were its front hooves. A giant pair of scissors broke through the bone. A hook then hoisted the two-footed corpse in the air from its hind hoof. The skin was pulled off its face and the entire hide stripped – Riverlands has a contract to supply Air New Zealand with leather for seats in business class. The head was cut off.

The foreman charged on with his tour. He'd seen it a thousand times before, and that was only yesterday: Riverlands had the capacity to butcher 1,250 cattle per day. 'There's our lung room,' the foreman said. And: 'This is the large intestine turned inside out. It goes to Korea.' Also: 'This is what we call the jawbreaker. He takes the jaw out, and makes it easier to get meat out of the head.'

There were tables piled high with tongues, kidneys and hearts. There were red offal and green offal. There were the cattle beast's four stomachs – the third is called the bible, because its flesh ripples like the pages of a book. And there, too, were first-class and delicious steaks, which I ate for lunch in the Riverlands' boardroom.

It was a memorable day. But it was even more vivid standing on top of the ruins at Hicks Bay and watching Lance re-enact where the killing was done. 'There was a ramp just there,' he said, pointing to the edge of the killing floor. 'They'd bring the sheep up it. So what happens is, when you catch your sheep you dump it down against the pole there, and you grab its bloody head and pull it back and cut his throat with your bloody knee down on his head.

'As soon as you've done that one, you get the next one, and put it up hard against the first sheep you've killed. But you can cut the head clean off if you pull the knife too hard. That's a bugger. You want the head on so you can put the boot down on it and pull out the brisket. That's one of the tricks of the trade, you see.

'So after you've cut its throat you leg it up. You take the trotters off and hang it up on the hook and you pelt it off, and after you pelt if off you gut it out, and there's the finished product…'

All the while he was moving along the rooftop, a small and nimble old buzzard in his gumboots and ripped jersey and black neck, miming the slit of a throat and the pulling out of a brisket – he was bringing the dead back to life and killing them all over again. He was dragging New Zealand history out into the open.

And then he snapped back to the present. A man called in on him on Saturday afternoon. 'Got a goat for you, Lance,' he said. His name was Rick and he'd parked up by the beach in his caravan. He said he'd been watching a fishing show on TV when he saw a flash of white in the bush. He grabbed his gun, rushed outside and shot the goat in the head. He hoped Lance could butcher it.

We went out to the yard. There was the dead goat. Big flies had settled on its bloodied head. Lance got to work with his knife.

'You shot him in the right place, Rick. Good stuff, boy.'

He took off the pelt.

'He'll cook up well, that bloody goat.'

He tied the goat's insides into a knot.

'That's so when you take the guts out, the liquid won't run into the rib cage.'

He cut the head off.

'Now I'll do the bloody brisket.'

He cut its legs off at the knee.

'It's a bugger of a joint to find.'

He hung it up on a hook, and got to work on the guts.

'Look at the bloody stomach bloat.'

Rick said, 'Sorry. Couldn't get it to you any sooner, mate.'

Lance said, 'No, she's right, Rick, she's bang on. Just what the doctor ordered.'

He took out three grey stomachs, and inspected his handiwork.

'Oh, that's as rough as guts, Lance,' he said to himself. 'You'll get the boot, boy. You'll get the bloody boot.'

Rick crouched at Lance's feet, inspecting and admiring the work of the master. The pigs and cats snuffled closer as blood and bits of goat flesh fell from the hook into the grass; the butchery had taken place by the wing of the meatworks where Lance had been working on the engine of his beloved Komatsu bulldozer, which he'd bought in 1967 and still took out now and then to cut tracks for neighbours in return for firewood.

The sun was sinking; there were long shadows, and the light in the sky was golden. It buttered the ruins, crept into Lance's bedroom. He slept on a single mattress. The blankets were old and rough. He'd pinned photos of his past beside the bed. When night fell, he'd think about the men who looked after him when he left school at fourteen and went out into the world. He had been motherless almost his entire life.

The shadows lengthened. The castle of the meatworks looked as dark as a tomb. Hicks Bay, Calliope Bay: like young Harry Baird, Lance hoarded a cargo of home-made ginger beer. He'd poured the precious fizz into about a dozen empty Sprite lemonade bottles and written the bottling date on each. They were on the floor of his bedroom. Outside, he completed his dismembering of the goat. The sharp knife doing its work, the goat in pieces on the grass, dinner ready to store in the fridge and freezer – I could have watched him all day.

# 02 PEGASUS
## NEWEST ZEALAND

They damned it at the Saturday morning flea market in horsey Rangiora, where the stink of horsehair clung to jigsaw puzzles and alarm clocks and books about horses. They mocked it, insulted it, wished a pox on it. Most damagingly of all, they pitied it. They said: Poor bastards. They got specific. They said: It's too windy, the summer easterly'll dry up the grass, and the whole place'll look like a desert. They said: It's too damp, the mould'll be halfway up the ceiling before you know it. They said: It's too cold, the winter westerly'll blow off the beach and make life miserable.

Such scorn, so many heads shaking from side to side, during a weekend in spring when I visited the Canterbury Plains and asked about Pegasus, New Zealand's newest town, out in the open in the middle of flat featureless nowhere on 400 hectares of virgin swamp, 25 kilometres north of Christchurch.

They damned it on Sunday afternoon at Kairaki Beach, where black dogs sniffed the driftwood, a little boy played with a black toy gorilla in the sand, and whitebaiters sifted for creatures in the black lagoon. 'Caught half a dozen,' said one baiter. He scowled. He had been at his spot since six in the morning. The subject of Pegasus appealed to his sour mood. He rubbished it, predicted nothing but woe, and concluded, 'I wouldn't give you two bob for it.'

The town, dreamed up by property developers Infinity Group, was yet to be built but a lot of it had already sold: it had set a New Zealand record when $122 million worth of sections sold at auction in one day. It was strange walking around. The whole place felt odd, obnoxious, soulless. It didn't feel like New Zealand.

The population of Pegasus was sometimes projected as 5,000, other times as 7,000. When I visited, the population was precisely two. I walked around the empty streets and stared at the empty sections. Pegasus was under construction, a work in progress. The signs read PEGASUS SCHOOL COMING SOON and PEGASUS TOWN CENTRE COMING SOON.

On the corner of Tutaipatu and Waireka Streets there were four park benches on which no bum had yet to rest. The only restaurant was the Grub Hub takeaway van for onsite workers. With its new streets driven on only by vehicles marked NORTH CANTERBURY CONCRETE CUTTING and PETROTEC 24-HOUR EMERGENCY RESPONSE UNIT, its rubbish bins as clean as whistles, its rows of bare spindly scarlet oaks and American sweet gums, its weeds of red, white and blue electrical cables sprouting out of the ground, Pegasus was perfectly lifeless.

What to make of this town of the future, this barely formed blot on the landscape? I should have damned it, too. I wanted to. I tried my best. I scoffed at the homeowners' covenants: clotheslines and letterboxes had to be of good quality, garden statues and fountains had to be approved, no caravans or tents were allowed, and no more than two cats or two dogs per household.

I attended a sales meeting in Auckland. The reps said, 'It'll be like Noosa.' Their fantasies grew more intense: 'Some people say it's the perfect town.' And even more intense: 'It'll get kids away from their PlayStations.'

I interviewed Bob Robertson, CEO of Infinity and, I suppose, the town father of Pegasus. He wore black from head to toe, set his watch fifteen minutes ahead, and tried to interview himself.

'Is it about money? No,' he said.

I hadn't asked, but seeing as he brought it up I interrupted him and said, 'It is so.'

He said, 'Sorry?'

I said, 'It is so about money.'

'Yes, it is so,' he said. 'It is so, to a level. But sometimes you pass that level.'

He got back to interviewing himself. 'What am I going to do with the money? What am I going to do with it? Okay, there's inheritance for the kids and money for my staff. But if it was about money I wouldn't be doing it. For Pegasus, I'm acutely keen to create what I would like to consider would be as close as possible to an ideal town.

'My vision of Pegasus is based on the perception of what I would want – and I treat myself as a guinea pig – if I was going to live there.'

But Robertson lived on the shores of picturesque Lake Wānaka.

Sometime later I saw Pegasus on TV. Current affairs show *Campbell Live* lingered on images of red, white and blue electrical cables sprouting out of the ground. The signs read PEGASUS SCHOOL COMING SOON and PEGASUS TOWN CENTRE COMING SOON.

Reporter Natasha Utting trudged back and forth across the footbridge over the artificial lake. The bridge and lake were new but I recognised the special ambience of Pegasus in an instant – an ambience of dreariness, of purgatory. It looked miserable and hopeless. No one was around. It looked as though no one would ever be around.

In fact the population had reached about three hundred. A café had opened, and a general store. But where was the school and where was the town shopping centre? Infinity put it this way: 'The effects of the global financial crisis have necessitated a carefully managed approach to the staging of the town's development.' Resident Steve Fleet told *The New Zealand Herald*, 'We moved here thinking there was going to be a whole new town and we wouldn't have to keep going into Rangiora or Christchurch.' He didn't sound too fussed. 'The kids love it. They just wander around and do their own thing. … It is quite nice with it being quiet.'

Silence in New Zealand has regional qualities. I thought back to the kind of silence that spring weekend when I mooched around north

Canterbury, with the wind in the willows and the shadows of poplars falling in long thin stripes across country lanes. It was silent as a grave in Tuahiwi, where the clumps of wild daffodils were beginning to fade and fray in the graveyard. There was only the shushing of the surf at Leithfield Beach, where the burger van was open from five to seven, Thursday through Sunday. There was not much more than the snip of scissors at Woodend, where the scrapbooking club met every Thursday over chocolate muffins.

I lingered on the footpath outside the Woodend bakery and waited for Karl Mason to emerge. I had seen him pull up in a fabulous 1974 Camaro painted canary yellow. A builder from Christchurch, he belonged to the Garden City Rodders Club and was taking the Camaro up to Kaikōura 'for a hot-rod run'. That, and 'to perve at the waves'.

He said, 'Pegasus? You couldn't pay me to live there.' The town was the least of his worries and he didn't appear to have a worry in the world. He was in great spirits, a lean lithe surfer whose haircut was narrowly avoiding the onset of a mullet. He was travelling with Karen Lewis. She said, 'Show them your baby.' Karl took out his mobile phone and proudly brought up a photo of a black 1952 Ford F1 pickup truck.

Graham Turner at Woodend Motor Camp owned a 1963 Leyland converted into a house-bus. He lived in it with his wife Claire, who was making a vegetable stew with barley on the woodstove while their two young sons Isaak and Leo lay on bunks watching *Toy Story* on DVD and munching on a snack. Isaak said, 'I got nachos!' Graham said, 'Pegasus? I hope it'll be good for the area.'

Graham worked as a carpenter. What was he doing in a motor camp? Before Woodend, he and Claire had run a café in Westport. She said, 'It was great in summer, but come winter – pffft! It just died. We made a huge loss.' They had rented their house and bought the Leyland for $5,000 on TradeMe. Their corner spot in the camp was nearest the beach and a pine forest. They had been adopted by a cat they found under the bus one night and called Smoochie.

Before Westport there was England. Graham's mother had become friends with two New Zealanders who picked potatoes and drove a converted ambulance they called Mabel. Their stories about New Zealand inspired her to emigrate. 'Then she rang me up one night and said, "I'm not very well." I said, "What do you mean?" She said, "I've got cancer." So of course I came. That was twelve years ago. Mum's still alive. She's got great willpower. Amazing woman.'

Then he talked about working on a plastering job at the home of a widow in her seventies. 'Amazing woman. She can hardly walk but she's out there in her garden digging up a patch ten foot long for two weeks with a spade handle she's attached to a trowel. She said it was like doing it with a teaspoon. She planted celery and broccoli but the cows got in and ate it.' He finished his story, and then he and Claire sat down outside the bus at a table and drank wine in water glasses. The good sharp scent of pine needles filled the air.

'Pegasus? I'm not happy about it,' said Annette Finlay. She was riding a bike in a fetching pair of black gumboot slippers – $12 from The Warehouse – while her dog Boss, a blue heeler cross, ran beside her along a country road that bordered Pegasus. She'd planned on a holiday in the Cook Islands but her husband couldn't wangle enough leave from work. It didn't seem too great a hardship. Boss chased a pine cone. All you could hear were sparrows.

'It's lovely here,' she said. 'We moved from Christchurch for the peace and quiet but along comes Pegasus. The people I know – none of us are keen on it. We go past and just cringe.' She rode away, possibly cringing.

There was a red-brick cottage set back on the road. It belonged to Alan Nordmeyer. I said, 'Nordmeyer?' He said, 'Yes. Arnold Nordmeyer was my father.' Sir Arnold Nordmeyer, Labour MP under Savage, later minister of finance, eulogised by left-wing political commentator Chris Trotter in his book *No Left Turn* as 'the political leader the New Zealand working class had been waiting for', and here was the revolutionary's son in Woodend, in a house built from red brick shipped over from Norfolk in 1865.

He was really quite benign about Pegasus. He said, 'I'm neutral now. Originally I was against it. How to put it that seems fair? I always considered it wasn't a good place to build a township. Too prone to flooding. The other thing I was never too sure of was the logic of starting up a new town from scratch instead of expanding an established town like Woodend, but I can see the sense in starting something new and not inheriting roading and sewage.'

On the wall there was a striking black and white photograph of a tussock range. He said it was a 1960 National Publicity Studios' picture, taken in the Mackenzie Country. 'It's the transition where the pale yellow festuca tussock grass meets the brownish chionochloa snowgrass, so it must be at about 3,000 feet.' He talked about his work as an agricultural and forestry scientist in Bhutan, Vietnam, Turkey and Pakistan, and then about his involvement in a gas exchange laboratory that measured $CO_2$ levels in trees. He was warming to a subject: global warming.

He said, 'I don't mean to rave but sea levels will rise and coastal communities are going to be hammered. Woodend has been there for 140 years but will Pegasus still be there in another 140 years?' He had his doubts. His own future? He was going to cultivate his cornfield any day soon and plant potatoes that afternoon.

The planting of spuds, the bright weekend in spring, the fresh air. For sale: alpacas, fennel bulbs, organic eggs, horse manure. Cherry blossom floated on the side of the road. The plains were low and the sky high and wide: north Canterbury was like a ranch with riverbeds and a coast. Idyllic little villages, each with their quality of silence, were tucked behind windbreaks of macrocarpa and pine. There was sand on the pavements. There were cribs called Briar Cottage and Driftwood Cottage. No one was doing anything more stressful than waiting for the burger van to open at Leithfield Beach.

All this now feels quaint and faraway, like something dating back to a long-lost past, an age of innocence. It *was* an age of innocence: it was before the Christchurch earthquakes. Kaiapoi and Kairaki were among the worst hit settlements in north Canterbury. Damage was extensive in the first quake, on September 2010. An aftershock on June 2011 caused further destruction. Only one town was left entirely and absolutely unscathed: Pegasus. Planners had wisely invested an estimated $20 million engineering and compacting the earth. They had brought out specialised equipment from Dubai and employed a method known as vibrocompaction – loose sand densified to create stable foundation soils. There were no instances of liquefaction, no rising sickly gloop.

The town wooed quake refugees wanting a safe harbour. According to *National Business Review*, Infinity had been able to assist buyers with deposits of just one percent.

Vibrocompaction, the end of chaos, deposits of just one percent – but what about the life force of Pegasus, of any town, of any place? I tried to hate Pegasus but failed: people got in the way. When I went there in that innocent spring I paid a visit to the household at 172 Infinity Drive. Retired couple James and Biddy Gardner – the first Pegasus homeowners, the town's early settlers – were wiping builder's marks off the windows and hosing down the outdoor tiles.

What sort of name was Biddy? 'My parents nicknamed me that and it just stuck,' she said. 'My real name? It's heinous! And it doesn't bring out the best in me. Maxine Juanita. Yuk! No, it's Biddy, thank you.'

How did she and James meet? She said, 'I was flatting with nurses, and he took everyone else out and then he got to me.' James said, 'It wasn't like that.' She said, 'Oh yes it was.'

They were full of life, giggly and giddy, brimming with a sense of adventure. James said his builder had got the bit between his teeth in the last few weeks of construction to make sure they would be the first to move into Pegasus.

It was their fourth day in their new home. The night before they'd had family and friends over for a drink. 'Oh, it was ripper,' said Biddy. 'I've felt better,' said James, through a hangover fog. They were a retired farming couple – sheep, beef, barley – from up the line in Waiau. 'We were there 47 years,' said Biddy. 'Seventy-three for me,' said James. 'I was on the same farm all my life. I said I'd retire at 60 if I was ready, but I was still enjoying it. I was still pretty fit at sixty-five. By 70, 71, I had had a gutsful of farming. Been there and done that.'

Biddy said, 'We didn't want to retire into the Waiau village. We knew that. It didn't appeal at all really, did it?' As they were talking, cars drove past their house in a slow procession – the curious and nosy, drawn by the strange spectacle of a nascent town.

Biddy: 'All the time! And they bring buses from the old people's home, and a walking group goes through.'

James: 'Back and forth, back and forth, especially in the weekends. What'd they say – 150 people, I think it was, came through the information centre last weekend.'

Biddy: 'Mind you, we did that too, didn't we? We drove in one day and looked at the model of the town and we just thought, "This feels right." And that was that for us. We'd thought of retiring to Rangiora and we weren't so keen on Kaiapoi and we didn't think we were centre-of-Christchurch kind of people, so…

'People say, "How are you ever going to live with neighbours all around you?" But the beauty of it is it's going to happen gradually. We should be acclimatised by the time Pegasus is chocka, shouldn't we?'

James: 'We've as good a view here as we had at home.' Beyond the neighbouring golf course was the Southern Alps. Inside the house there was a macrocarpa bookcase, a set of plates hand-painted by Biddy's mother in 1929, coasters on the coffee table; the curtains hadn't been put up but 172 Infinity Drive was shaping up as a home. What did they make of the petty covenants placed on each resident – no caravans or tents, all vehicles with commercial signage to be parked inside the garage, no garden statues or fountains without prior approval?

Biddy: 'One Christmas James bought me a lovely concrete gnome doing a brown-eye. Where do I put that?'

James: 'I've actually got permission to put it on the letterbox. I told one or two people about it and they laughed like hell. Mind you, they did say, "I don't think so."'

James remembered the summer holidays they used to take in the Marlborough Sounds. 'The beauty of it was we would sit up on a hill, and there was a wharf down below – we'd sit on the hill at night and have our drinky-poos, us and four other couples. Oh, we had marvellous holidays there for 27 or so years. We'd watch the wharf, and the world go by, and all the people...'

James and Biddy, the early settlers, had brought their history with them to Pegasus, invigorating the empty unloved town with their laughter, their ridiculous gnome, their drinky-poos, their heirlooms, their warm welcome. Effortlessly and triumphantly, they had brought New Zealand to Pegasus.

# 03 WAIŌURU
## OPERATION DESERT ROSE

T he half-moon above Waiōuru on an afternoon in the middle of
winter looked nothing like as remote or unearthly as the town
itself. New Zealand's only army garrison town, Waiōuru operates
as a defence zone. It looks very defensive. It looks low down, crouching.
The temperature had dropped to six below; even the sky looked as though
it were trying to burrow itself under the ground.

The army camp is cordoned off, out of sight, just about out of range.
From a helpful brochure welcoming new residents: 'Broadcasting
Communications Ltd have supplied Waiōuru with a TV translator due
north of the town on Waitangi Hill. This broadcasts TV1 and TV2 only
and if you wish to receive TV3 you will need to have an aerial directed
at Mount Taranaki.'

Waiōuru, pop. 2,000, is more or less in the middle of the North Island,
a kind of dead centre. It doesn't support a lot of life. The surrounding
Rangipō Desert looks raw, mugged. Waiōuru translates as 'The place that
all must pass through'. The passing is more memorable than the stopping.
New Zealand's most intense highway, the Desert Road, twists and rises
through the blonde tussock and red scorched earth on the high volcanic
plateau dominated by Mount Ruapehu. Ice and snow seal it off every
winter. There are two standing headlines in New Zealand journalism:
TRAMPER LOST and DESERT ROAD CLOSED.

It closed, opened, closed and opened again all in the same week in July. The clouds hung thick and low. You couldn't see the mountain, or much above the desert floor of tussock and pumice. Creeks and streams did their best to nudge through – the prize exhibit on the wall of Waiōuru's pub, the Oasis, was a quite obscene length of eel, weighing 32 pounds and going by the name of Hector. Even in death, Hector looked hungry.

Waiōuru is the compulsory training destination for new army recruits. The teenage boys are housed in small bedrooms in small wooden huts with cracked windows and peeling paint. They are sent out into the Rangipō Desert to shoot live ammunition, run when told to run, sleep when told to sleep, and freeze without any instruction.

Major Chas Charlton said, 'Waiōuru is our college and our university.' The army camp's policy is to place ten recruits into each bedroom: was Waiōuru also a boarding school? 'No,' the major said, and returned to the solemn duty of eating his hot lunch in the officers' mess. The plate of chilli con carne was piled so high it might have defeated Hector, but the major, a trim, taut man with a trim, taut haircut that stayed close to his head at all times, spooned down the lot.

He said, 'I'm a patriot.' What did that mean? 'No matter where I am, I feel a swell of pride in my bosom about New Zealand. I will do anything for my country.'

We were being eavesdropped by 1979 portraits of the Queen and Prince Philip on the far wall; they could rest assured their corner of the Commonwealth was in safe hands. Major Charlton spoke of the importance of tradition, loyalty, service. He knew his military history. He was about to go – armed with replicas of two 1861 Colt 44 open-top revolvers, an 1873 lever-action Winchester 44 rifle, and a 1905 side-by-side hammer shotgun – to a pistol contest at the Taupō Gun Club.

He conquered his lunch and marched to the elevator. His departure halved the number of officers in the dining room. With its stiff-backed chairs and its conveyor toaster, its white tablecloths and its royal portraits, it looked like the restaurant of a hotel that might have been considered upmarket in a provincial New Zealand town in 1982. It looked civilian but the armed forces were in the details – purple napkins for ordinary officers, red napkins on one table set aside for top brass.

The officers' tower block was built in 1982. It may well be the weirdest building in all of New Zealand and is probably the masterpiece of an architect whose work I saw throughout my travels. You could never mistake his buildings as the work of anyone else. They were a particular New Zealand aesthetic – grim, deranged, bitter.

His material was concrete, a lot of concrete, great big slabs of it, thick and bare, unpainted and grey and easily stained, sometimes stippled, always insane. The buildings looked like pavements built upright. Two of the best examples were the district council offices in Greymouth and a lookout with stairs and turrets smelling of urine on State Highway Three near Palmerston North. The biggest and most creative structure, his masterpiece, was the tower at Waiōuru. Its seven levels were designed like steps; it looked less as though it were leaning back than staggering backwards.

It also looked haunted. 'Funny you should say that,' said Second Lieutenant Gwyn Macpherson. He was the other 50 percent of the officers at lunch that day. He talked about the ghostliness of the mess, and of the entire camp, especially at night – the silence, the dark, the wind in the gum trees. There was talk, too, at the Oasis of ghosts and spirits who popped in for a visit. A woman who had been killed in a car accident many years ago was sometimes seen driving the Desert Road. Someone said they saw – through fog, near dawn – soldiers dressed in First World War uniforms marching in line towards the army museum. Waiōuru remained afraid at all times: the gates to the army camp advertised that the security alert level was black. It has stayed that colour since 9/11.

It was a town of ghosts, but also of the brilliantly alive. Macpherson, a handsome blue-eyed blonde, 28, described himself thus: 'I'm six foot four and I look like a Viking.' This was only the first part of a sentence. It continued, 'But there's a young recruit here, she's like four foot nothing, and she can do what I can do.' He was proud of the recruits. They probably worshipped him but he was without vanity, and very easy company. He talked about the house he had bought in Hīmatangi. 'It's got a 10 by 12 shed! I couldn't turn it down.' What was the house like? 'Oh, it's all right. But the shed's great.' In his spare time he sews. He bought an industrial sewing machine, set it up in the shed, and runs up camouflage webbing for army packs. 'Something always needs improving,' he said.

He grew up in Kaitāia, skinny and long-haired, 'wayward', a surfer. 'The army lit a flame under me.' He joined at eighteen.

When he was born, his father was sixty-two. He had been a sergeant with the 27th Machine Gun Battalion in Crete when the island fell to the Germans on May 20, 1941. 'He had nightmares to the day he died. He had twin brothers, and they were killed within 24 hours of each other, one in Crete and the other flying in the RAF. His mother blamed him for not bringing his brother back home from Crete.'

The Germans landed by parachute. For a long time they made easy targets, shot as they drifted in the sky. 'A shot paratrooper landed at my father's feet. My father always said he looked exactly like his twin brothers. That might have had something to do with his nightmares.'

Every desert has its rose. Where did it grow in Waiōuru? I went out into the Rangipō Desert with Lieutenant Macpherson in an army jeep that bucked like a ship in a storm. The ground was hard and bumpy; there was a lot of ice and clots of snow, and a lot of bits and pieces of shrapnel. It all looked the same, nameless, but the army had names. Macpherson took out the map he kept in his jacket and said, 'Over there is The Wall. That's the Sea of Boulders. And we call this one Ghost Bush.'

More ghosts; but the desert moved with life, in the shape of recruits in the ninth week of their standard thirteen-week basic training. As their platoon commander, the lieutenant talked about how satisfying it was to see them develop into soldiers. They were out in Zone One, as the army called the desert, wrapped up tight in their uniforms. The day's exercises included target practice with their Steyr rifles. Also, they had dug holes in the tightly packed desert earth. What with? 'An entrenching tool,' said Nick Josephson, eighteen. What? 'A shovel.' Steve Devantier, nineteen, from Te Atatu in Auckland, said they were about to charge over a hill and fill up a hole. Why? He said, 'So it isn't there anymore.'

They were boys with pinched faces and a Waiōuru tan – white as ice. They slept under coarse grey blankets. They mopped floors, cleaned toilets, got haircuts. Reveille was 0545 hours, lights out at 2215. The louvre window in their room was kept open day and night. They could not ever sit down on their bed. 'It encourages idleness,' said Lieutenant Macpherson. A whiteboard in one of the barracks was headlined SAYINGS FOR THE DAY. That day the saying was FIFTY. What did that mean? A staff sergeant said, 'That's how many times they've fucked me off today.' Lieutenant Macpherson talked about punishments. 'Once, I made a soldier carry an iron jack everywhere he went. It weighed 18 pounds. Everyone knew him as Jack. It's a term we use that means he wasn't helping out his mates.' What had he done wrong? 'His bed was in an absolutely shocking state. It's funny, when one person is slack it spreads like a disease.'

The recruits said 'Go hard' and 'Sir'. They had straight backs and were learning about service, tradition, self-respect. Also, they were having the time of their lives. 'Today,' said Steve Devantier, 'I got to go out and throw some grenades.'

Was he encouraged to join by his father? 'I haven't seen him since I was ten or something. Dunno where he is.' Teahu Peters, 18, said, 'I joined up just to change my life and that.' When asked for his name, he gave his full name, complete with three middle names. It was as though he were giving an interview to the police. He said, 'I had a bit of a record.' What offences? It was as though he were reading from a charge sheet: 'Unlawfully taking a motor vehicle.' He was very serious, very alert. Lieutenant Macpherson said, 'He's one of my star pupils.'

Boys from broken homes, boys who had been 'wayward' – were these the typical recruits the army took in and sorted out? Who else in New Zealand would volunteer for army life? 'I was a Honda consultant,' Oosa Tuala said.

Everything about Oosa was surprising. For a start, he was twenty-nine. He said, 'I've always wanted to serve New Zealand.' He had nearly applied to join the army in 2000 but decided against it because he had a young family. He had three children: two daughters, aged five and seven, and a son aged fourteen. 'Yes, fourteen,' he said. 'I was a fourth-form dad.'

He had left school at the end of that year and found work at KFC. 'I worked as many shifts as I could to raise my family.' He got other, better jobs. He was responsible, mature, level-headed, warm; also, he was articulate, spoke intelligently and well. He gave credit to his teachers at St Mary's Catholic Primary School in Papakura. And then he said, 'You can tell where a person is from by their slang. There's North Shore slang, Māngere slang, Ōtara slang. I've never talked in slang. I'm glad I don't.'

It was approaching 1730 hours: time for dinner. The recruits' menu was a choice of sirloin steak or braised sausages with roast potatoes, peas, cauliflower and carrots, and a hot pudding. The tables were set with cartons of Primo. Up on the seventh-floor dining room of the nearly deserted officers' mess, conversation was as stiff and carefully folded as the red napkins. Life, loud and beery, was outside the camp, at the Oasis pub, where there was a fire in the wood burner and country music on the jukebox. As the night wore on and the good times rolled, Hector the eel seemed to smile behind his glass case.

Don McLaren, a small, neatly dressed carpenter, explained how he had fished up in Waiōuru. He was living in Central Otago when he saw an advertisement in *The Dominion* for contract work. He put in a tender and won. He phoned up the employer. 'I said, "Well, whereabouts in Wellington is the job? Is it the Hutt Valley or in town?" Because what was I supposed to think? The advertisement's in a Wellington paper, for Christ's sake. The employer said, "It's in Waiōuru." I got the shock of my life when I ended up here.' And when was that? 'Eleven years ago.'

Friday night in Waiōuru, in the middle of winter, and the wind didn't whistle – it wailed, the loudest ghost you ever heard, haunting the small dark frontier town. I looked at my watch. It was midnight at the Oasis. Seven drinkers were still on their feet. They ordered jugs, smoked on the front step, gossiped and laughed. They talked about snow, how appealing it was for visitors and how unappealing it was to live with it.

They talked about how cold it got. The water mains constantly froze – one time, concrete in the mixer turned black. They talked about firewood and coal and chimney-sweeping. From the brochure for new residents: 'Fire ashes are collected in winter on Tuesday mornings. Ash will only be collected if in a metal container with handles, e.g. an ammunition box.'

They had to drive to Palmerston North or Taupō for groceries. They always missed Waiōuru whenever they left. Always wanted to get back. It had a hold on them. They said, 'The mountain.' What mountain? I took their word for it. Nothing was visible in the dark night or the grey murky day.

The next morning, the sky once again grey and murky, Don made big hot steaming mugs of instant coffee in the house he shared with his mate Bill Cupples, a house-painter from Ireland. The two codgers – Don was 54, Bill 66 – lived on a street of ghosts: 300 houses, considered surplus to army requirements, had been put up for tender and taken away by truck. The driveways had been grassed over. In the 1970s, when it operated at its peak, Waiōuru had a population of 7,000; now it felt as reduced as the restaurant in the officers' mess.

Don and Bill were showing me around their ghost street when the cloud lifted. 'Look,' said Don. 'Aha,' said Bill. There it was, magnificent and brazen, creamy. With its sides of luscious white snow, the mountain looked as if it were glowing. It was like a power source, energising the town, giving some of its power to the army. It burned in the sky and blossomed out of the ground: Mount Ruapehu, the desert rose.

# 04 ST BATHANS
## WIND

**E**verywhere, wind. Not whistling, not howling, no music or drama
to it at all, just something always pushing and shoving, lunging. It
got up early. It stayed up late. It carved trees, it herded clouds, it
did whatever its brute force felt like during an autumn weekend on the
Maniototo Plain.

Highway 85 is one of New Zealand's great drives, nothing to look
at but sky, hawk, rock, creek, tussock, and thistle and wildflower, and
sunlight and shadow running their hands over the beautiful mountain
ranges. It was a Central Otago pastoral, yellowish and empty, smooth
and short-haired, good for sheep and bicycles. Driving was a waste
of gas. All you needed was a sail on the roof. You could have cut the
engine and merely steered off 85 to navigate the side road that leads
to St Bathans.

The permanent residential population of St Bathans is seven. More
than half the town had dinner together on a Saturday night when Grahame
Sydney and his very young wife Heidi acted as hosts to Graye and Wendy
Shattky, who walked from their house armed with a bottle of wine and
a torch.

Jay and Jewell Cassells were also in attendance. They lived in Queenstown. Well, someone had to. Poet and golf caddy Brian Turner completed
the line-up. He had thought he'd be busy caddying for Peter 'Chookie'

Fowler at the New Zealand PGA at Clearwater. He said, 'Chookie failed to make the cut.' He had tucked his shirt into his pants. Jay said, 'It looks as though you ironed that shirt.' Brian said, 'No, I drip-dried it.'

Heidi walked into the kitchen with a basket of vegetables from her garden. Grahame grappled with a champagne cork. There was a card on the bookshelf. It read: 'Bryan Brown and Sam Neill invite you to partake in a beautiful, bewildering and astonishing event.' The art on the walls included two of Grahame's pencil drawings; the closest you could get to his celebrated landscape paintings of Central Otago was to look out the window at the wonderful view. 'I've had to sell all my own paintings just to survive,' he said. The cork popped open.

He moved into the house in 2003. 'When I first came into Grahame's life,' Heidi said, 'all his books were just lying on the floor.' She argued for a bookcase; he wanted to keep the walls for art; she won. One entire shelf was stocked with books about the South Pole. Grahame has twice visited the white continent, is besotted with its look and shape and light and shadow – Central Otago is an Antarctica with vegetables in it, and marginally less wind.

Drinks were poured. Grahame got to work on his homemade pâté and Heidi prepared a toasted bread snack topped with grated zucchini, garlic, basil and lemon zest. 'It's out of an Annabel Langbein book,' she said. It was early evening. The sky had softened, paled.

Heidi laid the table. The centrepiece was red roses and rowanberries. The drinks included a bottle of San Pellegrino sparkling water. Grahame said, 'Where did that come from?' Heidi said, 'The fridge.'

The dinner party served a serious purpose: it was the gathering of the tribe. All were united by a common cause. All were devoted to a subject of consuming interest. They knew they had gained a reputation as dreadful bores, that friends were sometimes too afraid to phone for fear of an earbashing.

I took Jay and Graye aside and said, 'So.'

'Right,' said Jay.

'Okay,' said Graye.

The tribe operated as Save Central Otago, a pressure group opposed to Meridian Energy's two-billion-dollar Project Hayes scheme to vandalise the Lammermoor Ranges in the Maniototo with a wind farm. A very big wind farm: 176 turbines, white and whopping, chopping at the air to generate what Meridian claimed would be 630 megawatts of electricity, more than the Clyde Dam.

Jay said, 'We're fighting world-class spin. It's formidably good. I give Meridian credit for that. They'll tell you that wind turbines are green, use renewable energy, don't burn fuel. And all that's true. But what about the carbon footprint of producing these damned things and getting them there?'

Graye said, 'You have to ask how this came about in the first place. The answer's simple: Helen wanted it. Helen Clark, when she was prime minister, wanted to show that New Zealand led the world in renewable energy. Meridian said, 'Well, Helen wants it; let's do it.' Then they told the public that wind farms would help solve the energy crisis, that they'd be efficient, and cheap. We've raised significant doubts about those claims.'

Jay said, 'Our case has always only been about the landscape. That puts us in tree-hugging territory, doesn't it? But we've always just stuck to explaining how valuable the landscape is.'

Graye said, 'If this wind farm goes ahead, the landscape will be destroyed.'

Jay said, 'Irreversibly. A wind farm – that's such a bullshit term. Spin. Call it what it is. It's an industrial estate.'

Heidi said, 'Here's another one. It's turbine-ised.'

Grahame said, 'That's right, turbine-ised.'

Jay picked up a ukulele and plucked at it. Graye said, 'Jay has provided us with strategic direction. We've been lucky to draw on his expertise as a former environmental lawyer.' The group had also been able to draw on Graye's expertise as a former SAS troop commander. He'd served in Vietnam, later gone private, and was now director of a security firm providing protection for oil companies and other multinational corporates in Iraq, Nigeria and Yugoslavia. Fit, alert, tidy in manner and dress, he gave only one hint of his military background. He asked, 'What's the latest information?' The subject in question concerned what Heidi was cooking for dinner.

The tribe had taken their fight against Meridian to the Environment Court. They estimated that legal fees would be at least $150,000.

Graye said, 'We didn't bank on it being this expensive.'

Jay said, 'I did. I knew from the start. It's big, big litigation.'

From the kitchen, where she was washing prawns under a cold tap, Heidi said, 'Grahame has lost six months' income by devoting his time to this. It's the same for all of us.'

'Until we agree that the natural world is a community to which we belong, and stop seeing everything as a commodity for us to use and exploit as we see fit,' Brian Turner once wrote, 'we're fucked.' But Meridian's wind farm had a lot of support. Graye said it had wrecked the community. 'There's been violence. People have sold up and gone, just to get away.' Then he added, 'There's a dartboard at a farmhouse that has a photo of Grahame in the bullseye.'

I asked whether this was a rural legend. 'No, no. These friends of ours went fishing for trout at the Loganburn. One of them was – should I say who, Jay?'

Jay shook his head. Graye said, 'Well, let's just say he was a significant player in our enterprise. The others thought they should do the right thing and go the farmhouse and ask the farmer if it was okay to use his land. The farmer invited them in for a cup of tea. They glanced around and saw the dartboard with Grahame's photo – and next to it a photo of the guy who I'm not going to name. They went outside and told him to lie low in the back of the car.'

Heidi said, 'That's how personal it's got.'

Graye said, 'That bitterness persists right now.'

Grahame said, 'I'd go so far as to say they've been bought off.'

The first course arrived. It was a green salad with feta, stilton and pears. Heidi said, 'You're welcome to have some, Brian.' The significant player in the Save Central Otago enterprise said, 'No, thanks. I ate on the road. Cooked up half a tin of peas and a poached egg.'

There is an amusing, mistaken notion that Turner is a curmudgeon, an incurable pessimist, a grouch muttering into his beard, but he told long funny yarns and sometimes couldn't talk for laughing. There were stories about rabbiting as a young man with his uncle Jack. Jack shot anything that moved. Once that included a car that wouldn't let him pass – he drew level, fired a round from his side-by-side over the roof, and roared, 'That'll cramp your fucking style!'

The good old days. As a poet, and also as New Zealand's best nature essayist, Turner has written firm lyrical lines about his love of the timeless land and his loathing of glibly defined progress. He said, 'When I was a boy...' He talked of wide open spaces, now despoiled. The 176 turbines would be 176 blots on the landscape, 176 obscenities, 176 insults that too many New Zealanders ('peasants!') took without flinching.

'We have a duty to look after nature,' he said. 'This talk that Meridian's scheme is in the "national interest" – I hate that term. I hate that cringing acquiescence people have to the "national interest". What really pisses me off is that the attempt to sacrifice nature is beyond any so-called benefits.'

Dinner was served – a French-Vietnamese seafood bouillabaisse – with French and Central Otago wines. The conversation turned to the Blue Lake in St Bathans. Grahame said, 'I tried to stop it from being motorised. Keep it quiet. Feel the serenity. I loathe jet skis. But I lost that fight.'

Then he talked about plans to dam the Clutha, and how they had to be opposed.

Graye said, 'That's not my fight.'

Grahame said, 'How can you lie down and let that happen?'

And then he clenched his fists and seethed about his failed campaign to stop the introduction of a street light in St Bathans.

He was a strange fellow. His paintings and photography strongly suggested he possessed genius. Nothing in his art was ever out of place. The clipped voice with well-rounded vowels, the straight face, the deliberate movements – he was more military in his bearing than Graye. He spoke with such intense dogmatic fervour; he followed a path of moral certainties.

Environmentalism seemed the least of his passions. It was as though he was ruled by fury. He'd once said that nuclear power was preferable to wind farms. Equally, though, there was nothing equivocal about his generosity. He was the kind of man who would think nothing of giving you the world.

The world was outside his front door – Rough Ridge, Old Woman Range, Hawkdun Range, Dunstan Peak. Above all, the highest peak, was Mount St Bathans, where 'the wind shakes the sparse grasses / water runs, stones rattle unexpectedly / and the land speaks', to borrow from Brian Turner in 'Under Mt St Bathans', a poem included in his collection of essays *Into the Wider World*. The book features his address to the Otago District Council in June 2007, when he presented his case against 'Meridian's application to build a giant windwhatever'. The speech is his magnum opus, ringing and defiant, tempered with grace notes: 'Our economy should be required to serve the natural world, not the other way round. ... This landscape, raw in winter, expansive, golden and rhythmic in summer ... Our finest natural glories can't take any more major assaults. ... The tyranny of apathy ... When I was a youngster in the 1950s...'

The wine flowed, and so did the Pernod. Dessert was a choice of chocolate gâteau or stewed stonefruit. Brian said, 'I'll have both.' The table experienced a rare silence as dessertspoons were put to work.

Jewel said, 'Beautiful, Heidi.' Grahame liked the sound of that. He decided to improve it by getting rid of the comma. 'Beautiful Heidi,' he said. 'That's you. That's what you are, my love. Beautiful Heidi.'

The next day I ran into Graye and we drove to the home he was building on the other side of Dunstan Creek. It was to be off the grid and rely on solar power, with a back-up generator. It had nice stone features made from rocks he and Wendy had pulled out of the creek. 'And this room,' he said, 'will be for when the grandkids visit.' The thought made him very happy.

He and Wendy were house-sitting a cottage in St Bathans owned by their friend and Save Central co-conspirator, All Black legend Anton

Oliver. Even given that Oliver is widely known as a gentle soul and a conscientious, intelligent man studying environmental policy at Oxford University, it seemed an unlikely house for a hulking former All Black hooker. It was small, quite dark, almost feminine; there were fruit trees in the little garden and bees in the lavender outside the front door.

Wendy put on the jug, rustled up a plate of crackers and spread. She said that when Graye left on his first tour of Vietnam in 1968, she was left at home in Papakura with their first child, aged six months. Graye talked a bit about Vietnam, the SAS, and his private security work. But the story I liked most was what happened when he and Wendy decided to sail around the world.

They bought a yacht. It was called *Supremacy*. What an awful name, I said. Yes, they said, but it's bad luck to change the name of a boat. Their luck could hardly have been worse. They planned to sail to Tahiti, then follow the trade winds north to Alaska. They didn't get very far. The steering broke. They couldn't move; the yacht was taking on water. They radioed for help. They were a thousand miles from land, marooned and at serious risk.

That night they saw something amazing: a city, its lights blazing – a container ship. The sea was rough and they were told rescue was impossible until the morning. They woke up when they heard the massive iron sides of the ship bumping against their yacht. A rope ladder was thrown down; they had only minutes to pack their most precious things in a shoulder bag. For some reason Graye took a set of knives, a Christmas present from his daughter. The ship took them to the United States. All hell broke loose at Customs when officials detected the knives. The date was September 12, 2001.

They never saw the yacht again. 'And now here we are,' Graye said, 'two shipwrecked mariners as far away from the sea as possible.'

A year later there they were, Graye and Grahame, standing next to each other and smiling very widely on the front page of *The Otago Daily Times* beneath the gigantic headline GONE WITH THE WIND. The news was stunning: the Environment Court had upheld their appeal against Meridian's wind farm and refused Meridian consent to do its worst on the Lammermoor Ranges. Graye wore a jersey. Grahame was dressed in jeans and T-shirt. They were photographed on the side of the road in St Bathans. All you could see was blue sky and tussock grass, ruffled by the wind.

# 05 ŌHINEMUTU & WHAKAREWAREWA
## HOW TO COOK A FISH HEAD

The mist parted and there were a couple of drunk people. Heriata Porter was 49 years old with slender legs, a sensual, blurry face, and a man's hat jammed on her head. Her partner, Nathan Rayner, 36, stood behind her wearing baggy grey track pants and a loose grey top. His head floated like a balloon above her shoulder. They were outside their caravan, which was parked on a scruffy patch of gravel next to a cabin. 'That's our bedroom,' Heriata said. 'We pay $50 a week to whoever we hire it off of.'

A garden table and chairs were set out in front. A mob of garden gnomes squatted in the dust. The couple walked inside the caravan and resumed drinking from cans of Brenner, a cheap German lager brewed in Papakura. They crushed their empties into a plastic bag hooked over the door handle.

It was getting on to tea time. Dinner: fish heads. Heriata's recipe: 'You boil them in fresh water with onions and salt. That's it.' But that wasn't it. They had no electricity – no TV, no lights, no fridge, no stove. They watched the sky, lit candles, kept their beer cold in a chillibin filled with ice water, and cooked outside. Heriata said, 'We live off steam.' The pot of fish heads sat in a thin trickle of hot springs that bubbled and steamed out of the earth in one of the most amazing places on Earth.

Rotorua, world-famous for its geysers and its mud pools and its dancing, painted Māori; Rotorua, New Zealand's battered old shopfront, fuming and humid, rampantly erotic, with public pools for many and private tubs for two. It attracts an estimated three million 'visitor arrivals' each year. They come to boil their flesh in hot pools, to marvel at and possibly eat shrimp cocktails. They come from Korea, Australia, Germany, England, Japan, America. Mostly they come from the principality of Auckland.

On this Friday afternoon in January, under a grey drizzling sky, every visitor looked the same: limp and disappointed. Misery is a great leveller. International tourists caught on fast to the distinctive melancholy of a lousy summer's day in New Zealand.

The wind flew up and tore at the surface of Lake Rotorua, shredding it with its claws. The water looked foul and cold, like a bucket of suds. In the distance Mokoia Island assumed the shape of a fat dark lump. At the lake's edge, a colony of feral black swans bobbed up and down, screaming and shitting. The wind gained strength, rain began to fall in fat dark lumps; two days later residents would emerge to find unusual carnage and a death toll of about three hundred.

Glyssa Bosworth told *The Daily Post* she was strolling downtown with her one-year-old daughter when they noticed a dead sparrow. 'I could smell something absolutely horrific.' She turned around and saw a great many dead sparrows at the base of a tree. 'There was a humongous pile of them. It was gross.'

She immediately thought of bats, which had been seen in nearby trees a few years earlier. There had been no recent sightings of bats. Council staff blamed the storm but that didn't account for the slaughter. Later, the SPCA accused person or persons unknown of poisoning the sparrows with the pest control agent alphachoralose, but the birds had already been destroyed and with them any evidence. The file remains open.

Death, humongous and gross; a suspicion of bats and poison; meanwhile, tourists driven inside, puzzling over the contents of motel and hotel libraries, with their ancient paperbacks by Catherine Cookson, their never-opened volumes of *Reader's Digest* condensed novels ('Call me Ishmael. The end.'). The heavy overnight downpour uprooted trees, raised the river, and spilled dishwater out of the lake. Playing fields were flooded. Already desolate playgrounds were deserted.

But rain never stops the giddy, happy play of mist, steam and warm thermal smoke. Everywhere, the lovely sleepy scent of sulphur escaped from the earth. Money is well spent at Te Puia cultural centre to gape at the famous Pōhutu geyser fizzing at the bung, but it's just as bizarre and astounding to be simply walking along a road and noticing a drain smoking its head off. There was a drain smoking its head off in the lakeside village of Ōhinemutu.

Much about Ōhinemutu is bizarre and astounding, including the fact that people live there. It's one of only two so-called 'living villages' in New Zealand, open for tourists to wander around and gawk and point and photograph while locals go about their business. The other living village, Whakarewarewa – duly astounding and bizarre, and smoking its head off on the raised banks of Puarenga Stream – was at the opposite end of town. As in Ōhinemutu, the silica looked as though it were melting.

I traipsed from one village to another. In places, the mist was as thick as a scrub fire, as slippery as fog, sliding along the street, lingering upon the pools that stand in drains. And then the mist parted and I stepped into another, stranger underworld. Heriata – Ata for short – opened the door to her caravan.

She took off her hat. The caravan had a view of the lagoon, the lake, the island. The storm began to build; unsuspecting sparrows were on their last legs; big fat raindrops sizzled on the pavements. Ata said, 'I'm a chronic alcoholic. We drink every day, bro, that's the truth. We do 36 cans between us. But it doesn't kick for me no more. I don't get no buzzes no more like the younger days, eh. It's just a bad habit now. To wake up to a drink – it's just a bad habit. And that's what I do. As soon as I wake up I grab me a can, and then I go for my bath with my can of beer. No, two cans of beer.'

At six every morning she went for a bath in a shallow, steaming pool in a dark bathhouse behind the caravan. 'I live in it,' she said. 'Go in four times a day. I'm the cleanest Māori in town.' She was funny and vivid, brash and shrewd, drunk and tidy.

Outside, where the garden table and chairs pretended to be in a garden, there wasn't a single discarded cigarette butt. I didn't notice that: Ike Mitchell pointed it out. He gave Ata high marks. To Ike, cleanliness was possibly above godliness.

Jandalled and singleted, no spring chicken but as agile as a boxer, Ike moved at great speeds and with serious purpose around Ōhinemutu in his role as caretaker. He said he got by on four or five hours' sleep every night. The marvel is that he managed to sleep that long. He talked quickly, non-stop, cursing and laughing, adamant. 'I love history,' he said, 'and I hate bullshit.'

Most people lose their voice when they're quoted in a newspaper – they don't sound like themselves – but I instantly heard Ike's voice when I googled him later and found a *Daily Post* story from 2004. He was responding to a thin-lipped little government booklet that presumed to instruct Māori how to prepare and cook hāngī hygienically. Ike was asked to comment. He was insulted by the booklet. He said: 'You show me a bastard who has died from eating hāngī.'

He spoke exactly like that. He mentioned the funeral of former Ōhinemutu resident Sir Howard Morrison, and how a female journalist had wandered over and asked him an impertinent question. 'I said to her, "Lady," I said, "if you had a pair of balls I'd put you on your arse."'

He was standing on the forecourt in front of the meeting house. He decided to give a quick tour of the kitchen. 'Spotless,' he said. 'You could eat off every inch of the floor.' He banged the side of the three enormous metal steam cookers. 'Can do 1,790 meals in an hour and a half.' He turned on a tap. A roar of hot thermal water squirted out, and then he turned it off and sped towards Ata's caravan. On the way, he was moved to give a speech about a civic official who lived in Ōhinemutu. 'There was a sewage leak here last year and it was going straight into the lake. Well, he walks up and down and he sees it but pretends not to notice. Too much like hard work to try and fix it. He doesn't give a shit. He's just in it for himself and his overseas trips. Fucken arsehole.'

As Ike passed by in a whirl of passion and oaths, Ōhinemutu hissed and bubbled, steamed and blew smoke. Daylight packed it in and the colour of Lake Rotorua turned to dishwater. A few limp and disappointed tourists wandered around. They were cheered by Ōhinemutu's picturesque Anglican church St Faith's, built in 1910. Inside, they saw the frosted figure of a handsome, daintily bearded Māori Christ on a window overlooking the lake – when they parked their bums on pews they could see Christ's brown feet walking on the water. They photographed the church and the cemetery. 'When we die,' Princess Te Puea once said, 'the Earth folds us in its arms.' But it doesn't do that at Ōhinemutu: the bodies are put in whitewashed tombs above ground.

Ike briefly directed his wrath towards the city council ('Dickheads … mongrels … pricks') and then he arrived at the caravan. 'Spotless,' he said. 'Never throws a single butt on the ground. See? Nothing. There's some other people here live like animals. Generations of druggies. But I don't worry about the bastards. I live my life. I'm happy.'

I was exhausted. Ike made introductions then left on some fresh mission. Inside, the caravan was very tidy, and also very narrow. The couple's very old dog Sooty lay on the floor. It didn't look as if he were ever going to get up. He was more like a species of rug than a dog.

It was good to get out of the lousy weather and sit in the caravan. 'Some people says it's an eyesore,' said Ata. 'They've tried to kick me out. Well, how come all the tourists come to photograph my pretty place? But it's hard being stuck in here sometimes. We don't have no car. No toilet. We do a mimi in a bucket, and go to a cousin's house for the other.'

Her living conditions were somewhere around the halfway mark between Third World and First, more or less as primitive as when Ōhinemutu was settled. Strange to imagine the village in an earlier century, because it would have looked much the same: the moonlight glowing the same way on the surface of Lake Rotorua, the mist rising the same way out of the Earth's crust.

Army officer Herbert Read described Ōhinemutu in 1825 in his racily titled memoir, *A Ride through the Disturbed Districts of New Zealand*: 'In an open space in the middle of the settlement stone flags have been laid down, which receive and retain the heat of the ground in which they are sunk. This is the favourite lounge, and here at any hour of the day, but especially when the shades of evening are closing round, all the rank and fashion of Ōhinemutu may be seen wrapped in their blankets, luxuriously reclining on the warm stones.'

Steam is the constant fact of Ōhinemutu life. The modern trimmings as enjoyed by Ata and Nathan were beer, smokes and WINZ. Nathan said he got about $180 a week on the dole. He spoke in a thin quiet voice, as though he wasn't used to forming words out loud. He said about the dole, 'By the time you pay your bills and that, it's bugger all.'

Ata laughed and said, 'What bills? Stop lying! We don't get bills, darling. We've only got one bill and that costs us $50 a week.'

Nathan said, 'Yeah, that's what I mean.'

Ata said, 'And that's for our cabin. But we're gonna… we're trying to set ourselves up, 'cos I wanna get rid of it. Our friend – I've got this friend – is looking to find me a cottage. He's a demolition man. He knows what I like. He can pick one up that no one wants and put it beside the caravan. And then I can get rid of the cabin and pay him the $50 a week.

'I tell you, man, I wouldn't mind a bloody two-storey home. But hey, that's just a dream. We gotta get real. You know. But hey, we're happy with what we've got anyway. We don't sit here and wish for anything more. Eh. I say to my tane, "We be grateful for what we've got, darling."'

'What we've got,' repeated Nathan. 'Yeah.'

'And don't think, eh, we need this and we need that 'cos we don't,' said Ata. ''Cos we got it all. We got a lot more than anybody else. Some of them out there are homeless, eh. But we're happy. We never starve. And Ōhinemutu is full of life, tangis going 24/7.

'You know, I'm in paradise, bro. I don't even go to the city much. I can't be bothered. If we want anything in town, my tane goes to get it.' Her tane stared at the floor. 'Plus,' she said, 'I caregive a house. I don't just sit at home and drink all day; I drink on the job. And we always put in our ten cents worth of mahi at the marae. Do the cleaning, whatever. It's only next door, and we're doing jack. I take a can with me but I don't advertise it. I'm discreet.'

From the big bay windows of the Lakeside, an old wooden shack posing as a pub directly above Ōhinemutu, I watched a young woman run out of the bathhouse with a towel wrapped around her, unlock her car and speed away. Three teenage boys lifted their bicycles on to the front wheel and rode through the village. Tourists with bare legs and backpacks pointed and recorded. The ground smoked.

The pub was large and semi-deserted. Two tough bastards with bruised faces – one Pākehā, one Māori: violence often attracts racial harmony in New Zealand – kept ducking outside to take some kind of drug and returning to lean against a wall, grunting and frowning, their eyes behind wraparound dark glasses. They must have been really stoned because on the jukebox they selected 'Moonlighting' by Leo Sayer. It blasted out at deafening volume.

I shared a table with a couple of old boys. We stood and drank in silence. We had no choice: it was impossible to talk. When the song finally finished, Henry Webber, 83, talked about the time the great Australian pool player Eddie Charlton walked into the Lakeside. 'Must have been, oh, about five, six years ago. He was in his prime then. We played at that table just there. Just a frame. Eight-ball. It wasn't a one-sided game, it was a close game. Very close. But I beat him.'

'That's right, he did!' said Peter Garlick, seventy. Henry was dark, solid, stocky; Peter was pale and thin with slicked-back hair, and wore a pair of shiny silver polyester pants. He had turquoise eyes and a long nose that dipped into his glass. He stood in the doorway, hunched against the wind, lit a rolled-up cigarette, and took just two quick puffs before coming back in. He was economising. He said his pension paid $617 a fortnight. I asked where he lived. 'Upstairs,' he said. I asked how that had come about. 'It's quite funny, actually.' But it wasn't, really.

He had lived in a comfortable pensioner flat for ten years. 'I'd have stayed another ten if I'd had my way. I was happy as Larry. I had TV, a stove.' Then a woman from South Africa bought the flats and evicted him. It had something to do with his drinking. The room in the Lakeside was small and cheap. 'I sit up there and read cowboy yarns,' he said.

The shabby pub left to rot, the weak sunlight, the two tough bastards probably on more than dope – I felt nostalgic for Ata and Nathan's snug caravan, their friendly company, their bond. 'Together,' sang Leo Sayer. 'They're gonna make it together.'

'I was brought up in Catholic schools,' Ata said. 'My mother told me I was going to be a nun. I was like, "None at all." They made us pray so hard it wasn't funny.'

Nathan said, 'I go up to St Faith's sometimes.'

Ata said, 'I haven't been to church for years.'

'I go up and have a listen, eh,' Nathan said, staring at the floor.

I asked Ata whether she had been good at school. 'Nah. The only class I liked was typing.' Was she fast? 'Oh, yes, tweet, tweet… Everyone calls me Tweety Bird.' Tweety Bird's hands were covered in faded tattoos. She said, devastatingly, 'I knew I wasn't going nowhere right from day one.'

She said she had two children. 'The eldest is 34 but I don't know him. He got taken away from me. The father took him away 'cos I was sixteen when I had him. He was thirty-one. He kidnapped my baby, actually. I say to the family, "Tell him to come home. Mummy's waiting."'

No one said anything for a while. I thought about the stack of ancient paperbacks at my motel, where I'd flipped open *Fenwick Houses* by Catherine Cookson and read: 'I was just sixteen when I realised that you don't go to hell because you sin but because you love.'

The love story was in the room. The older woman, the younger man: she was wise to the ways of the world; he seemed confused, hesitant. They were gentle with each other, protective, tender, patient. The long hours in the caravan with their cans of Brenner… They had been together ten years.

'I was boarding with his mum,' Ata said. She brought out a plastic folder that contained news clippings. She had been photographed for a story about smoking. He had been photographed talking to a police officer about his mother's death – the cops had viewed the death suspiciously but concluded the poor woman had just fallen over and cracked her head.

Ata continued, 'His mum used to go with one of my cousins. So yeah, I'm boarding there and next minute he rocks in and I'm like, "Hey, he's got a job! Fuck, he's making good money! He can fucking keep me going!" Hah, hah, hah!' Her raucous laugh tailed off and she said, 'No, it wasn't like that. I just fell in love with him.'

Nathan stared at the floor. He was thinking about his job as a scrub-cutter. 'I just got laid off this year actually.' And then: 'No, it was last year I got laid off.' I asked about employment. He said, 'There's no jobs around Rotorua. The mills and that, they've all laid people off.' I asked about his dealings with welfare offices. He said WINZ made him attend 'senimars'. They weren't much help.

While Ata wrote and read phone texts about the house she was caregiving, Nathan held up his beer can and said, 'Up to me, I can stop just like that, eh. I just *choose* to carry on. But I can give up drink if I want to, if I had to. But she won't stop.' He said it without rancour or judgement, just as a hard little fact.

Ata held up her beer can and said everyone called their caravan the 'canavan'. Who was everyone? The friends who liked to visit and, as she put it, 'rock'. Then: 'But any men try to rock here, I stand in my doorway. That means they can't come in. 'Cos they think they can come here and drink our beer and smoke our smokes.'

'And spot on the stove,' Nathan said.

'There is no spotting in here, eh,' said Ata. 'I don't mind people having a joint, but hash oil – nah. It stinks.'

So all the friends who came to rock were women? 'Yeah,' said Nathan. 'Bee-atches.'

'They're not bee-atches,' said Ata.

'I go next door when they come over,' said Nathan. 'Just sit in there by myself.'

'Nobody's around me, I'm bored,' said Ata. 'I'm a crowd person.'

'I'm a loner,' said Nathan. 'I haven't got any friends.'

'Hello!' said Ata.

'I haven't got any mates.'

What about his scrub-cutting crew? 'Nah, 'cos they're all recovering alcoholics,' he said.

Ata received another text and said to him, 'Do we want to go to Di's?'

'Who's that?' he asked, nodding at her phone.

'Auntie Eru,' she said. 'Yay or nay?'

'Nah.'

'Can I?'

'Yeah.'

She got up to leave and put on the man's hat. Nathan got up too. He said he'd go for a walk and when he got back he'd either sit in the caravan by himself or in the cabin by himself. I waved as he walked off. His grey tracksuit was the same shade as the lake and the sky.

When night fell, Rotorua's main drag, Fenton Street, glowed from one end to the other with the neon force of its motels. The lollipop reds, emerald greens, golden yellows – the names made for happy reading. La Mirage. Bel Aire. Golden Glow. Emerald. Geneva. Havana. Baden. Rob Roy. Four Canoes. There were so many. They were like TV shows, little extravaganzas, points of light shining and twinkling in the dark, with their heated pools in private courtyards.

In motels you have paperbacks by Catherine Cookson. In hotels you have ham steaks with pineapple on the restaurant menu, and a $45 buffet complete with pavlova, ye olde shrimp cocktails, and Māori cultural performances – the small stage, the acoustic guitar, the painted faces under a spotlight. In broad daylight, the window frames of the motels and hotels were chipped and flaked, because nothing stands in the way of Rotorua sulphur, chewing its way out of the earth and invading every surface. There was talk of having to change bath and sink taps four times a year. Sulphur had a particular appetite for electrical appliances. It even corrupted the alphabet: the sign for the Regal Geyserland had been reduced to REGAL CEV ERLAND. Imogen, a guest, posted a bad review with a happy ending: 'The furniture is shabby and tatty, the mattresses saggy and ancient. The blankets are just rough cuts of material … appliances don't work … the shower is disgusting …The staff are friendly and helpful.'

I thought of another sour-faced visitor to Rotorua, the writer and harridan Lynn Barber, who visited in 2002 and commented: 'The town centre consists entirely of burger bars, massage parlours, tourist tat shops and Māori nightclubs offering evenings of haka and hāngī (war dances and barbecues) to be avoided at all costs.'

War dances and barbecues! Still, she got the 'avoid at all costs' right. But there was so much to see and do. There were the spa baths and mud baths, a fast jet-boat ride and a slow gondola. Haka World taught the haka, but not correct use of apostrophes ('Learn the word's and actions!'). And visitors could immerse themselves in an authentic pre-European experience at Mitai Māori Village, or Tamaki Māori Village, where guests were invited to 'browse through the marketplace to view designer clothing and much more'.

Mitai and Tamaki weren't living villages. No one lived there. The population at Ōhinemutu was about 300. I asked Polly Morgan, 71, of Whakarewarewa, how many people lived in her village. She started counting the people in families: 'One, two, three, four … five, six, seven … eight, nine, ten, eleven…' She got to 53 and then said, 'No more than a hundred.' We sat next to each other on a bench outside the meeting house. Tourists walked by. Polly smoked a cigarette and wore a soft tracksuit. 'We never used to lock our doors,' she said. 'We'd play and then go to the auntie's for bread and jam. It's a business now. Tourists all the time. It doesn't bother me.' Asked what she thought the difference was between Ōhinemutu and Whakarewarewa, she came up with an incredible answer. 'My own opinion is that they're more commercialised than we are.'

However, it cost nothing to visit Ōhinemutu. Visitors arriving at Whakarewarewa entered a ticket office and were greeted with $29 general admission, $31 general admission plus cob of corn cooked in steam, $59 general admission plus hāngī lunch, and so on. Punters then set foot on the bridge over Puarenga Stream and were immediately asked to pay another tariff by 'penny divers', young boys and girls who swam in the river and called out to passers-by to throw them coins. 'Please, sir! Give us some money! Lady!' etc.

It was easy to submit to the hand-wringing liberal within and ask yourself what kind of message it was sending that Māori children were encouraged to beg. It hardly seemed plausible that this nineteenth-century custom was still in existence. It made New Zealand look distinctly Third World, but the divers could earn about 30 dollars a day in the high season. Liberal anxiety is no match for that much hard cash.

Whakarewarewa had souvenir shops, and Neds Café specialising in hāngī meals. It was dusty and tiny and lovely. Hot mineral water melted the Earth's crust, colouring it yellow and orange and bone-white. Houses were obscured behind clouds of delicious steam. A man leaned out the window of his car and asked Polly, 'Any mail, Auntie?' None of the houses had letterboxes; all mail was sent to post boxes and picked up from there.

Another man dipped a plastic bucket into a hot pool and walked back to his home. 'Water to wash the dishes in,' he said. That morning Polly had put a pot of chicken soup in her steam box in the ground. She was about to have her 'nanny nap' and would eat the soup at about seven-thirty.

Chicken soup and village life, lovely, peaceful, quiet. 'Any mail, Auntie?' Tour guides telling attentive Germans about the apparently smooth impact of the first Christian missionaries on Māori: 'What was written in the scriptures coincided with our beliefs.' The sun was gentle and a tūī sang in a gum tree. But the ground was sinking, caving in, eroded by geothermal acidic fluids.

And it seemed no one knew where they stood in other ways – Whakarewarewa was in the midst of an ongoing land dispute among Ngāti Wāhiao, Ngāti Whakaue and Tūhourangi. Part of the dispute was based on the widely held view that Tūhourangi were squatters. They had only come down in the last shower: they arrived after Mount Tarawera erupted in 1886 and were 'gifted' their land. The message was: Gift it back. What was a mere 120 years of settlement? They were even later on the scene than Pākehā.

Polly's iwi was Tūhourangi. She said, 'People have called me – what was it? – an overstayer. No, not overstayer. Something else.' I said, 'Squatter?' She said, 'That's it! "You fellas are just squatters." That's what some people say.'

She laughed. 'The honest truth is that some of us here couldn't care less about who owns what. As long as I've got food in the cupboard and I have my smokes…' She threw away her cigarette butt. It landed in the brown grass. She stood up; it was time for her nanny nap.

Nanny naps and village life; the tour guide saying to the attentive Germans 'Repeat after me, "haka"', and the Germans grunting 'Huck-ah'; the wonderful smell of the mineral water, and the gorgeous clouds of steam flung this way and that in the air – and then the mist parted, and there was a Māori chief. 'I live in chaos, as you can see,' he said, in his very strange house in the village. I didn't see much chaos. Perhaps his paperwork needed arranging, and it's true there were a lot of cobwebs up in the extremely high ceiling. The real chaos was the fact he was there in the first place. I had stepped into another underworld.

His name was Jim Dennan and he was eighty-eight. He had lost the hair on his head and he moved slowly, creakingly, on his two new knees. He was large, fleshy, pale. The immediate and dominant thing about him was his sardonic nature. Resentment kept him alert, smoothed his skin; he had quite a youthful face and he didn't waste unnecessary energy on smiling.

He was true to himself, but who was he? It was bewildering to place him in Whakarewarewa: an aged sardonic Englishman who spoke in a fairly posh accent, living by himself in a dark timber home with exquisite Māori panelling.

He said, 'You don't know much about me, do you?' That wasn't true. I didn't know a single thing about him. And so he revealed an epic family saga. I had come in at the end, and found an exile from Oxfordshire living in a beautifully carved whare in Whakarewarewa.

You could see the whare as you entered the village. It was up on a hill. It looked like an abandoned meeting house; there was a beat-up couch on the floorboards of the front porch. If you squinted, it looked haunted. Jim Dennan was its ghost.

It had been built in 1909 for Maggie Papakura, high-born descendant of Te Arawa chiefs, subject of documentaries and biographies, one of the great beauties of her age, intelligent, entrepreneurial, independent, a celebrated guide at Whakarewarewa who left New Zealand in 1912 to marry a wealthy English landowner and live in his stately home, Oddington Grange, in Oxfordshire. She is buried there. She was Jim's grandmother.

This partly explained the presence of her unlikely mokopuna, the only son of her only child, in the whare in Whakarewarewa. But there was more to the family saga, other crucial subplots. Jim's mother died when he was a child; his father was made bankrupt, had to sell the Oddington manor, shooed Jim and his sisters away to live with relatives in England, and returned by himself to Whakarewarewa, where he married the legendary Guide Rangi. When Jim's father died, Guide Rangi inherited the whare. Guide Rangi, Guide Maggie – during their lifetimes, they were among the most famous Māori in the world. Jim was a unique link to the two women, the two celebrities.

And here he was, living in obscurity, off his wits. He had a souvenir shop in the village; it sold his paintings and carvings, and a selection of second-hand wristwatches. The shop was merely his latest business venture. 'You name it, I've done it,' he said. 'You give me a foolscap sheet of paper and I'll write down a different job on every line.' He looked around for a foolscap sheet of paper, gave up and sighed heavily. 'Chaos.' He sat there, resentful and posh, in the dark gloomy whare with his shirts hung over the frame of his single bed. But why was he here? It was the classic New Zealand answer: land.

In 1992, he said, he was sorting through family papers, read about the whare where his father, stepmother and grandmother had lived in Whakarewarewa, and decided to come out to New Zealand for a visit. He popped into the village and made himself known. 'And that was when I was told, "Well, it's all yours. Why don't you come and live here?" So I thought, "Well, I've had a bloody good time in NZ for two months so I will."

'It took three years to get passport and citizenship papers. In the meantime they were writing to me – I've letters saying, "Hurry on back, we're waiting for you" and all this crap. So I arrive back in 1995 and they say, "It's not yours. It's ours."'

Eventually 'they' let him live in the whare. 'But I don't own it. I don't own a blade of grass in Whaka. Not a single blade of grass.'

It was the cause of his bitterness. I asked whether he was regarded with the respect due him as Rangi's stepson and Maggie's grandson. He said, 'Well, I am a chief when all's said and done. They tolerate me in that sense. But I don't walk around with a feather stuck out of my head and all that sort of crap.

'I was brought up in Pākehā land and consequently I think Pākehā. But when you try and put Pākehā thoughts into people's heads here they don't want to know, do they. They say, "We want to do it the Māori way." Well, the Māori way is hold your hand out and get some free money and don't do any work.'

Earlier in the day, I had talked to Dardin Heretaunga, a strong, solidly built 36-year-old who lived a few doors down. He wore black jeans and a black T-shirt. 'Yeah, heavy metal, that's right, bro,' he said. 'Iron Maiden, Black Sabbath, a bit of Floyd…' We sat on his porch. The lawn had dried up because of the geothermal heat beneath the topsoil. He said he was unemployed.

'I was in the bush for a little while, eh. Logging. Silviculture. But I got out of there and started working on my uncle's dairy farm.' He said the word 'uncle' a few other times, and always pronounced it 'oncle'.

He continued, 'Then I was in a relationship for three years, but that…
Anyway, I went to Sydney and got a job as an autoglazer.'

I asked whether wages in Australia really were heaps better than in
New Zealand, as people always said. 'Yeah, nah, it adds up about the
same when you take expenses into account.'

But was life in Australia heaps better than in New Zealand, as people
sometimes said? He said, 'Yeah, nah, to be honest I couldn't wait to be
home. I partied hard and had a lot of fun but the food's better here.
Way better.'

Like what?

'Mutton,' he said.

He hadn't found work since he returned to Whakarewarewa. 'Still
looking, but there are no jobs in Rotorua.' So what did he do with himself?
'Just stick around the village,' he said. 'It's my home, eh bro.' Some of his
relatives were buried on the side of the path that ran through Whaka:
I noticed the name 'Heretaunga' on a number of the tombs next to the
pretty Church of the Immaculate Conception.

Further up the path were large monuments to that wandering bankrupt
who deserted his children, William Francis Te Aonui Dennan, and
his widow, Rangitiaria Dennan, Guide Rangi. There was also a wordy,
windy memorial to Maggie Papakura. It stuck to the old false European
narrative of the arrival of the Māori in New Zealand. 'A chieftainess, the
first-born of the eldest line of the noble and sacred ancestors. Related
to seven of the eight canoes which arrived here about 1350, and from
which all Māori tribes in New Zealand are descended…'

But what to make of Jim Dennan, the Māori chief who arrived in
1992? I asked him, 'When you first saw Whaka, did you actually want
to live here?' But I'd asked the wrong question, missed the point. It
wasn't about wanting, it was about what he thought he was entitled to.
'I wasn't allowed in the village until my seventieth birthday. The day I
was allowed in we had a chief's welcome on the bloody marae and all
that crap. You know, big fuss, big birthday party, and everybody made
me welcome.'

I asked him, 'Well, now that you're in, do you enjoy living in Whaka?' He answered, 'Very much. I enjoy the tourists, especially the English.' He didn't socialise much with the villagers. 'I go down to the RSA sometimes.' He didn't share the public hot-spring baths: 'No. Would you? You would? What, after 20 bloody people have gone in? Good luck to you. I wouldn't.'

He was acting the full-time snob. He said, 'The people here don't like me because I say it straight.' But there was a frailty about him, something vulnerable and anxious. He said about his life: 'I've written it all down.' He brought out a scrapbook. It was his illustrated memoir. There were snapshots, and a commentary written in blue pen. The many and varied business ventures, a busted marriage, ending up in Whakarewarewa selling second-hand wristwatches – it told the story of a self-unmade man.

I flipped backwards. There was a photo of a white Volkswagen van taken two years before he came to New Zealand. His caption: BUSINESS VENTURE (FAILED). 'I had a smoke alarm business,' he said, very nearly smiling, 'but it failed when the van caught fire.'

There were more photos of vehicles. Caption of a picture of a yellow Leyland truck: FIRST TRUCK IN THE SAND AND GRAVEL VENTURE. Caption of a green Ford van: FIRST DAY ON THE THRAPSTON LAYBY. See damp Thrapston and die; the van was his mobile snack bar, selling hot dogs and other merriments wrapped in fat.

On the same page, the narrative of his life included this remark: 'Shirley got a job in refrigeration and soon found a "boyfriend".' Who was Shirley, and what was with the sardonic inverted commas? There she was, a few years earlier and a few pages back, a lively, bright-faced brunette posing with a hail and hearty Jim behind a bar. The caption read THE MILTON ARMS, LUTON, WITH WIFE SHIRLEY 1968. He said, 'Shirley fell out with Vic Roffe, one of our customers, and busted his glass in his face. He was very good about it, but we lost all our customers. Shirley's why I'm living 13,000 miles away.'

There were photos of Jim in the war, and then photos of Jim as a pampered child of the gentry. There were photos of his two sisters and photos of his mother. Jim's comments read: 'I remember spending our days with a governess. ... Prep school. ... Mother died in Radcliffe Infirmary on February 16, 1932. It was Barbara's birthday. The party was held in mother's bedroom.' One of his sisters had added her comments: 'I was awakened by father at two a.m. and told mother was now with the angels. ... I remained in bed for two weeks.'

The death of one parent, and the other parent abandoning his children to remarry and live in a strange house in an amazing village on the other side of the world... Te Aonui Dennan died in 1942, but the way Jim told it he didn't even know for four years. 'It was after the war, 1946, when I got a letter and some bits of paper to say my father had died.' The papers were on behalf of Guide Rangi, asking Jim to sign documents that would give her the right to live in the whare. He said, 'In those far-off happy days I believed that marriage was due to all the good things of love and passion and all that crap, so I thought I'd better give her a hand. I signed a paper saying she could have the use of our land for her lifetime. That's what I thought I was doing, but I wasn't. I'd gifted the land to her.'

I flipped the pages of his memoir until I got to the beginning, where there was a faded photo of a serious little boy perched on a tricycle in 1925. The three-year-old from Oddington Grange in Oxfordshire had the same round anxious face as the man who was a year away from turning 90 in the whare in Whakarewarewa. I closed the scrapbook. His life had passed before his eyes. 'So here we are,' said the author, 'and here I die.' He said his ashes would be buried between his father and Guide Rangi, beneath the monument to his spectacular grandmother.

Jim sat in front of the window while we talked. All the while, tremendous gusts of white steam whisked past, danced and played and teased, lighter than feathers, mocking his silly tirades. It came in thick and hid the view from the window, and then it ran off and you could look out beyond Jim's head and see the bridge where tourists threw coins to beggars.

Beyond was the city, which got on with its business while the tourists stopped and stared. Beyond was The Grumpy Mole Saloon next to the army recruitment office, and the Matariki Cultural Centre (hāngī, painted Māori, tea and coffee) next to Pizza Hut; massive Chinese radishes and bags of the world's tastiest popcorn, Ka Pai, made by Rotorua man Carl Neville, at the Saturday markets; the one hundred and second annual Rotorua A&P show at Riverdale Park, with the headline attraction: 'Sheep Racing!'

Beyond was the big screen at Shed Bar for live coverage of the fight in Newcastle, Australia, between All Black boxer Sonny Bill Williams and Scott Lewis. Beyond, at the supermarket, were boneless chicken breasts for $2.49.

At Kuirau Park there were shocking things going on beside the hot springs. A grandfather and his two children had seen men engaged in sex acts in broad daylight. 'All I wanted to do was throw up and run like hell,' Grandpa told the *Daily Post*. Rotorua district councillor Charles Sturt said, 'Sexual activity seems to be rampant and needs to be stopped.' The newspaper's editorial said, 'It's a terrible look for a tourism town.' Also at Kuirau Park were rampant, unstoppable workings of tūrutu, a flax-like plant with starry white flowers and deep blue berries that oozed an inky juice.

Rotorua, forever humid and fuming. Rotorua, drunk and stoned, hanging in as one of New Zealand's most popular tourism attractions, with the occupancy rate of hotels and motels 53 percent, the third highest in the country behind Auckland and Queenstown. Did that make the town half full or half empty?

After I said goodbye to Jim Dennan I looked in on an outdoor concert down the road from his house. A crowd of about 300 had gathered to watch. The performers poked out their tongues and rolled their eyes. The audience roared with laughter. When the performers did it again, the laughter rose like a wave. Braying and paying tourists had reduced Māori culture to a comedy act. I looked at my watch in case time had moved backwards, to about 1950.

And then the audience was told the love story of Hinemoa and her lover Tūtānekai, how she swam across Lake Rotorua to Mokoia Island to be with him. When the story finished, a young man and a young woman sang 'Pōkarekare Ana'. The audience went completely quiet. They were entranced by the slow beautiful song, the beautiful crystalline singing. I wept. I stood in the sunshine, wanting to rub the music and the smell of sulphur into my skin, to have it always, to keep some trace of the rare loveliness of the moment. Standing in the sunshine at dusty steamy Whakarewarewa I thought back to bubbling lakeside Ōhinemutu, to the love story of Ata and Nathan, a modern Hinemoa and Tūtānekai, swimming in alcohol, afloat.

# 06 HAURAKI PLAINS
## COUNTRY ROADS

**K**eith Berry turned his teal-blue 1972 Ford Falcon 500 into the driveway of the dairy farm in Elstow he had worked for 38 years. The satisfying crunch of gravel, the deep breathing of the motor: it had 150,000 kilometres on the clock but was in beautiful working order, plush and polished. He had bought it brand new in Te Aroha. For 30 years it had sailed the long straight roads of Piako County and the Hauraki Plains.

On family holidays the Falcon hauled a lightweight Chevron caravan. Keith and his wife Lesley, whom he met at a table tennis club in Walton, had six children. Their eldest daughter belonged to a Baptist church, and her daughter, who was to turn sixteen in October, was going to Ethiopia to perform missionary work over Christmas.

Keith talked about the storms of late July and early August, which uprooted six native wattles on the farm. Then he told a story about his neighbour, Cliff Strange. As a boy, Cliff had planted oak trees on his farm. He was 78 during the storm of 1972, when the wind dropped off Mount Aroha, dived down, and whirled around the oak trees like a corkscrew. The trees popped out of the ground. Next day Cliff drove his Leyland tractor to have a look. Hundreds of oaks, an entire fence line, had been ripped out – a lifetime's work destroyed. No one knows how long he sat there and surveyed the damage. He switched off the engine and died.

Keith, 74, told this story in the kitchen. He had put his car keys on the dining-room table, which was actually a round snooker table with pockets, an oddity bought at an auction in Waihī. It was a cold Friday afternoon. Lesley, 67, planned to drive next afternoon to Morrinsville with her neighbour Lyn Pendergrast, 78, so they could catch a bus to go to the National Country Music Awards at the Founders Theatre in Hamilton.

Keith said he'd rather stay home. 'He doesn't tie me down,' Lesley said. She admitted to an independent streak; while raising their six kids she had always set aside time to enter baking contests at the Te Aroha A&P show. Her portfolio included scones, muffins, shortbread, melting moments, iced biscuits, sponges and fruit cakes. The results were spectacular and legendary: she won the baking trophy every year from 1975 to 2004. Rhoda Rosewell dared to win in 2005 but Lesley fought back and won in 2006, and then retired. She took her pikelet recipe from the 1961 Country Women's Institute cookbook, which advises, 'A tablespoon of hot water and a tablespoon of soft butter is the secret.'

Lesley's interest in country music started when her 14-year-old granddaughter Kyla, who sings and yodels, joined the Morrinsville Country Music Club. 'I follow her everywhere; there are a lot of clubs.'

Morrinsville, Whangamatā, Pirongia, Tokoroa, Te Awamutu, Cambridge, Matamata, Te Aroha, Morrinsville, Cambridge, Paeroa, Ngāruawāhia, Kerepēhi – country music is vital to the New Zealand way of life. It was the music I heard most during my travels, a high, lonesome, warm sound, twanging in the telephone wires, as rural as floods and saw doctors. Country music clubs travelled like a subterranean river all over the land. There were handwritten signs on bakery and library windows for the next meeting, the next event: in Golden Bay, where yodelling was strong; in Hastings, where the annual awards would be held in October at Lindisfarne College – accommodation available in the school dormitory, $25 per night, please bring own bedding.

It was the music of recession, company, loneliness, broken promises, good times, truth. It swept across the plains and filled the valleys. It was homely music, road music. Death notice, 2011: 'Condolences from the

Fountain City Country Music Club, the Mt Pirongia Country Music Club and the Te Awamutu Country Music Club.' Graeme Fitzsimons had died instantly when his car was sliced in two by a double-decker truck in Taranaki. Half of the car was jammed between the bank and the truck; the other half was further up the road. Fitzsimons and his wife Janice were described as regulars on the New Zealand country music scene. They sang harmonies, and travelled to country music club meetings in their mobile home.

Other regulars worked behind the scenes. Merle Howarth, QSM, 84, a life member of Te Aroha's club, could be found behind a stall at the Paeroa market, selling her plum sauce and grapefruit marmalade for three dollars. Vilma Berger, treasurer of Paeroa's club, said, 'That's V–i–l–m–a. I've met one other lady with that name. She said, "D'you know where it's from?" I said, "No, but if I ever find out, I'll tell them to put it back down from wherever they found it."' The name of Ngāruawāhia's club secretary was Daisy Rangi.

But the country music river was changing course. Bernie Eva wanted it to go 'mainstream'. As president of the Pro-Am supporters club and convenor of the national awards, his great mission was to eradicate the word 'western' from country music. Last week, he said, he'd called a special general meeting in Morrinsville and got approval from members to change the club's name from Morrinsville Country & Western Club to Morrinsville Country Music Club.

He was a stocky man, 62, with a broad gentle face and a fear of flying: 'A pity. Aeroplanes fascinate me but I won't fly in them.' His son Paul had just gone in for his seventh skin graft – he'd burned 70 percent of his body in a roadworks accident and had no sweat glands in the lower half of his body.

There were two freshly baked and iced carrot cakes by the front door of the house: Bernie's wife Rita was one of the caterers for the awards night. The couple had met when Rita was waitressing in Hamilton. 'She's a Mormon. Both our kids were brought up in the church. I'm not a believer but I harm nobody.' Their bookcase included *The Lives of Our Prophets, Trucking 2005 Diary, Rugby Greats* and *Living Well in Retirement.*

For over twenty years Bernie contracted a trucking business to a mushroom producer. 'Only small trucks, six-wheelers, 14 to 17 tonnes, single units. We had very comfortable trucks with air suspension and parabolic springing, because mushrooms can't vibrate around on the back of the truck. Mushrooms have to be looked after.'

There was a falling-out with management. 'I packed it in under principles, and then I paid the price. My loyalty and service never mattered a razoo to the new CEOs. It was very disappointing. I was angry. I was angry for nearly two years. We argued over $35 in the end. I drove both trucks off the yard that night. Told them to go get stuffed. And then I couldn't sell my trucks, and I struggled, and… Awww, that's another story.'

Now he worked in liquid fertiliser. 'I like the product,' he said. 'It's interesting. I did an adult apprenticeship in golf course greenkeeping, so I appreciate that greenkeepers deal with the biology of the soil. They put a lot of selenium, molasses and sugars into it.'

It was Friday morning. He had already driven to Hamilton and back to deliver stage gear to Founders Theatre for the awards show. He said, 'It's an amazing amount of work. Thirty-five or so people are involved with running the show. It's big, *big*. Our show is budgeted up to $67,000.

'Money like that never gets spent on country music! Country music club people will not spend money on country music. Country music club people get their country music very cheap. We want the general public. The Golden Guitars show in Gore – they do an extremely great job. Gore is acknowledged as the home of country music, and rightfully so, but basically that's amateur. We consider ourselves professional. We're the next step up.'

He talked about the Pro-Am supporters club. 'We want two thousand members. It's around two hundred at the moment.' He had dreams, good intentions. The awards show had the Hamilton City Council on board, funding from Creative New Zealand, generous sponsorship. He was making country music respectable; as such, he had to stay vigilant and remove all trace of country and western. 'We do not want the word "western",' he said. 'We do not use the word "western".' He urged, cajoled, nagged clubs to drop it from their name.

The word frightened people, he said, put them off. The general public looked on country and western music as a joke, kitsch at best, ridiculous at worst – 'the whole cowboy thing, yee-ha and all that'. Country and western music was old hat. Country music was new hat. I asked what sort of artists wore the new hat. 'Shania Twain,' he said.

The drinking mood was stern and stand-offish at the Grand Tavern in Te Aroha, but merry at the RSA. There was a good-sized crowd under the bright lights; a poster read, 'We are looking for a guitar that can be kept behind the bar for those party nights.'

Club president Russell Smith stood at a table near the bar. A former army man, he still had a military bearing. He worked as a purchasing officer for Fonterra. His sons Greg and Shane were outside on the smoking balcony. Shane was in the navy; he had returned home for his twenty-first, which was the next night at the RSA. Greg had stayed in Te Aroha as a training jockey. His hours were six a.m. to ten a.m., racing 20 or 30 horses, contracting his services at ten dollars a horse. He said, 'Mum's into country music.'

Mum was Jean Smith, tiny, blonde, very pretty. She had an unusual quality about her. It was as though she carried a secret, was hiding something. Russell said Jean had a story; he suggested I come to their house in the morning.

The next morning Jean said, 'We were brought up on country music. We had a family band – banjo, piano accordion, mouth organ. It was just part of our everyday life. As a kid I thought, Oh god, here we go again! The instruments would come out, and so would the booze. But boy could they play. Country music is a beautiful thing. I realised how special it was as I got older. The melodies, the words – I often think country music can relate to your own life.

'But it was my adopted grandfather who got me into it. He was an amazing old man, George Scanlon. He took me all over the countryside – talent quests, country music clubs. I really liked to sing and I started writing songs.

'I was spotted one night at a club and taken to see Jack Riggir, Patsy Riggir's dad, who was a singing tutor in Cambridge. About fifteen of us went to him for lessons. He would listen and give advice. He was a quiet, well-spoken man. Blind, but you could walk into a room and he'd know who you were, just like that.

'At fifteen I was chosen to make a record in Australia. It was a contest: I made a demo tape at 1ZH in Hamilton and I was the one they picked. People had so much faith in me and that was really important because I was quite shy, had low self-esteem and all that rubbish. I had been raised in foster homes. Mum had died when I was five. Dad's whole life had crumbled and he had turned to the bottle, but he took me back when I was eleven and he got a job at Waitoa.

'When I won the contest, he said, "Wonderful, wonderful!" But then he had one of his moments and decided that no, I wasn't going to do it. "Waste of time." Maybe it was resentment. Jealousy. His drinking. I don't know.

'I lost all my confidence. He crushed my whole world. A month later I left home and that was that. I've never played in public since. I sing for my daughter and I sing for myself.'

Russell said, 'Go on, Jean.' He handed her the Epiphone acoustic guitar she had owned since she was twelve. She said, 'No. No.' But her husband persisted, gently, and she picked up the guitar and sang in a pure beautiful voice for three intimate and exquisite minutes 'Dust on Mother's Old Bible', a sentimental country ballad about a child who has lost her mother: 'The night the angels called her…'

That afternoon, while Bernie Eva and his crew were running around backstage setting up the national country awards show for the benefit of the general public, the Hauraki Country Music Club held its monthly show at the war memorial hall in Kerepēhi. Kerepēhi has a marae, a general store, a creek. A little boy said, 'I go eeling, eh. They like sheep guts.' The dairy factory closed down about 20 years ago. There were boarded-up shops, abandoned houses, an empty fertiliser shed. But it was hard to find a park outside the war memorial hall. The club was hosting South Auckland country music club members, who had chartered a bus. Inside, the hall was packed, every seat taken, only a bit of room at the back for four women who line-danced, scuffing the wooden floor with their boots.

The door fee was three dollars, the raffle tickets two dollars. First prize was a small hamper that included saveloys, a packet of chicken coconut rice, and dishwashing liquid. It bore out the unkind words of Bernie Eva: 'Country music club people get their country music very cheap.'

On the low stage, a tight five-piece backing band played behind a succession of nearly 30 singers. It was amateur hour for about four hours, music from the wide open spaces inside a hall full of workers and beneficiaries. The applause was vast and noisy – it was an afternoon of country and western. Kerepēhi raucously defied Eva's edicts and yee-ha'd. There were rhinestone and rawhide, cowboy hats and cowboy boots, plus a lot of black.

First up was Dave Carson, 85, in black hat, black trousers and black checked shirt, who wheezed out a melody from his squeeze box. He said from the stage, 'This'll set you right for the day. Or wrong. One of the two.'

There was John Randolph, 62, a large, sombre man dressed entirely in black, who said, 'I sang with a rock band. Then a mate asked me to look at country music. I never looked back. That was 35 years ago. The way I see it, he introduced me to the fellowship.'

There was Brendon Ramsay, 29, who worked as dairy products inspector for Progressive supermarkets. He held on to his guitar as if it were a church icon, something precious and dear. 'I'm on the road most of the time. I'm always playing country in the car. Hank Snow, Joy Adams, Hamilton Bluegrass Band – did you know they're originally from South Auckland?'

There was Eddie Reidy, 90, who arrived with his third wife Irene, fifty-seven. She said, 'All except one of his six kids are older than me. He's had a full life, New Zealand national umpire for bowls, a calf judge, St John's volunteer. When he gets up singing in the morning I know he's happy.'

There was P. J. Wallace, 60, who stood out as a Māori with a shaved head in a wheelchair. 'I lost my leg a year ago,' he said. 'Diabetes. Flared up so I took it off.' He had toured the world as a musician with Prince Tui Teka's show band and wore an enormous crucifix. He said, 'My ancestors were all psychics. They gave me the cross for protection. I don't know what from.'

Afternoon tea was served. A guest from South Auckland had murmured, 'I hear they're quite frugal', but there were three tables of scones, pikelets, cakes, sausage rolls, and spaghetti sandwiches on white bread. It looked like a very generous spread. There was a great deal of elbowing and snatching, and in 20 minutes the tables were picked clean.

And then there was more music, New Zealand music, an expression of good times and struggle on the back roads, in the small towns. I sat back, tapped my foot, clapped, enjoyed the show, soaked up the happy ending of my travels in the flatlands.

But the memory and the sound of something else ran beneath the entire afternoon, and into the evening, and the days that followed: small, hurt Jean Smith, strapped into her childhood guitar, perched on the couch in her Te Aroha home, very nearly making a comeback into public life, her lovely voice caressing every true word as she raised the dead and sang 'Dust on Mother's Old Bible'.

# 07 MIRANDA BIRDLAND

T here is a field of maize on the side of the road in the sunny croplands of Mangatangi Valley near Thames, where a flock of twenty Australian galahs – gorgeous on the eye with their rose-pink breasts – arrive for a feast when the maize is harvested. The parrots are probably escaped cage birds, like the sulphur-crested cockatoos that also make cameo appearances, although both species may have originally flown across the Tasman. No one knows for sure. All birds are a mystery. They never give up all their secrets, despite the attention and close scrutiny they receive from birdwatchers.

On a summer morning filled with bright light, I travelled through Mangatangi to Miranda, where thirteen birdwatchers trudged towards the sea with telescopes and tripods hoisted over their shoulders. They had come to the white-shell shoreline to identify Arctic wading birds.

They were led by Keith Woodley, who manages the world-famous Miranda Shorebird Centre. A handsome man camouflaged behind a beard and glasses, his tall long-limbed presence confirmed the first law of ornithology: there are few short birdwatchers. He confirmed the second law, too: ornithology demands acute vision and hearing, and an alert response. Keith was deceptively slow, even languid, but he could move fast. There was a bolt of beard and leg as he darted along the line of his thirteen students to train their telescopes on the sudden arrival of a red-necked stint. It's a small bird. It has short legs, and a short black bill pointing out of its fat brown face. It doesn't look as if it could cross a road, but it came to New Zealand from its breeding grounds in Siberia.

'It's the smallest long-distance migratory bird,' claimed Christopher Moses, twelve years old. He had signed up for the wader identification course with his mother, Joanne. They had recently returned to New Zealand after living for seven years in Tanzania. Christopher's father was a United Nations lawyer. Joanne said, 'He went from working on South Auckland murders to prosecuting the Rwandan genocide.'

Christopher said, 'Tanzania's great for birds. I've probably counted over 400 species. I marked down only the ones I could definitely identify. There were a few species of duck I wasn't sure about.' He talked about the day he spotted the rare Beesley's lark in short grass. Yes, but seven years in Tanzania – what was it like returning home? He was an amazing boy, possibly the future of New Zealand ornithology. He said, 'It's been hard. I mean, you've got some good birds, but you have to drive for an hour to see them. In Tanzania, you have to walk only ten minutes. It's cool coming here though. I've seen some waders today that I've seen on the Tanzanian coast – whimbrels, black-tailed godwits...'

Keith alerted his class to a sharp-tailed sandpiper 'just to the left of that stick'. There were quite a few sticks out on the shell bank, and over four thousand birds. The high tide pushed them closer to the shore, to the birdwatchers who peered through their telescopes and then sat down to consult the field guide.

There was a pathologist from Rotorua, and a brisk elderly woman from Papakura who said, 'I've seen things today I never thought I'd see.' Christoph and Tamara Wehrmueller were on holiday from Basel in Switzerland. 'Owls,' Christoph said. 'We get a lot of owls. Raptors – eagles, vultures. Crows, and ten species of raven.' It was their third visit to New Zealand. 'Birds,' Tamara said, 'are always the theme of our trip.' Back home, they stay in touch with New Zealand by subscribing to the centre's newsletter. 'We read everything and keep every copy.' The newsletters are filed by Christoph, who works as a university librarian.

As manager at the centre's office, Keith keeps a tidy ship. There wasn't a crumb anywhere in the vicinity of the six-slice Woodson toaster. The centre also has dormitory rooms and a library. There are guides to the birds of Britain, Japan, the West Indies. There are seven volumes of the Oxford *Handbook of Australian, New Zealand and Antarctic Birds* (*Volume five: Tyrant-flycatchers to Chats*). Naturally, there are copies of the 1966 *A Field Guide to the Birds of New Zealand*, co-authored by Dick Sibson, whom everyone knew as Sib. A tall well-built man with an urbane manner, he taught classics at King's College. He would read a line by Virgil about swans alighting on a lake and ask, 'Now, what species of swan did Virgil have in mind? There are three possibilities...'

Sib first saw Miranda in 1941, first saw the amazing sight of bar-tailed godwits, wrybills, oystercatchers and other waders parading on the shell bank. He bicycled from Auckland. Later trips were made with Ross McKenzie, who drove despite losing a leg in the First World War and suffering badly from shell shock. The author note in McKenzie's 1972 book *In Search of Birds in New Zealand* reads: 'After graduating from the bird-nesting of his early years, Ross McKenzie did a little game-bird shooting before going to France in 1916 in search of bigger game. He barely survived.'

Together, Sib and Ross inspired a generation of birders. One was Beth Brown, the first person to raise the notion of building some kind of lodge at Miranda. Stuart Chambers, in *The Story of the Miranda Naturalists' Trust*, writes that the idea came to her on a summer's day in 1973 'with an immense tide which brought in the birds and held them for ages'.

The idea spread. A trust was formed, funds raised. Richard Adams, the British author of the best-selling novel *Watership Down*, donated the proceeds of a public lecture; his book had been based on the research findings of trust member Ronald Lockley, related in his not-at-all-best-selling publication *The Private Life of the Rabbit*. The trust made good money from Adams' talk. When the novelist returned a few years later they repeated the exercise but it was a flop – door takings were only $93, minus $27.50 for expenses.

Efforts continued. The centre was finally opened in September 1990. It is now firmly established as a mecca for local and international birders. The birds ignore it all and just keep arriving. Thousands of Arctic waders return from Alaska and Siberia every spring. Knots, turnstones, plovers, sandpipers and, most famously, the bar-tailed godwits romp through the mudflats alongside less-travelled birds such as black-billed gulls, dotterels, wrybills and royal spoonbills. It's one of New Zealand's greatest sights.

The pleasure is all Keith Woodley's, day in, day out. 'I've succumbed to the passion that besets people who spend too much time around shorebirds,' he said. 'It just grabs hold of you and won't let go.'

It irks him that the local council has put up a road sign that reads SEABIRD COAST. He went with a colleague to ask them to change it to SHOREBIRD COAST. Keith, who has an abiding interest in military history, said, 'We were repulsed with heavy losses.' He added, 'They thought we were being pedantic, of all things.'

He has lived for the past 16 years in a cottage beside the centre, a kind of artist in residence. On a table in the cottage he paints gentle, careful watercolours of birds. He won't have a TV in the house. His CD collection includes Bob Dylan and Townes Van Zandt – he had arranged a lift to Auckland that week to see Steve Earle in concert. He was born in Invercargill, studied politics and history at Victoria. He said, 'I may have reached the northern limit of my range.'

Actually, he travelled north of almost no north in 2008, when he flew to Alaska and camped out for twelve weeks to study the same bar-tailed godwits that roost at Miranda every spring and summer. His book about the epic migration is called *Godwits: Long-haul Champions*.

I visited him at the cottage on a Friday night. We ate fish and chips, and he talked about camping out on the Alaskan tundra and seeing the first godwit arrive on May 6. 'A single male came in at about five-thirty in the evening. That was a big moment for me – watching a godwit arrive over its breeding ground, having come all the way probably from New Zealand.' Winter snow and ice gradually cleared and countless flocks of birds began arriving. Keith talked about the flattened tundra landscape, its mosaic of lichens and cranberries, its sedge meadows, the huge swathes of bleached logs carried down the Yukon River.

Sooner or later all birdwatchers catch hold of a sentence that sounds as if they're talking in their sleep. When Keith spoke of a research trip he took to Europe on the way home from Alaska, he said, 'I went to Vienna specifically to see a godwit that had been dead for 204 years.'

The bright light, the shell banks as glaring as snow, the pale misty view of the Coromandel ranges over the water, the wide estuarine tide mooching in and out over the mud… Were any creatures moving, apart from birds? Kingfishers perched on flame trees surrounding the cemetery. Miranda holds the promise of a long life: Betty Wills died at 91, Una Harris at 92, Janet Frederick at 93, Sylvia Graham at 94. There was another suggestion that Miranda existed as a kind of wonderland: one gravestone was marked LEWIS CARROLL.

Miranda used to have a post office, a school and a cheese factory. It still has hot pools and a holiday park. There is a stall in front of an organic orchard. 'This place used to be littered with orchards,' Annie Wilson said. 'I'm the last one.' She talked about returning to New Zealand after living in Seattle for fifteen years. 'It was a terrific culture shock,' she said. 'My work in this world is to convert all the dairy farmers in New Zealand to organics before they completely destroy the soil and the rivers. It's dirty dairying around here, I'm afraid. I hate to say it but it's phenomenal greed. They can't squeeze any more out of the ground. They'll go to the wall, most of them.'

Her speech was interrupted by a neighbour who dropped in for a cup of green tea. 'This is Ben,' Annie said. 'He built the loo.' I shook hands with a merry Dutchman. Ben Beemsterboer asked if I would like to look at his loo. We walked around the back of the section. He'd built it with bricks. I was carrying a glass of Annie's delicious organic apple and grapefruit juice. I took a long drink and looked at Ben. He said, 'Do you get it? It's a brick shithouse.'

It was time to leave. The closest village was Kaiaua, which had a fish and chip shop and a pub. In the early 1990s a nutcase shot and killed the publican. A man at the door said, 'What the hell did you do that for?' He was shot and killed too. The nutcase was murdered a year later in Pāremoremo Prison.

This story was told by Jack Hema in his motorhome called ON THE MOOVE. 'Come on in,' he said. ON THE MOOVE was parked alongside 27 other motorhomes on a reserve known as Ray's Rest. The collection looked like a travelling circus. Keith Woodley once counted 93 motorhomes during a Queen's Birthday Weekend, a record. The parking fee: nothing.

Who were these migrant waders? With their fold-up dining tables, their awnings, their solar panels, their Freeview TV boxes, pot plants and terrible novels, they represented middle New Zealand on the fringes, fantastically social, fanatically house-proud, wading in leisure.

They were also public enemies. The line-up of motorhomes was my first encounter with the species who would become known as freedom campers. Their fame and notoriety increased during my travels. They cropped up everywhere, attracting headlines and statistics. Motorhome users doubled in the past decade to 110,000 international visitors and 40,000 New Zealanders, but they said they weren't the same as freedom campers. The issue was shit, and how it was stored. Motorhome users shat in their own nest. Freedom campers drove vans and shat on the side of the road. Motorhome owners, said the president of the New Zealand Motor Caravan Association, were responsible Kiwis. Freedom campers 'should be shot'. Being burnt alive was another option: in Nelson a man tried to set a campervan on fire while a couple slept inside it.

Motorhome owners didn't want to be lumped in with freedom campers. They just wanted to be lumped in with each other, as closely as possible, going by the way they parked up at Ray's Rest. I stepped inside ON THE MOOVE and talked to Jack Hema. He said he'd been on the road for two years. 'Was in Little Waihī recently. You been there? Pipis there. Flounders there. Good place.' His opinion of Kaiaua: 'Good. Heaps of snapper.' His plans for the following year? 'I've done the whole of the

South Island but I didn't see everything so I'm going again. Westport. It's good, that Westport.' I expected him to mention fish. He said, 'There're wekas there. You seen 'em? Awesome bird.'

Manu Taitoko and Bev Ross said, 'Come on in.' They were in their motorhome, Dolph Inn. Also, they were in love. They had met at Paeroa police station – Bev worked in the watch-house, Manu served as an officer for 24 years. They quit, sold up, and had been on the road for four years.

Manu recalled the day Dolph Inn came into their lives. 'It was at a motorhome sale. We just went to have a nosy – nothing else to do on a Sunday afternoon. By the time we came home we knew exactly what we were going to be doing.'

'It was weird,' Bev said. The moment I hopped on I thought: This feels like home. It wasn't the fanciest bus, but… yeah. Strange, eh.'

Manu went outside to check on his kitset gazebo. He had lashed it down with big hulking ropes; it looked as if it would survive a tsunami. He looked along the line of other motorhomes and said, 'We'll take a chair and walk along a bit later. You always find someone to have a drink with. Friendly people everywhere.'

Percy and Dale Edwards were in Rusty Snail. 'Come on in,' they said. They were from Whanganui and had worked in the catering business. They quit, sold up, and had been on the road for twelve months. 'Best decision we ever made,' Dale said. She writes updates of their travels on a group email called *The Rusty Report*. The report is relentlessly enthusiastic.

Sitting in the front of Rusty Snail, Percy and Dale laughed and talked about the jobs they'd had in the past year – planting grapes, staffing fairground stalls at the A&P show in Gisborne, working the night shift at the freezing works in Paeroa, where Dale was on the slaughter floor. 'I do the offal, the guts. Nothing goes to waste.' Percy said, 'My job is to cut out the diseases – pleurisy, things like that.' Where to next? 'Whichever way the bus is pointed,' Percy said. 'Sometimes we flip a coin: north or south?'

Dale said, 'So many people, other motorhome owners, have said their only regret is not doing this before.' Percy said, 'Yeah, it's a skins holiday.' What? 'Spend the Kids' Inheritance Now.'

Outside, five white-faced herons poked for food in the mudflats. You could hear skylarks and oystercatchers, and inevitably there was a pair of spur-winged plovers. They were fighting off an Australasian harrier in the air – it was probably circling over a nest. 'The closest interest I'd had in birds was KFC and muttonbirds,' Dale said, 'but since coming to Miranda and seeing the godwits – oh, man. I'm absolutely intrigued. Do you know how far those birds come? It's amazing.'

A fine sea-spray mist smudged the view of the Coromandel. It felt as though the bright light in the sky and on the water would never go out. An immense tide brought in the birds and held them. Everywhere, birds. Around late March the godwits would leave Miranda for Alaska.

# 08 SCOTT BASE
## SMOKING IN ANTARCTICA

The first sign of life I encountered when I got inside the low long tunnel of Scott Base was a mohawk. It was attached to a Scotsman. It took me a while to put the two together.

Outside was the frozen white nightmare of Antarctica, with all its incredible geologies and absolute detachment from civilisation. On the day I arrived it was minus five degrees, which the natives considered benign. The sky was entirely blue. The sun glared on two mountains. There was Erebus – in Greek mythology, the god of Darkness and son of Chaos. The other, smaller mountain went by the less threatening name of Terror.

New Zealand clings to Scott Base as its presence in Antarctica, and Scott Base clings to the hard black edge of Ross Island. The base operates as a fridge in reverse: the cold is trapped on the other side of the door. Once inside, you feel as though you are in an underground tunnel. It feels subversive and exciting, but after a while the walls seem to close in. I estimated it took about seventeen seconds.

Fortunately, I located the door that led to the smoking deck. It offered a view of the frozen sea. Currents form a pressure ridge close to the shore, forcing up the ice in spectacular and mesmerising shapes, as though a surf wave is about to crash with a hiss and a roar but remains suspended. The sea under a thick lid of ice, the wind and the cold and the silence – awe is compulsory, but I opted out. The standard line about Antarctica is that it's beautiful. I have no idea how that standard line came about. Antarctica was as awesome as death. Antarctica looks as though it's in a state of shock. It looks like Hell has frozen over. Day after day, it looks like a cold day in Hell. In short, it's hell.

It may be the case that I had misgivings about Antarctica. A few days before I left – flights operate from Christchurch, on fat, rumbling Hercules aircraft – I'd said to a friend, 'I'm worried that I might fall into a deep–'

'Crevasse?'

'No, depression.'

It was the thought of all that wide white waste. It was worse than I thought. Antarctica obliterated signs of life, annihilated it; the whole stupid, merciless place was a vacant lot. The very best description of the sullen planet was recorded in December 1773. Cook's second voyage took him south in search of the Unknown Southern Continent; his passengers included Hitihiti, a young aristocratic islander from Ra'iatea who hitched a ride on the *Resolution*. He toured New Zealand. He didn't like it much. He was in for worse as Cook left Queen Charlotte Sound and crossed the Antarctic Circle.

Historian Anne Salmond provides a wonderful account of Hitihiti's polar exploration in her book *Aphrodite's Island*. 'On December 12 at 62 degrees south,' she writes, 'Hitihiti saw his first iceberg. During his visit to New Zealand he had gathered a bundle of little sticks, one for each island they had visited since leaving Ra'iatea. … Now he added another stick for this "bright star", which he described as "white, evil, useless".'

Among the happiest sights I saw in my fortnight was morning tea at Scott Base. About a dozen men steamed up a small room with their mugs of tea and coffee, and crowded around a magnificent plate of freshly made sausage rolls. You can take New Zealanders out of New Zealand, but we had arrived at the ends of the Earth and immediately colonised it. We were domestic, suburban, worshippers of tea leaf and pastry, happy to while away the hours at indoor pastimes – all that fortnight, person or persons unknown worked in silence in the library, patiently piecing together a thousand-piece jigsaw of hot-air balloons floating in summer skies.

There was a social divide between the university scientists and the ground staff of carpenters and electricians. In summer the population at Scott Base hovers around 85 when academics arrive to measure, monitor, sift, sample, prod and poke the continent. I rarely saw them have anything to do with the working guys. They spoke a different language and kept their hair on. As well as Alan Williamson, the mohawked engineer from Dundee who now lives in Dunedin, four other ground staff had taken a razor to their heads. Chris Knight, a mechanic from Palmerston North, had chosen to scalp the back of his.

A core of ten ground staff would stay on after the last flight of the season left at the end of February. Their tour of duty would last for thirteen months. 'Wintering over is the reward for summer,' Alan said. The working week goes down from six days to five; when the last plane leaves, the roller doors on the bar go up and stay up. Sixteen more staff would soon be arriving to winter over, and Alan wondered whether it would create a split camp of two tribes – the core who all knew each other, and the fresh faces. 'It could be a bit like *Survivor*.'

Chris Knight would notch up one thousand nights on the ice. 'It's my third winter and my last,' he said. 'I don't want to get institutionalised.' He talked about the drag of routines. 'Breakfast served at the same time, lunch at the same time. The trick is to keep your own pace, otherwise it can be a long winter. I've seen people walking around the base at two a.m. looking like zombies. They just couldn't cope with it.'

In summer, the Antarctic observes an exaggerated version of daylight saving. The sun sets in February. After it creaks below the horizon in April, the continent experiences weeks of midnight black. Chris Knight was auditioning for the great New Zealand understatement when he said, 'June is definitely pretty dark.'

Damian Thorn, who would winter over as base cook, was looking forward to that. 'I can't wait until it gets dark. I hate the sun. This constant sunlight is doing my head in, to say the least.'

It also did his head in to work a 17.5 hour shift to prepare a dinner at Scott Base in honour of Prince Albert of Monaco. The principality had signed up to the Antarctic Treaty and the monarch had decided to tour all 27 bases on the continent. I saw him after his meal – a short, tired man who spoke with an American accent. Thorn could be found on the smoking deck, biting down on a cigarette at midnight, in the full glare of that cursed sun. The next day he was given the wrong numbers for lunch and had to face diners holding empty plates, and that morning there was a mad rush to supply packed meals for a departing flight – no one had notified the kitchen. He was not pleased. Outside, there was the terrible poetry of the mystical, ancient Antarctic; inside, there was the actual stuff of life.

It was a happy ship, run with generosity, kindness and humour. Scott Base operates as a government agency, set up to provide scientific access with minimal environmental impact. It runs on a tight annual budget of eleven million dollars. Ground staff suffer the usual joyless dictates of OSH – Occupational Safety and Health – and put in long hours. After work, they get outside, skiing, climbing, opening themselves to the amazingness of the elements. They sometimes received unexpected gifts – a hike up Mount Aurora led to the discovery of a discarded 35-kilogram jet rocket. It was nabbed, put in a backpack, and taken back to base to send home for conversion into a potbelly stove.

Country music pitched its high, warm, lonesome sound throughout the base, courtesy of Steve Locke, a Telecom technician from Christchurch who operated the radio station, among his various duties. He first came to Scott Base in 1999 'to upgrade for Y2K. We all knew it was cobblers but who'd turn down a trip like that?' He had prior experience of living in obscure corners of the Earth: in 1984 he had gone to the Chathams for six months and stayed thirteen years. This was his third summer at Scott Base and his eighth visit but he wasn't game to winter over. 'There's a saying here. The first time you do winter is for the experience. The second is for money. The third is because you don't fit in anywhere else.'

And then he quoted another saying. 'Americans come here for booze and we go there for sex.' He meant the Americans over the hill at McMurdo Station. He added, 'There's probably more action when people come in for events.' He meant the scientists who arrived for field trips. You had to watch your step on Scott Base; according to legend, the shared dormitory bedrooms meant private assignations were held in the library, the drying room, the first aid room. For most, though, sex conformed to the governing ethic of Antarctica: absence. No night, no trees, no humidity, no scent, no TV or cellphone reception, no hunting, no fishing, and – most artificial of all – no children, anywhere.

All else was the presence of nature, the weather and, possibly, God. At the terribly pretty Chapel of the Snows at McMurdo, I found Wellington priest Father Phil Cody. 'A lot of people get involved in a spirituality down here,' he said. 'They are struck by the awesomeness of the place, and also its isolation – they need something to sustain them.' I asked how many people attended Sunday service. 'Fifteen,' he said. McMurdo has a population of about a thousand.

God was in Hell. Death had dominion. You saw it every morning from Scott Base, looking upon Erebus, knowing what happened there. As Mike White wrote in *North & South* magazine, 'We don't even say "Mount", we leave out "plane" and "crash" and just say "Erebus" and everyone knows what we mean.' It didn't look much from Scott Base, just a small white lump. From the air in a helicopter it looked vast and awful. Even that close you couldn't comprehend the impact and the horror of what happened there at 12.49 p.m. on November 28, 1979. In his Royal Commission report into the annihilation of all 257 people on board Air New Zealand flight TE901, Justice Peter Mahon was moved to describe Antarctica as a 'white silence'.

I have a copy of the report I bought second-hand. The previous owner had left in it a clipping from the *Listener* – a column by Tom Scott, published on May 16, 1981 in response to Mahon's shocking report, which blamed Air New Zealand for the tragedy. 'The frailty of human judgement is a persistent, if unwitting, theme to the Royal Commission findings,' Scott wrote. And then, with some prescience: 'Mahon's central conclusion just might be subject to the same frailty.'

Air New Zealand has always refused to accept any blame. It also refused to apologise to families of the victims until Mike White's *North & South* cover story appeared in November 2009, headlined: 'Erebus: No peace, no apologies, no end to grief. Will the 30th anniversary be any different?' A week after the magazine went on sale, Air New Zealand got around to answering the question: it apologised to the families.

Swedish vessel *Oden*, regarded as the world's best icebreaker, docked at McMurdo. It was a big brutal thing that coughed black smoke and added to the impression that this corner of America in a foreign field looked like a dark satanic mill. It took about an hour to walk there, up and over the hill from Scott Base. There was something intensely satisfying about being able to walk from New Zealand to America. It would have felt even more intensely satisfying were it not for the sheer agony of walking for an hour in the cold air, which made you feel ten years older with every step.

McMurdo turned out to be a lively dump of a place, roaring with heavy machinery and boasting three bars, a Wells Fargo ATM, and an excellent library. Scott Base's library was desultory – old rubbish like *Death is Late to Lunch* by someone called Theodore DuBois, new rubbish such as the biography of a newsreader, Angela D'Audney. McMurdo's library was generously stocked with titles by Haruki Murakami and Robert Fisk; it had a complete set of *Granta*. It also had a librarian, a beautiful girl with dark hair and glasses, who looked like Lisa Loeb. The quietness in the library had a softer, lovelier quality than Antarctica's white silence. The rooms were dark. There was a couch. Outside, friendly and enormous Americans waddled the dusty streets. The first guy I met was smoking a cigarette as he crossed the road. I told him that smoking was permissible at Scott Base only on a narrow smoking deck. He smiled and said, 'Welcome to the land of the free.'

I spent a lot of time at McMurdo. It had a smoking room. It had a very big cafeteria that did chicken pie, chicken and lentil stew, and barbecued chicken, but the South Polar skuas tore down on anyone foolish enough to attempt a takeaway chicken. Other main food groups such as popcorn marshmallows were on offer. But protein was in short supply: no one had solved the audacious Christmas theft of 250 kilograms of steak.

There was so much of everything else. McMurdo had more people than Scott Base, and there was more of them, with their big American necks and their big American bottoms, taking up room with their big American confidence. Returning home to Scott Base was a reminder of modest and droll New Zealandness. The buffet trays in the dining room at lunch one day were marked SAUSAGES, SAUSAGE PIE, SAUSAGE PASTA and CHICKEN CURRY WITH SAUSAGES. The salad selection was marked NO SAUSAGES.

Craig Cary, an American professor of biological science at Waikato University, greeted his overnight guests at his camp in the Dry Valleys on the mainland of Antarctica and immediately asked, 'Where are the frozens?' He meant the box of frozen meat, bread and cheese. The helicopter had left without delivering it.

'This is third time it's happened,' Cary said. He recounted the history of the two previous failures, then said, 'I mean, shoot! We had three chillibins of beer came in from McMurdo. One of the guys asked and in it dropped. No problem. But what do we have to do to get frozens out of Scott Base? They keep promising and nothing happens. Nothing. It's bad for morale. It ain't right.' And so on, a litany of complaint about another Antarctic absence – no frozen food in a frozen continent.

Cary talked a lot, about everything. As well as giving detailed impromptu lectures on his project in the Dry Valleys, he delivered a dissertation on Germany's military advance on Russia in the Second World War. I can't remember whether this subject occupied his thoughts during the trek past a frozen lake to locate a mummified seal, or whether it was on the five-hour round journey to the top of a steep ridge to inspect the fabulous and grotesque shapes caused by the wind in rocks known as ventifacts.

'I think you've got a pretty good handle on what it is we're doing here,' he said to me. I didn't. I'd lost the plot of his 'important study'. Meaning had got buried beneath his load of words. All I knew was that it was international, led by Waikato, and had something to do with a great many cross-discipline Earth scientists studying microscopic life in the arid desert of the Dry Valleys.

Cary took samples of earth beneath the seal. There were another 500 sites where his team scratched around in the soil. Walking inside a large blue tent, I found scientists from universities in South Africa, England, Australia and New Zealand quietly sorting through ten-centimetre bottles of collected soil samples while listening to *The Dark Side of the Moon*. As well as lichens, algae and various assorted bacteria, the organisms under inspection were springtails, the largest terrestrial animals in Antarctica. They are two millimetres in length and lie dormant 300 days of the year.

I couldn't wait to leave the Dry Valleys but it was heartbreaking to leave Cape Bird. I went there with Kerry Barton of Landcare Research, who was monitoring a colony of Adélie penguins. A helicopter flew around Erebus and touched down on a rocky beach. A lot of steps led up a cliff to a two-bedroom hut.

I came to look on the hut as a luxury resort. It was built in 1966 by carpenters Ray Greeks of Lower Hutt and Roger Bartlett of Warrington, Otago, who survived an Antarctic storm there and wrote in the logbook, 'The roar of the wind and rattle of stones on the walls...' Later, back in New Zealand, I got an email from Greeks, who now lives in the Far North; he wrote as though the Antarctic storm were still howling around his ears.

'We flew all the gear up in three loads and as the chopper departed for the final time we could see bad weather brewing to the south. We worked furiously for many hours, levelling the site, erecting the walls in order to get the tie-downs in place before the storm hit.

'We had a pile of plywood sheets for interior lining, all nicely pre-cut and painted; we stood two full 44-gallon drums of kerosene on top of these to stop them blowing away. By the time we had the tie-downs drilled into the rock it was nearly impossible to stand up outside, so we grabbed a box of tucker and hunkered down inside.

'We were looking out the window as one shrieking gust came through to see our full fuel drums picked up like they were empty and just disappear. Plywood sheets filled the air like confetti. We never ever found a trace of either them or the drums again.'

When Greeks returned to New Zealand, he went hunting with Bartlett in Te Anau. 'I met his sister, married her in 1967, and am still happily married today. We have just had a great three weeks at Rakaia fishing, with Roger joining us, so the friendship forged in that stormy environment has lasted as well as the hut obviously has.'

The hut was snug and warm and solid. Kerry Barton, as an old Antarctic hand, supervised the laying down of provisions, established radio contact, and got the stove working. We were a party of five. We drank tea at the dining table in front of the hut windows with a view of the beach, icebergs and grey sea. Penguins fished in the water and hitched rides on ice floes. Skuas performed dazzling swoops high in the air.

'I have a surprise for you,' Kerry said. She led our party out of the hut and along a walkway to the top of a mound. The scene below was outrageous: a colony of fifty thousand pairs of squawking, gargling, hooting, barking penguins sitting in their pink-hued excrement of krill in a valley formed by a glacier that stood in the sea. A colony of fifty thousand penguins makes a lot of noise. The constant din, the unbelievable numbers of birds – they were everywhere. The colony went for miles, along the beach and up the valleys, stuck there, flightless.

Soft, furry, gormless, the chicks had nearly fledged, and stood – or slept together face-down – in protective crèches. The protection was from the only bird of flight. The penguins had strength in numbers, but it was their only strength. South Polar skuas were their worst nightmare and they lived that nightmare every second. Closely related to gulls, skuas are monogamous, have a life expectancy of 35 years (one banded skua at another cape on the island has reached 40), and can fly vast distances:

Scott saw a skua on his doomed expedition to the South Pole, making it the most southern bird in the world. In winter it migrates as far away as the North Atlantic, to feed and sleep entirely at sea. It's large, with a lightly tan body, a sharp hooked black bill, and webbed feet that it uses to scoop up krill. In summer its other main source of food are penguins.

To walk through the valley of Adélie penguins was to walk through a valley of death. The ground was a boneyard: every step revealed another headless skeleton of an annihilated penguin, only its three-toed feet and flippers uneaten. This, surely, was Hell, preserved through the ages. For an updated version, I watched the final seven minutes of a penguin's life. Two skua had succeeded in isolating it from the crèche and the adults. One skua planted a foot on the chick's head and plucked out its feathers. The other bird ate it from behind. The chick beat at its assassins with its flippers, but it may have felt like just a gentle caress. On and on they ate it alive, and continued eating it when it finally, mercifully, stopped moving.

'Cape Bird is about the best place anywhere in Antarctica to study penguins versus skuas,' Euan Young said. Like Ray Greeks, Euan wrote to me after I returned from Antarctica; like Greeks he was familiar with the huts and the cape, where he worked as one of the world's leading researchers of Adélie penguins. 'As you saw, it is possible to sit above them and record their lives so perfectly with minimal disturbance.'

Yes. From one of his scientific papers: 'Twenty-five hours' observation of foraging skuas was carried out, in which 42 attacks on penguin chicks were recorded, and over 40 feedings observed. ... Feeding was a desperately frantic business with the head and neck buried within the carcass to gobble up the soft internal flesh. ... In some cases, skuas were drenched with blood over the forehead, neck and breast...'

As well as skuas vs. penguins, Young has observed skuas vs. skuas. 'Siblicide is the major cause of chick mortality. ... Very few survive more than ten days. ... In five seasons at Cape Bird, monitoring approx. 250 pairs each year, only three pairs of chicks survived.'

I had stood for about 15 minutes watching the two skua eat the penguin chick. Feedings were going on all over the shop – in the centre of the colony and at the margins, skuas were attacking lone chicks, greasing their heads with young blood.

I kept watching. I watched in the days and I watched last thing at night. I was happy. It was here at last, on a beach beside a glacier, among fifty thousand pairs of penguins shitting pasty pinkish krill, among skuas getting on with the 'frantic business' of eating penguins alive, among New Zealanders who carried on the work performed by other New Zealanders for nearly 50 years, that I knew peace.

# 09 APIA NEIGHBOURS

What happened on my first night in Samoa is that I got bitten by a wild dog, so next day I decided to call on the prime minister to ask what he was going to do about it.

The dog had been lean and swift, and had made a bad first impression, especially on my leg. My appointment with the dog had been sudden and short. I waited three hours to see Prime Minister Tuilaepa Lupesoliai Sailele Malielegaoi. His office was on the top floor of the only tall structure in downtown Apia, but how to get inside the building? The glass doors at the front wouldn't open. I angrily shook the handles and glared at a man sitting inside the lobby. He glared back and angrily shook his head. He shouted something I couldn't hear through the glass. He walked slowly towards the doors and pointed at a handwritten piece of paper Sellotaped to the glass. It directed visitors to elevators in the ground-floor car park.

The elevators in the ground-floor car park were beside a stall selling cream doughnuts and pineapple pies. The stairwell was blocked by an old metal safe with a sheet thrown over it. There were vacant spaces beneath parking signs reserved for the deputy prime minister, the minister of natural resources and other government officials, but the attorney general had come to work – there was his big shining Toyota Hi-Lux 3.0, with its licence plate AG01.

A man sat with his legs wide apart on a hard wooden chair inside the elevator. This didn't leave a lot of room, and it seemed rude to travel in silence in the intimate box. 'How are you today?' I asked. 'Busy, uh,' he said. He was very good at pushing the button. He made it look easy.

That was at two o'clock on Friday afternoon. I didn't have an appointment to see Prime Minister Tuilaepa Lupesoliai Sailele Malielegaoi. I had something more powerful: a grievance. My leg throbbed. I limped out of the elevator. A man sat behind a desk. There was a sign above his head on the wall with an arrow and the words PRIME MINISTER. I hobbled towards the sign but stopped in my tracks when I caught the view from the large bay windows, the wide blue yonder of Apia Bay. There was so much of it that it looked as though it could be the entire Pacific. There was more of it than sky.

I eyed it with wild surmise. What was out there, beyond the sea, over the horizon? What promised land glittered, signalled, lured, over the rainbow? New Zealanders look to Australia for that answer; Samoans look to New Zealand.

Where there's a Pacific Islander in New Zealand, there's a statistic. In 1921 there were 164 Samoans in New Zealand. In 2006 there were 131,103, more than half the total population of Pacific Islanders in New Zealand. The browning of New Zealand continues: it is officially estimated that by 2051 sixteen percent of children under fifteen will be European, 30 percent Māori, and 33 percent Pacific Island.

One final statistic: more than half of New Zealand's Samoan population live in South Auckland. All I needed to do to go to Samoa was catch a bus, but I had decided to go the long way round and fly to Apia.

It was the end of the wet season. Muddy water collected in the potholes and slowed traffic to a bumpy crawl of about 35 kilometres an hour. Samoa was lush and squelchy, gorgeous to behold with its coral reef and blue lagoon, its plantations of taro and coconut. I stayed on the main island of Upolu. The other island, Savai'i, was just beyond the reef.

The *Lady Samoa II* passenger and car ferry left from a wharf near the airport. I wandered over on Sunday afternoon to have a look at the boat, with its two yellow chimneys. Motorists queued at the wharf, and now and then got out of their cars and strolled across the road to buy a cold drink. Earlier, for about two hours from midday, the heat had chased everyone on the island into shade. The roads had been even emptier than in the morning, when the churches opened for singing and business. God is a nosy, constant presence in Samoa. A sign at the ferry terminal shop read GOD BLESS THE HAND THAT GIVES TO THE POOR. I needed a cold drink. The most delicious and also the cheapest on offer – for two tala, just over one New Zealand dollar – was a coconut. It took up room in the fridge alongside Coke and Fanta.

Nutty, palmy Samoa. In downtown Apia, dragonflies touched pink and gracious water lilies on the surface of an open drain. There were stores specialising in providing supplies for the popular drug of bingo. There were a lot of buses – old, brightly painted jalopies that bounced up and down like toys on a trampoline. There were a lot of taxis, churches, barefoot children, and empty coconut shells scattered on the side of the road. There was a lot of diabolical food cooking in large vats at roadside stalls – chop suey, mutton curry, soup bones. There was one McDonald's, packed at lunchtime; its nod to local cuisine was the Samoan Burger. At 17.80 tālā it had 'everything', which possibly included mutton curry.

There was a lot of gold and black – the colours of Western Union's money transfer bank. Just about every village had a branch to handle the $128.2 million of remittance money sent to Samoa by families who had emigrated to New Zealand. 'Remittance money' – it was a difficult piece of English but every Samoan had mastered it. It accounts for 24 percent of Samoa's GDP and is the country's biggest source of income.

There were a lot of dogs. I didn't see the one that went for me until it was too late. I didn't see the one that went for me because it was dark, about ten o'clock at night, and the dog barked once, from beneath a tree, then ran out fast, its jaws open like scissors.

Sending Samoans to New Zealand is a trade. I knocked on the door of a travel agency in a dimly lit shopping arcade in Apia and talked with a consultant, Lotu Auapaau. Slender, welcoming, 22 years old, he said he dealt on average with three people moving to New Zealand every week. Right now, though, he was waiting to see a family who just wanted to fly over to attend a wedding. They'd already paid for the fare from Apia to Auckland. 'Most people pay one way and get their family in New Zealand to buy their return ticket.'

I asked when the family was due to see him. 'I don't know.' How long would he wait? Lotu wore a red T-shirt and smiled happily. 'If they don't turn up,' he said, 'I'll just sit here and watch people walk past.' How long had he already waited? He said, 'I expected them to come in yesterday.'

The linoleum floor had peeled away like an orange skin, and his pamphlets included a stained and tattered copy of *Life in Australia*, published in 2007. Yes, Lotu smiled, he'd been to New Zealand. 'I went there on 3 April, 2008.' The date lit up his face. His first thought on seeing Auckland: 'Wow.' He was there for two years as a volunteer for the Mormon Church, knocking on doors from ten a.m. to nine p.m. in Henderson, Ōtara, Manurewa and Waterview. It was strange listening to him recite the names of unglamorous Auckland suburbs with real enthusiasm in his office in tropical Apia. He was so fervent. 'I love New Zealand,' he said. Why? He thought about it, smiled with even more enthusiasm, and said, 'It's the best for food, uh. I miss the Chinese takeaways. KFC! Oh, man.'

I left Lotu's offices and headed for water. 'I rest,' Lealafia Tolai said. He was sitting by himself in a lovely green reserve by Apia's sea wall. 'On 13 September this year I am fifty-two. Is too old, uh.' He had a heavily bandaged foot and was blind in one eye. He wore an All Blacks cap. 'A souvenir from one of my uncles. He go New Zealand.' He took it off and stroked it, loving his only possession. It was early in the morning. What was he going to do all day? He said, 'I rest.'

Further along the sea wall I was apprehended by 20-year-old Asofa Suti. 'Don't miss this one chance,' she nagged, over and over, as she harped on about the wonders of the Samoa Worship Centre Church. Her manner was sharper and more anxious than anyone I met in Samoa; in fact, she was an American Samoan.

She was with two 18-year-old girls from Apia, Hattesah Saseve Sellsin and Leala Kaisara, both born-again, both lovely and happy and round-figured. Asofa was thin-lipped, unsmiling, unhappy. 'This is a bad place,' she said. She meant Apia, with its beautiful harbour, its two or three sets of traffic lights, its boisterous nightclubs. 'Drinking. Smoking.' What else? Hattesah and Leala giggled but Asofa, pious and simmering beneath the coconut trees, ignored the question and opened her bible.

I had cause to remember her a few days later when I stopped and talked to Isaac Warren, 29, who was sweeping leaves from the mango tree in his front yard. His kids played at his feet. Their names – Benedict and Nelda Andronicus – were clues to his mania. 'Right now I'm clean because I gave my life to Christ,' he said. 'I tell you, sir, it was either die or go to jail for me. I'm telling you this from my heart, uh. When I drink, I destroy everything. Very bad. Violent. I was working as bartender. I was in fight. An accident happen to me. I use sepalu.' He put down his broom, picked up his bush knife, and swished it through the air. 'Oh, man. I nearly am sent to jail. But my wife was telling me the good news, uh. And then I listen and have been saved for two years now. Do you know the Worship Centre Church?'

The biggest news story of the week was the appearance of anonymous pamphlets, billboards and newspaper ads stating that the Second Coming was just around the corner. The end, yet again, was nigh. Or, as the front page of *The Sunday Samoan* put it: HOW WORLD WILL END?

The exact date being put about was May 21, 2011. The alarmist was apparently Christian fanatic Harold Camping, 89, of Colorado. Camping's prophecy was the subject of sermons throughout Samoa. Ministers sought to soothe their anxious congregations. I went to hear Reverend Nu'uausala Siaosi Si'utaia at the downtown Apia Protestant Church. He called his sermon 'Resurrection of the Dead'. He advised against panic. He called for reason. He said there was work to do. Last Sunday the church had collected $2,026; today's target was $3,300.

How did parishioners afford to give as much as a tālā? When I ambled into the waiting room in the prime minister's department I met

Sina Setefano, 49, and Grete Purcell, 21. The two women had been at a job interview. The position was for a cashier. It paid an annual salary of 7,000 tālā. 'I wish, I wish I get the job,' said the voluptuous Grete. 'I live in village in the east. We lose eight people in the tsunami. My nephew. Only three. So sad.' A panel of three government officials had conducted the interview. How did she think she had got on? She said, 'Ahhhh! I was panic.'

Sina, the older woman, who lived on Savai'i, was calm, mature, sad. I asked about her New Zealand accent. She said her parents had sent her to Lower Hutt when she was ten, and she had been adopted by a Presbyterian minister and his wife. 'I miss New Zealand. I call it my home.' She talked with real feeling about Panmure.

What was she doing back in Samoa? 'I left my husband. He had an affair with a girl in Wellington. I couldn't have children. But I came back because my mum was sick. I look after her. Poor Mum! But it's hard for me to live the village life,' she said. 'It's difficult. Very difficult.' What did she do all day? 'Good question. Well, I get up at six a.m. and cook breakfast for Mum. We have an electric oven, but the power bills are too high so I chop firewood and burn leaves to cook. Then I do the washing and...' She patted her hair. 'There are a lot of unpaid hours in a day.'

The prime minister's department was an assortment of cracked wooden desks and antique computers, and the paintwork was chipped and smudged. I followed the women downstairs. It was lunchtime and they were partial to the pineapple pies on sale in the underground car park. Through the stairwell I saw a sign for the attorney general. Remembering his Hi-Lux in the car park, I walked to his floor and asked a woman whether I could meet him. Ming Leung Wai, 37, appeared and led me to his office, past a handwritten sign that read: TODAY'S CANTEEN SPECIAL – BOWL NOODLE $3.

He was an elegant man, charming, smiling, half Chinese and half Samoan, sleekly built, with immaculate hair. We chatted about more or less absolutely nothing for ten minutes. He said he had studied at Waikato University. He reckoned he had the best job in the world. He walked to the window and pointed out his house in the hills. He said he worshipped at the Assemblies of God. Then he looked at his watch and I looked at my watch. He stood up and I stood up. Simultaneously, though, we shook hands, and as we walked back past TODAY'S CANTEEN SPECIAL I asked about the possibility of meeting Prime Minister Tuilaepa Lupesoliai Sailele Malielegaoi. He said the PM was due back in his office at two o'clock and I should come back at that time and wait. 'He sees everyone,' smiled the attorney general of Samoa.

I had a bit of time to kill before returning to have more time to kill so I mooched downtown, where I starved rather than tackle the Samoan burger, or eat at a food hall where the menu advertised something called PUMKIN MUTTON. In the waterfront reserve I made out the figure of Lealafia Tolai, still at rest; Asofa Suti and her gang of Worship Centre missionaries were nowhere to be seen. The midday heat chased me out of the sun, and soon I was in the air-conditioned offices of law firm Kruse, Enari and Barlow, talking with the office manager. Aigaga McNeely was coy about her age. I told her she couldn't have been more than forty. She immediately rang her husband to pass on this minor flattery and then she passed me the receiver. 'I'm a Kiwi,' the voice said. 'I went to Rongotai College.'

Aigaga said New Zealand was a nice place to visit but she'd never want to live there. She had lived in Australia for twelve years and been most homesick for the Samoan sense of humour. 'Typically, what happens is that someone will start with a little detail and build on it, and then someone else will add to it, and it will grow and grow, and before you know it you've totally lost the plot and the whole thing just becomes completely absurd.

'It's all in Samoan. I'll translate it for my husband, who sits there looking gloomy while we're rolling around with laughter, but it doesn't work in English.' I thought about the ex-pupil of Rongotai College puzzling over Samoan humour. 'Anyway,' she said, 'that's what I missed most in Australia. The food, no, I didn't miss the food at all. It was the chat and the laughter. That's the way we live.'

I imagined these great farces being played out as a feature of village life. She said she wasn't all that interested in village life. She gave a speech. It began, 'Okay. Here's a story. I've made my commitment to a certain kind of life; I've made my choice about it. I shouldn't be telling you. My father was an ex-prime minister.

'Okay. We grew up on Savai'i. My father had a cocoa plantation. That was his wealth. We were very advantaged as children. We had a generator – electricity, you see. We had lights! We ate with knife and fork! What I'm saying is, we were brought up palagi. We had the big Her Majesty's Voice gramophone. We had a flush toilet!

'Okay. And my father read books to us every night. We had shelves and shelves of books. We had *Treasure Island*! I don't know where he found them all. He was a gentleman, my father. We never saw or heard him beat our mother. It was a privileged life, a civilised life. So what I'm telling you is that he believed an education is more important than,' she concluded, 'this village thing.'

I spent all afternoon with her father. A photograph of Va'ai Kolone, twice voted in as prime minister of Samoa in the 1980s, stared down from the wall in an anteroom set aside for visitors waiting to see Prime Minister Tuilaepa Lupesoliai Sailele Malielegaoi. There were photos of all Samoa's prime ministers from the time the country achieved independence in 1962. The gallery ended with a portrait of Tuilaepa Lupesoliai Sailele Malielegaoi. He looked to be in his forties, dark-haired, healthy, mirthless.

The walls were done in wood panelling. There was a wilting pot plant in the corner, big, comfortable, cracked leather chairs, and a quartz clock from Japan. Two o'clock … three o'clock … four o'clock … His secretary on the tenth floor said, 'He sees everyone.'

I waited with nine businessmen who had made prior appointments. We sat in silence. The secretary opened the door and said, 'Mr Benjamin, please.' A small Indian who wore a gold watch jumped to his feet. The door closed. I wore a watch from the $2 Shop and dozed. When I woke up I was alone. I killed the next hour by rifling through a metal filing cabinet behind the pot plant. There was a request from a primary school for two additional classrooms. 'The village has access to electricity and piped water.' It asked for $58,760 from the Samoan Government Small Grant Scheme funded by the Australian Government. There was a proposal for operating a 60-cabin, double-hull, twelve-million-dollar cruise ship that had come to nothing, and a letter from a thirteen-year-old girl in Esko, Minnesota, asking for souvenirs from Samoa to present to her social studies class.

Next, I read an internal memo headlined A WORD FROM THE PUBLIC SERVICE COMMISSION. 'Following the melancholy reflection of Good Friday, many of us may still be pondering the hideous evils of the world...' It went on to recommend that public servants uplift their spirits by reading *Desiderata*. I started reading the dozy platitudes and dozed off again.

I was woken by the prime minister's secretary. She led me into a gigantic office stuffed with toys. A large white-haired character wobbled like a jelly behind a desk. Some fat men defeat age and maintain the bright smooth faces of their childhood, but this character's immense size created another illusion: he looked like a woman. I thought I might have been shown into the wrong office. Was this a set-up, an elaborate Samoan joke? Who was this overweight drag queen who signed papers and didn't look up?

I stood in front of the desk in my jandals and togs.

'Prime minister,' I said, hoping it hadn't sounded like a question.

'Uh,' he confirmed.

What happened is this: the quick brown dog went at the lazy palagi idling along a narrow street after dark and took a bite out of the back of my leg. It felt like an electric shock. I squealed like a girl, and ran away. I was staying at Eden's Edge Hotel. 'Help,' I said to the receptionist. 'Sit,' he said, and then he ran away.

I heard him talking to Mepa Apelu, the lovely funny woman who managed the motel.

'A palagi has been bitten by a wild dog!'

'What palagi?'

'A guest.'

'Where?'

'He's over there.'

'No, where was he bitten?'

'Leg.'

'How bad?'

I craned my head around the corner. Mepa, the receptionist and the cook were at the open-air bar. Smoke curled from Zap mosquito coils on the floor. Geckos fled along the ceiling.

'Bathe his wound in water.'

'Boil the water.'

'No, from the tap.'

'That's too hot!'

'Now it's too cold.'

'Salt! Add a pinch of salt.'

'Here.'

'That's too much.'

'What else?'

'Vinegar.'

'Really?'

A woman joined the conversation. I recognised her boozy voice; she was a guest, a Samoan woman staying with her eight-year-old son. They were expecting his father to arrive from Australia. While she waited she drank heavily, and screeched vile abuse at her son in the middle of the night. Another of the guests, a lesbian from Canada, gave the boy swimming lessons in the motel pool. She gave him a mask and snorkel, and he learned to dive. He was quiet, sensitive, anxious. He adored her. She was in Apia for a week. Everyone at the motel braced themselves for the boy crying his heart out when it came time for her to leave.

His horrible drunk mother said, 'What's happened?'

'A palagi has been bitten by a wild dog.'

'Where?'

'Leg.'

'No, where'd it happen?'

'Why?'

'Because you need to find the dog.'

'What for?'

'You've got to take out a hair of the dog and put it on the wound. Old Samoan remedy.'

'Okay. Is this ready? Feel.'

'No. The water's too hot.'

'Here.'

'Now it's too cold!'

'More vinegar?'

Samoa was somewhere between First World and Third World, leaning to the latter. It was rows and rows of tins of Oxford corned beef, it was St Joan of Arc Primary School, and Robert Louis Stevenson Secondary School, where the initials RLS were spelled out on a lawn in bright flowers. It was shops selling enormous dolls with white skin, taxi drivers hissing in the shadows, 'Want a girl?' and a young guy with peroxided hair sweeping banyan leaves off the pavement next to a van marked WONDERFUL TAKEAWAYS. It was the glow of leaves burning in clumps on the side of the road at night-time, and signs at the airport and throughout the island that read NO TO RAPE AND INDECENT ACTS. It was eels, roosters, dogs.

It was the loneliness of Leota Laki Sio, manager of the grandly named Galusina Village Resort on the coastal road that circled the island. You couldn't go anywhere near the water. Big waves exploded against rocks. The road was bombed with potholes. The resort had 22 rooms; when I called in it was entirely empty and Leota was sitting all alone in the restaurant. He opened the resort in May 2010. 'We're still growing. We've had our ups and downs, uh.' I asked about the ups. He said 30 people making a New Zealand film stayed at the resort for ten weeks. He pointed to a table. 'Nat Lees sat there, staring out to sea day after day.' It's possible the Auckland actor was blissed out, but it sounded more like a case of clinical depression.

There were a lot of wonderful places to stay on the beach all through Samoa. Galusina Village Resort wasn't one of them. Sio said, 'It's a different experience from the normal sand and sea resort.'

He kissed his small son good night. The boy trotted back into his house, past the resort's swimming pool, which was the size of a home pool. It *was* a home pool. Leota had built the resort on his own property. He said, 'There's room for improvement.' He needed an occupancy rate of 40 percent to begin to make a profit, but the rate was about 30 percent. The rooms were basic, there was a boring playground, and the sea smashed angrily at rocks. He said, 'It's a very nice view, peace and quiet.' He was right about it being quiet. A sign on the road advised happy hour at the resort bar between seven and nine. It wasn't happy. I left Leota sitting alone as dusk gathered around his sea-sprayed folly.

At the nearby village of Fagali'i I heard claims that Leota had built the resort with money – as much as 28 million tālā – he had won in a lottery in Australia. What did they make of the resort? 'Crazy!' Tanielu Pololua, 39, joined in the laughter. It was the sight of Pololua that had drawn me to the village. He sat in his open-air fale and washed blood off his sapelu. It was a poor village and the knife seemed to be more or less his only possession. He spoke about it with something close to reverence.

'When you got a sapelu, oh man, you can cut grass. It's a bread knife – it does all those things!'

Bits of chicken and onion were on a chopping board. 'If you don't have money,' he said, 'you have chicken. It's the cheapest.'

I asked if he had electricity.

'Yes.'

I asked if he had hot and cold water.

'No, just warm.' There was a row of about 30 beer and soft-drink bottles on the floor. His kids collected them to sell for money.

'It's good to talk,' he said. 'I've been sick the last few months.'

He breathed heavily when he talked. I asked if he had heart disease.

'No, pneumonia.'

His weight was the elephant in the fale, so I asked how much he weighed.

'I think it's 468,' he said.

He wore a lavalava and no shirt. The lavalava revealed the classic build of a sumo wrestler, even two sumo wrestlers. But he was also a matai, a chief, with gentle eyes and a soft voice, and I thought of him as holy. His five young children crowded around him, eager for his touch. He picked them up like kittens and stroked their arms. I asked what he wanted them to achieve in life.

'To serve God,' he said.

The womanly prime minister was hospitable and rambling. We chatted about more or less absolutely nothing for 20 minutes. Just to get things rolling I remarked that Samoa's situation seemed perfectly hopeless.

'Well,' he said, 'there are always ways people can earn more and make a future for their children, but a lot of people don't know or understand how to work the land. I know why people go to New Zealand. A salary is an attraction for them. But what a lot of people don't know is that there are lots of outgoings to life in New Zealand. There are church commitments, remittance money to send home, bills. People say children can get a better education in New Zealand. But you can get the same education in Samoa. People say there's a higher standard of living in New Zealand. But I encourage them to stay here and develop Samoa. We have the land. Opportunities are endless. We have lots and lots of coconuts.'

But there weren't any jobs. According to US State Department figures, only eighteen percent of Samoa's population were in salaried positions.

'We used to export cocoa to Europe,' the prime minister said, 'high-flavoured cocoa. Now we export none. We need people to work on the land. Taro ... bananas ... inter-cropping ... organic farming. ...We offer people incentives but they don't take advantage of them. People always grab the easier options.'

He seemed to be blaming Samoans for Samoa's predicament. 'I am giving you the view of a leader who needs all the hands he can use,' he said. 'We cannot speedily develop to give people jobs. Progress is being made but it's slow.' He mentioned Yazaki, a Japanese-owned auto parts company in Apia. 'It's the biggest one we ever captured.' It employed a workforce of 2,000, but jobs were cut to about 800 after the Japanese earthquake and tsunami in 2011. 'They're still here,' he said, 'but they probably regret it, and want to leave, and are regretful they ever came here in the first place.'

This fell a bit short of inspirational. He was similarly downbeat in a newspaper story a few months later on the subject of a proposed multimillion-dollar Chinese-owned hotel. 'I'll believe it when I see it,' he said. 'Nothing has materialised from the big proposals we regularly get.' The comments were made after he visited China on the way back from a United Nations Conference on Least Developed Countries in Turkey. The conference, too, aroused his temper. The UN had voted for Samoa to 'graduate' from Least Developed Country to Developing Country status. Samoa, the prime minister objected, wasn't ready. The conference in Turkey had been 'a waste of time'.

He had won three elections and been in power thirteen years. His ideas for changing Samoa's way of life seemed whimsical – switching traffic from driving on the right to driving on the left, and altering Samoa's position on the International Date Line, literally bringing the country up to date with the rest of the world. An opposition MP criticised the proposal. That MP, said Tuilaepa, was 'very stupid' and an 'idiot'.

He was just as dismissive of TV3's John Campbell's attempts to ask him about allegations of misappropriated tsunami aid money. He sent TV3 a semi-literate letter of complaint. He wrote: 'Please note I am signing this message and not by some other kind of idiot. Only idiots recognise and emphasise the importance of other idiots.'

You could say he threw his weight around. It was not a pretty sight. He sat behind his desk, massive and puffing, surrounded by toys. The gifts of leaders of many nations were displayed in cabinets and on walls.

It was Friday afternoon and he wanted to go home and watch rugby on TV. We made even idler chit-chat as he gathered his things. He kept his wristwatch on the desk in front of him 'so I can watch it all the time'. The politician he most admired was Bill Clinton, 'but of course what he did to that girl was very bad'. No, he said, he didn't believe that God created the world in seven days. 'He created the world instantly.'

I remembered to inform him that I'd been bitten by a dog.

'Where?'

I stood up and showed him the livid red bite on my leg.

'No, where did it happen?'

I told him.

'Well,' he said, 'we have a programme of shooting wild dogs.'

On my last day I stumbled across Hell. On the way to the airport I had plenty of time, so I headed off along the coastal road and into the jungly interior, up a steep dirt track and on to a long dipping road, empty of traffic and people, until by chance I came to a prison. I'd read a few things about Tafa'igata Prison. It sounded like a terrible place. It was built during the German rule from 1900 to 1914. In 2010 the US State Department released a damning report, noting that some prison facilities were nearly a century old. It continued: 'Only basic provisions were made with respect to food, water and sanitation. Diplomatic observers reported that each concrete cell held ten to 15 inmates. Most cells had gravel floors, no toilets, poor ventilation, and almost no lighting.'

Up until 2007 the prison punished inmates by locking them in solitary confinement for seven days, naked. Two years ago 41 prisoners staged a mass breakout and hijacked a bus; police shot out the front tyres and negotiated a peaceful surrender. The prisoners said they were protesting about being 'fed and treated like animals'.

A friendly guard sat in a hut outside the gates.

I asked him if I could come in and look around.

No, he said.

I walked over the road to the lost village of Falelauniu.

The government of Prime Minister Tuilaepa Lupesoliai Sailele Malielegaoi had ordered that Falelauniu stay out of sight and out of mind. I had not read about it when I walked over the road from the prison. I didn't know what it was. It didn't look like a village. It looked like what it was: a slum. It was a human rights abuse worse than anything alleged at the prison. It wasn't leaning towards Third World: it was firmly, blatantly, Third World.

I approached the shack closest to the road. Five or six young guys sat inside on the bare floor and glowered. They called out someone's name. Fesouaina Matalavea, a pretty 22-year-old, came over. Yes, she said, she could speak English – she worked in Apia as an information officer for an aid agency. The savage irony of it hung in the air. I looked around at the shacks, at the slum, and said, 'What is this place?'

'We were moved here by the government,' she said. 'We used to live by the sea in Sigo before the tsunami. They said, "It's better you move."'

'Was the village devastated by the tsunami?'

'No,' she said. 'Nothing happened to it. We were okay. The government just used the tsunami as an excuse to move us. They wanted the land back to put up a government building.'

'And they kicked you out?'

'They gave us 3,000 tālā to move out.'

'That doesn't sound like much.'

She laughed and said, 'It wasn't much.'

She wasn't bitter. She said, 'It's not really terrible. It's good because it's more like fresh air than in Sigo.'

It was in the middle of nowhere opposite a prison.

I read about it later in *Samoa Observer*, in a story about building materials donated to Falelauniu by Vaughan Simpson, general manager of construction company CaBella Samoa. Simpson is a well-travelled individual, and in the region has been involved with major international companies such as Fletcher Construction. The Falelauniu situation opened his eyes to the darker side of Samoa, a place he calls paradise. Driving around he couldn't believe what he saw. 'I've seen a lot of poverty throughout the Pacific and … I haven't seen worse.'

A businesswoman in town, who preferred not to be named, was shocked by the poor quality of life of people at Falelauniu. Lost for words, she looked around the place and cried; all she could mutter was, 'It's very sad. I don't know.' After spending half an hour talking with members of one family she offered to pay for the education of their children for a year and to 'help out in other areas where they're in need, such as dishes, clothes and housing. Whatever I can, I'll do it.' Driving back to Apia, she tried to describe the environment and daily living conditions but couldn't. All she could manage was, 'Oh my gosh, I can't believe this is happening in our country.'

There was another story about villagers forced to root around the Tafa'igata rubbish dump in search of expired tins of food. In response, a government official visited Falalauniu and threatened villagers with legal action if they didn't stop talking to journalists.

'He's a journalist,' Fesouaina said as she showed me into one of the shacks. One of the old men sitting on the bare floor got up and closed the door. A couple of old ladies sat on chairs in the main room. There were children playing on the floor, their skin covered in sores. There were flies everywhere, all over the floor, all over the bodies and faces of the kids. There was one decoration hung on the wall: a cracked mirror. The boys wore shorts. The girls wore skirts and no knickers. A baby was asleep on a pillow on the floor. He had a mosquito net around him; compared to everyone else he was living in luxury.

There was rubbish on the dirt outside the house. I pointed at a low wall built from concrete further down the hill. 'The bathroom,' Fesouina said. 'It's not finished yet.' A small taro plantation, dogs, chickens, flies, stench: it was just another day in the life of Falelauniu, the disgrace of Samoa.

The older kids lay on the wooden floorboards and did their homework, writing down sums with worn-down pencils in damp exercise books. It was good to think of them at school and away from their wretched hut for at least a few hours, but the bus fare to send the four kids to school was eight tālā a day. Fesouaina was the one person in the household who had a job. She said she earned 15,000 tālā a year.

I tried calling her a few months later. I was put through to the CEO of Sungo. 'She doesn't work here anymore,' the woman said. 'Her position was terminated.'

It was like being told she'd died. I thought of the pretty 22-year-old in clean clothes in the lost village, that disgrace and national scandal, that incitement to line up Prime Minister Tuilaepa Lupesoliai Sailele Malielegaoi next to a wild dog and know which one to put down first. I thought of when I stood with Fesouaina outside her shack on a beautiful sunny day at the end of the wet season and asked her if she'd ever gone to New Zealand. Yes, she said, once, when she was fourteen. What did she think of it? She looked so happy when she said, 'Civilisation.'

# 10 MT ROSKILL
## WELCOME HOME

And God created Mt Roskill. For years this dense Auckland suburb was known as New Zealand's bible belt, with more churches per head of population than anywhere in the country, the Christian cross rising above a low skyline of red slate roofs. It had its own special weirdness; its powerful concentrations of faith and ecstasy swirled in the air like a mist. Also, you could smell the fear of sex even when you drove through with the windows wound up. You still can, especially on Stoddard Road, where the traffic – freight vans, removal vans, cool-store vans, flatbed trucks, beat-up second-hand Japanese jalopies – runs bumper-to-bumper between the lights at Richardson Road to the east and Sandringham Road to the west.

The only break in the traffic is a zebra crossing that leads to the Masjid e Umar mosque. It used to be the Christian Congregational Church of Samoa; when the building was auctioned in 1996 it attracted bids from a Hindu temple and a fitness centre. It sold for one and a half million dollars to the Mt Roskill Islamic Trust. 'Very good price,' the trust's secretary, Muhammad Moses, said. 'They'd built it for three million.'

There was a sign at the mosque's front door. It read SILENCE! THIS IS THE HOUSE OF ALLAH. Inside an office, Muhammad and his brother-in-law Hanif Patel chatted loudly, merrily. 'Look at all these,' Hanif said. He scattered wristwatches on the desk. 'There must be 20 or thirty. Some of them expensive! This one's a Rolex – maybe fifteen hundred dollars. The men take them off while they're doing ablutions before prayer, you see. They wash their hands and then forget to pick up their watches. It doesn't matter. No one ever steals them. That never happens.'

Hanif owned a downtown convenience store. Muhammad said, 'I worked in a government department for twenty-eight years.' What department? He lowered his eyes, and answered as though confessing a sin. 'The Inland Revenue Department. I was an investigator.' He took early retirement. He is fifty-three. His family arrived from India 'a hundred and ten years ago'.

There are now an estimated 36,000 Muslims in New Zealand, the numbers boosted by waves of refugees from Iraq, Somalia, Ethiopia, Sudan. 'We have 41 different nationalities who come to the mosque,' Muhammad said. Hanif opened a cupboard to reveal stacks of the *Koran*. 'So many languages! This one's in Russian. This one's Turkish I think...'

The largest population of Muslims in New Zealand is in Mt Roskill. Their road to Mecca is Stoddard Road: build a mosque and they will come, late. As the clock ticked towards one o'clock on a Friday afternoon in winter, the pavement on both sides of Stoddard Road suddenly filled with bearded men in long white knee-length shirts, op-shop checked suit jackets, and lace-up sports shoes. Friday is Jummah, the holy day, the Islamic sabbath. One in the afternoon is its rush hour, the most popular of the five daily prayers. How many people today? 'Probably two thousand,' Muhammad said. The car park was packed. A beat-up Mercedes C180 had the licence plate UAE EMIRATES. About a dozen taxis advertised as DISCOUNT, AFFORDABLE and CHEAP. As the clock ticked ever nearer, the men put on their skates, hurried but never ran. Downstairs at the washbasins, watches were torn off wrists.

Prayer was about fifteen minutes. Afterwards, the men slipped their feet back into shoes and relaxed in the bright winter sunshine. Two thousand pious souls, laughing, chatting: Africa and Arabia had come to Mt Roskill, the bible belt was now the *Koran* catchment. But how much had changed? The fine mist of faith and ecstasy, the fear of sex – it was all still there, wrapped up within itself, as Auckland's heathen traffic hurried along Stoddard Road, heading east, heading west, dying to get Friday over and done with and enter the temples of home or bar.

The mosque publishes a newsletter. Its author keeps returning to a favourite theme. Sample: 'Music incites one towards adultery. ... The drum and tambourine are forbidden.' And: 'Abstain completely from cinema, television. ... Do not read love poems or novels.' Also: 'Avoid holiday resorts and shopping malls. ... They are choking in the toxic fumes of nudity.' A pretend letter from a reader asks, 'I have been promoted to a senior position and personally supervise 30 female workers. Most dress in a very immodest or provocative manner. I totally fear for myself. What should I do?' Answer: 'Never make eye contact.'

Newspapers are 'very dangerous ... A Muslim home should be free of such material.' Marouf Ahmadzai, 19, was standing outside the mosque with friends. He said he arrived in New Zealand six years ago from Afghanistan. 'When you went outside,' he remembered, 'you had no guarantee of whether you came back dead or alive.' What media did he rely on for information about current events in Afghanistan? He was a big strong lad and his manner was confident, very nearly belligerent. He said, 'I don't like news. I don't like bullshit. News is all false, all bullshit.' What did he miss about Afghanistan? He said, 'I miss the dogfighting.'

He wore the long white shirt, the tidy neat hat called a topai. Another teenager, Tariq Ahmadzai, looked glamorous with his luxuriant black hair and a purple shirt open at the neck. He was handsome, lithe, charming, ambitious. He said, 'I'm on the crew at Wendy's right now, but soon I'll be shift supervisor.' Friday night in Auckland beckoned. He talked about sharing a biryani dinner with friends. Nothing more exciting? Hanif Patel, the jovial owner of a downtown dairy, joined the conversation. He said on Tariq's behalf, 'He can look, but not touch.'

Touching, though, is good; besides, it's the Kiwi way. I made the comments in jest. Hanif said, 'I tell you what sort of bird the kiwi is. It's a bullshit bird. Can't bloody fly, sleeps all through the bloody day. Kiwi way is bullshit!'

His heated satire reminded me of something I'd read in the mosque's newsletter. Among various warnings against lust, temptation and shopping malls, it instructed readers: 'We have been commanded to oppose the ways of the Jews and the Christians.' Whose side were they on?

Muhammad introduced a vast bearded Māori. 'I trust this person more than anyone I know.' The trustworthy Māori said his name was Mohammed Aissa Hussein. He had converted to Islam in 1995. 'My pastor discovered that Jesus wasn't a god, he was a prophet,' he said. 'We had a fair idea the bible was more like a puzzle. He said for me to go to Australia to look for answers.

'I went to Sydney. I took a notebook and a bible everywhere. I met someone. It was revealed that he was a Muslim. He says, "Sit down." He showed me a couple of videos made by an Islamic scholar. One was *Is Jesus God?* The other was called *Is the Bible God's Word?* I went quiet for two weeks because of what I discovered.' What had he discovered? 'I knew who God really was.'

But who was Mohammed Aissa Hussein? He was 53, born in Whakatane. He said he came from a family of thirty. 'I was a very sickly person. I had a motor accident back home on the farm in 1969. People said I was a bit nutty. I was a mental outpatient. I was easily led; I didn't know what I was doing. Prison, gangs...'

His arms were heavily tattooed. The graffiti on his flesh included two swastikas. He was devout, softly spoken; he talked about 'how the Earth moves, what moves it'; he began to chant. He was in ecstasy. He could have it. The bright winter sun cast long shadows of bare trees. The traffic on Stoddard Road roared east, roared west. They were going to a better place.

Real estate listings for Stoddard Road and its avenues routinely advertise houses as CLOSE TO MOSQUE. The block of shops at the corner of Richardson Road includes the Khoobsurat Hair and Beauty Salon, which offers eyebrow threading, and Mohammed's Halal Meats ('The name you can trust!'), which offers tripe, beef soup bones, lamb testes, and $8.99

roosters. A poster on a shop selling Indian saris says: REMEMBERING EK YAAD RAFI KE BAAD. A TRIBUTE TO THE LEGEND AT AVONDALE COLLEGE.

Old Mt Roskill – the white, working-class suburb that gave the world Russell Crowe and Graeme Hart, New Zealand's richest man – maintains a presence at the corner of Sandringham Road in the shape of Giles Carpets. Established in 1981 around the corner in White Swan Road, it moved to its Stoddard Road showroom nine years ago. Entering it was like entering a family home. The three middle-aged Giles brothers, Kevin, Alan and Philip, were horsing around with each other and ducking into the staff kitchen for a hot lunch. A wall was covered with newspaper coverage of Sir Edmund Hillary's funeral.

They talked about carpets for a little while – the in-demand Feltex Classic range, the élite Axminsters – but they preferred to talk about sport. They had set up a bar, plasma TV and a competition pool table at their nearby warehouse. They played most nights after work, competed in tournaments. 'We're all serious about pool,' said Alan. 'I played the best in New Zealand recently.' He meant he had played national champion Glen Coutts. How'd he get on? 'He kicked my arse.'

Alan had his arm in a sling. 'Sunday before last I made a tackle and ripped the muscle right off the bone. I just walked off the field but I knew I'd done some damage. I've been around league since I was five. I've dislocated both shoulders, my elbow, broken my cheekbone, my hand.'

In his prime he played loose forward for Ponsonby. 'Pocket money really. There was a $1500 sign-on fee and you'd get between 40 and 80 dollars for a win.' Since turning 35 he had played masters, or seniors. 'And once you hit 50, you wear red shorts. That means you're not allowed to dump them – you just hold on to them. But they can run fast, some of those old buggers. Especially the Island boys. One in particular, Joe, he's a big solid boy. Perfect build. Six foot two. Lean and mean. Not an ounce of fat and runs like the wind.'

He dwelt again on his injury. 'I hit the tackle low with my left shoulder; I don't know why it was my right shoulder got hurt. I got put on morphine, had an operation. They drilled two holes through the bone to reattach the tendon, and stitched the muscles back.' And then he said, 'I've played my last game. Ever.' He shrugged with his one good shoulder. The words echoed through the showroom, crept over the carpet samples in colours of Aquatess, Cheshire, Hemisphere, Cayenne and Montoza. It was the end of an era.

Allah was bigger than Jesus on Stoddard Road but a cross remained visible on the low skyline. The mosque and a desolate Assembly of God behind a high fence – the two of them were like contestants in a show called *God Idol*. They cast their eyes to heaven. At street level, a homeless man sat in a parked car opposite the mosque, packets of food and a sleeping bag at his feet. He sprawled on the front seat in a pair of underpants. He squawked, 'Get away from my car!'

Stoddard Creek was in an even worse state. Black, sticky, odious, it looked as though it spent its days being mugged. It was the kind of sick, polluted Auckland waterway found throughout this city of harbours, bays and rivers, this city of water pouring in on the tide. One of my favourite passages about Auckland is by the historian and poet Keith Sinclair in an otherwise dull anthology *Auckland at Full Stretch*, published in 1977 by Auckland University's board of urban studies. Sinclair writes: 'Auckland is the gulf and the harbour and the mangroves and the mudflats. ... The authentic Auckland experience is a summer's day watching the yachts heading past Rangitoto. It is paddling a canoe up Meola Creek and landing on the reef and cooking fish on the rocks.'

Sinclair's vision of bright watery Auckland also takes in the wonders of his garden, where he grows 'guavas, feijoas, Chinese gooseberries, tamarillos, passionfruit, chokos, zucchinis, green peppers, aubergines, lemons, apples, cape gooseberries, tomatoes, peaches, nectarines, apples, sweetcorn, not to mention radishes and ordinary salad vegetables'. Not to mention he is so carried away with his abundance that he lists apples twice. And thus: 'This is the first thing about Auckland. Life here is lavish. Nature is kind.'

But the authentic Auckland experience is also semi-industrial Stoddard Road and black Stoddard Creek. Zeb Mohammed, the sombre Pakistani proprietor of Khyber Foods and Spices, strolled behind his Stoddard Road shop to feed the ducks. He threw slices of white bread into the creek. 'Quack,' said the wretched fowl. Just then the roller doors of his store clattered open, revealing an indignant African wearing a purple smock and holding a sharp halal knife. A cloud of thick toxic smoke rose from a business three doors down – a petrol and diesel importer. 'That's not right,' the African said. Zeb looked at the smoke, and watched it die down. He said, 'It's under control now.'

The meat counter at Khyber offers ox tongue and lamb's feet; the shelves offer Babaji milk toast, Tuc salted biscuits, Al-Rabih fava beans, Priya green chilli pickle, Thums Up cola, and CTC tea. You couldn't get liquor anywhere on Stoddard Road but you could get anything else your pure body desired. Next door to Khyber, on the window of Khaled Sab's barbershop, a poster advertised the services of Dr Wasfy Shahin: 'Dear brothers and sisters, I would like to bring to your kind notice that I have recently opened my own clinic and I have been doing circumcision with a latest technique.'

Khaled the barber, 48, came from Syria. His Stoddard Road neighbour, Khaled Barakat, 47, came from Egypt and operated the King Tut takeaway bar. He had two plastic tables and matching seats out the front. It was a great pleasure to pull up a chair, eat his $2 samosas, drink his $1.50 cups of sweet black CTC tea from India, and listen to him talk and joke.

'In Egypt, I was in the middle of everywhere. In New Zealand, I am in the middle of nowhere.' An excellent host, full of restless energy, smart, chatty, gentle, lascivious, he was very likely the most hilarious man on Stoddard Road. He was just as likely its only Muslim socialist. 'In the circle of production,' he said, 'you can take out capital, you can take out everything, except one thing: you can't take out the workers.'

Back in Cairo he worked as an accountant. His qualifications are no use here. The rent for King Tut was $1700 a month; he charged an Indian sari maker $90 a week for a small bedroom at the top of the narrow stairs.

The takeaway bar was about the size of a school satchel. He didn't have a complaining bone in his body. 'Sitting out here,' he said happily, 'I feel like I'm in a cafe in Cairo.' He stood up, and reappeared a few minutes later with a water pipe. He took a blast and then he said, 'I feel like I'm a Kiwi when I go to Pak'nSave.'

Khaled stood and smiled in the doorway; Zeb, the Pakistani spice merchant, returned from the creek. A radio was tuned to The Breeze. The Eagles sang, 'I guess every point of refuge has its price.' Another man appeared – refugee Loia Mouhmod, 43. He made the delicious semolina squares sold at King Tut. 'I am a Palestinian from Iraq,' he said. He put it another way: 'I am two problems.' He had arrived earlier in the year on a refugee programme with his family of 25 – his wife and children, his parents, his brothers and their wives and children. Back in Iraq he sold men's clothes. The shop was bombed. He lost everything. Now he wants to study English 'and then I can get idea for a job'.

He stood with his two daughters, Rana, ten, and Shatha, seven. They were lovely quiet little girls. He said, 'Everything is fine for my kids. They go to school, they learn English. We are safe, thanks to God.' He talked about the day he arrived in New Zealand. 'I come to the airport. I see my case worker waiting for me. You know what she said to me? She said, "Welcome to your new home." I am so happy I want to cry. I feel this is my country.'

He opened his arms. He embraced Stoddard Road.

# 11 WANGANUI, WHANGANUI IN ABSENTIA

You asked people about the virtues of living in Wanganui and they said, 'It's close to Wellington.' Even, incredibly, 'It's close to Palmerston North.' Wanganui, the littlest and furthest city in the west, keen to affirm it was within reach of the apparent civilisation of Palmerston North. Wanganui, population 42,600 and disappearing – down 10.5 percent in six to nine year olds since the last census, down 12.3 percent in 20 to 29 year olds, 9.9 percent in 30 to 39 year olds. Wanganui, with its numerous empty and abandoned downtown buildings and lights out early in the suburbs, not at all a ghost town but ghostly, tenuous, desolate, very clean, touched by phobias – it felt like a city that wasn't sure what to do with itself. Famously, it was a city that wasn't sure what to call itself, Wanganui or Whanganui.

On a weekend in spring the argument was running hot. Four teenage bogan chumps had formed a protest on the main street, Victoria Avenue, to register their disgust at the National Geographic Board's decision that Wanganui should respect Māori spelling and be renamed Whanganui. A passerby, Spencer Hall, languid, longhaired, 33, mocked their protest. 'You're a homo,' said one of the chumps and spat in Hall's face.

It was a city in transition, a new city about to be brought to you by the letter h, but it would always be the river city, clinging to the banks of all that amazing water, that central reason for its existence. In bright sunshine, with the river running high and wide, Wanganui is one of the most obviously beautiful cities in New Zealand, sitting prettily on the edge of a fertile emerald plain. There is the smooth white dome of the neo-classical Sarjeant Art Gallery shining on a soft green hill. There is the long empty coast, car tyres carving spirals into the hard black sand. There are all the attractive Spanish-style stucco houses low to the ground. Higher, and even more Mediterranean, there is the good cheer of hundreds of palm trees. And, always, there is the river with mud on its boots, running in a kind of ring around the city, disappearing into the mysteries and silences of native bush.

'I can't wait to leave,' said Ollie Shand.

'Yeah, I second that motion,' said his friend and fellow student at Wanganui High School, Sam Hicks.

Wanganui or Whanganui, the city will always be boring. Boredom is the New Zealand condition. Teenagers are most at risk. A front-page story in the *Wanganui Chronicle* itemised the evidence of lout rampage in Victoria Avenue on Friday and Saturday nights: 'Scuffles, fights, abusive language, vandalism, urinating in shop doorways, broken bottles, piles of vomit…'

Sitting around doing nothing on Saturday morning in Majestic Square, three 16-year-olds shrugged at the newspaper report and said, 'That's 'cos Wanganui's a shit-hole.' They looked away when asked their names. They preferred to go by nicknames, but it was hard to interpret their grunts – one sounded like Egg, the other like Nog.

Egg said, 'You always get two or three drunken dickheads come up to you and try to start something.' Where? 'On the street,' Nog said. 'Anywhere. It used to be outside the Red but that got shut down 'cos this girl there got killed. She got killed by this guy. My mum used to teach her.' Egg said, 'My brother chucked someone out the window there once.'

Were they planning on staying in Wanganui when they left school? Small freckled Nog, sitting on his hands, said, 'Fuckin' hope not.' Muscular mullet-haired Egg, who had folded his arms high against his chest, said, 'I go to Wellington sometimes.'

There were other ways to depart. 'Farming with the angels,' read the obituary for a man whose name really was Ray Death. But there were also interesting arrivals, and returns. Spencer Hall, the man spat at by chumps, had fled Wanganui after leaving school. Now and then he'd come back to visit, and always cringed. 'Sleepy little place. Almost lazy.' When he returned eighteen months ago, though, it felt different. 'I didn't cringe. Wanganui's getting there. It's finding its voice. I'd say it was stirring.' He gave a lot of credit to Stink Magnetic Tapes, the independent record company that had moved from Wellington in 2008, and was devoted to recording 'dirty rock 'n' roll' – local bands include The Death Rays, which consists of two sisters dating two cousins.

Music had also helped bring back Orrin Reynolds, 30, Sacha Te Utupoto Keating, 31, and Nigel Scanlon, 30, of Katipo Productions, devoted to recording Wanganui hip-hop. 'Wanganui's pretty sweet. It's a nurturing environment,' Reynolds said. Asked about the bylaw that made it a criminal offence to wear gang insignia in the city, he said, 'The perception is that we're under siege, but it's totally the opposite, bro. I've never felt unsafe here. I live opposite a gang house, got me a big-assed plasma TV, and always leave my front door open.'

They were about to drive to Wellington for a benefit gig at La Bodega for the widow and children of Tony Costa, 33, who had died in a surfing accident at Lyall Bay. Spencer Hall was about to drive to Pātea for the annual Yee-Haw Spring Hoedown. ('Pātea has an ATM now,' advised the party invite.)

Traffic was also headed *towards* Wanganui that weekend. The city was hosting two cultural events – a glass festival and a literary festival. The latter featured appearances by novelist Fiona Kidman, poets Kevin Ireland and Glenn Colquhoun, baking guru Alexa Johnston, and others. You could see the writers around town happily slurping on flat whites at sidewalk cafes, gazing contentedly at the river, admiring the hundreds of flower baskets along Victoria Avenue. 'Wonderful,' they said. 'Lovely.' The festival broke even on its $23,000 budget, attracting an audience of pensioners and that one age-group to show a significant population increase since the last census – 50 to 59 year olds, up 16.8 percent.

The event was organised by Joan Rosier-Jones, novelist and political firebrand – she once stood for the Socialist Party against Marilyn Waring. Among her volunteers was Jan Bullen, chair of the National Party's Wanganui electorate committee. 'North of here,' said Bullen, 'it's a different culture. Rural, basic. Wanganui's more sophisticated. I belong to a book club. At the moment we're reading about Jews and the Holocaust. I'm not that interested. I'd like to move on. One of our ladies was a POW of the Japanese in the Philippines. She had to knit white cotton socks for the kamikaze pilots. They wore them so they'd go to heaven, or wherever you go when you're Japanese.'

She said, 'I'm true blue.' It seemed reasonable to expect she hadn't much enjoyed the long years of Helen Clark's government. 'No. They made it all warm and fuzzy. In real life there are winners and losers.'

Who were the losers? Jan lived on St John's Hill, also known as Snob's Rock, where Wanganui's money was tucked away. The bottom of the heap was west at Castlecliff, home of Black Power, and east at Aramoho, home of the Mongrel Mob. Helen Ngapo, who attended the literary festival wearing quite flamboyant dresses, taught at Aramoho Primary School. The first thing she said was, 'It's decile one.'

The school roll was 70 percent Māori. Many of the parents worked at the Mars pet-food factory (airport sign: 'Wanganui, home of Whiskas!'). Many were unemployed. 'A lot of the kids are from gang homes,' she said. 'People think of us as a ghetto but most houses are still on a quarter-acre section. And we have 100 percent attendance on parents' day. I tell them, "It's a legal requirement!"' She laughed, and then she said, 'The reality is that parents at Aramoho care about their children as much as any parents.'

We were joined by her husband Henry Ngapo, the school principal. There was an immediate impression of dignity and calm, strength and mana. 'I'm originally from Waiheke Island,' he said. 'Pisshead for a father. No money. But I've got five tertiary qualifications, including a Fulbright. I tell that to the kids. We've got one girl who wants to be a doctor. Her parents are very supportive. Her father was one of the men implicated in the killing of baby Jhia.' He meant the Mongrel Mob drive-by shooting that killed the two-year-old daughter of a Black Power member in 2007. Henry said, 'It was a really horrific time. The kids were stressed to the max. But the guy I was telling you about, the father, something clicked inside his head after that. He doesn't drink anymore, stopped smoking dope. He wants the best for his daughter.'

Helen taught social studies. 'The kids said, "We'd like to learn about revolution" so I gave them a quote from Zapata – "Revolution is not a bed of roses" – and said, "Tell me what it means." This girl, the one who we're talking about, said, "Tears will be shed and hearts will be broken." A seven year old. Can you believe that?'

Other, similarly unofficial signs of life, hope and goodness in Wanganui ran riot at the apparently endless home of potter Ross Mitchell-Anyon. It was impossible to locate anything as prosaic as a front door or a back door in his ramshackle, sprawling house on the banks of the river. 'Built it myself,' he said. 'Wood butchery.'

It was more than merely chaotic. Ross was like a man who had declared war on blank space. His hair was all over the shop. He drove a big black bomb. The paintings on his walls included a portrait of David Bain. He threw planks on to an enormous outdoor brick fireplace; the warmth brought people from thin air. 'It's like a bloody hippie commune here,' he said, shaking his head. 'I seem to attract waifs and strays.'

He drove into town in his six-cylinder 1962 Vanguard 6. 'It's a portable blackboard,' he said. He'd chalked its side doors with the notorious letter H. 'I own that one,' he said, pointing to the former Ministry of Works building. It cost $75,000. 'That's one of mine,' he said, driving past the former *Wanganui Chronicle* building. It cost $115,000. Both are tenanted by local artists and musicians.

'To tell you the truth,' he said, 'I'm a poozler.' What? 'A scrounger, an arranger of bits and pieces. I'd always bought parts of buildings – windows, boards – and then I thought, why not buy the building?' I bought my first one dirt cheap. They still are. Wanganui's art scene is such because of the cheapness of the real estate: you don't have to charge much rent for studio space. I had someone wanting to buy the *Chronicle* building. They offered me a lot of money, but they wanted to knock it down so I told them to get fucked. I've got the glass artist guys in there. People like that keep the blood going through Wanganui.'

He parked the car near the Sarjeant Gallery. His public sculpture 'Handspan', which features over 5,000 casts of hands, was being dedicated in Queen's Park. He looked around. 'Oh, there's my hand,' he said. 'Haven't seen that in years. Ha! There's Helen Clark's.' The sculpture had been funded by a peace activist called Gita Brooke. Gita's husband Anthony really was the last White Rajah of Sarawak. His family held absolute rule over the Malaysian state from 1843 until 1945.

Later, back at his house, Ross and his posh sexy girlfriend Bobbi Magdalinos, a school inspector, stoked up the giant fireplace. Bobbi said she'd only recently moved to Wanganui. Her husband, Napier architect Paris Magdalinos, had died in July the year before. She said, 'There I was, the widow in mourning black. Three months later I fall in love with a bohemian potter in Wanganui.'

We looked into the flames, and into something even more compelling and primal: a dirty great big hole in the ground directly in front of the fireplace. It was art, a statement. Mitchell-Anyon had concreted the sides. A very, very long ladder stood in it. You could barely see the bottom. It looked like a journey into the centre of the Earth. Bobbi said, 'We were sitting here one night by the fire and Ross said, "I'm going to dig a hole." And I said, "Fantastic." Because that's what you say to someone like Ross.'

He said, 'You can go up, and you can go down. But not many people go down.' No. We continued looking at the hole. It was a void. It was an abyss.

# 12 MERCER FOG

The graveyard was across the road from the school and over the fence from a three-bedroom house on the edge of a paddock. It was raining hard at last; summer's drought had rusted the countryside. Mercer – exactly halfway between Auckland and Hamilton, a fast 40-minute drive in either direction – smelled of chimney smoke on a Friday morning in early winter. A thrush was singing above the dirt track that led to the gates of the primary school, which had a roll of 22 – seventeen Māori and five Pākehā.

A spade and a copy of Jehovah's Witness magazine *The Watchtower* were in a corrugated iron shelter in the grounds of the cemetery. Grave markings blamed the Waikato River, which flowed past the town: George Sellwood drowned at Mercer, 1900; Roy Carter drowned, aged 27, in 1920: 'Sometime we'll understand'.

The sky was almost black, and the dark outline of a man could be seen through the windows of his three-bedroom house. Paul Whitelaw, 53, had sat down for a cup of tea. He was a new face. He'd moved in exactly two weeks ago, packed a suitcase of clothes and shifted from Whitianga to run sheep and beef on an 1,100-acre farm. 'I worked up north as a carpenter building homes,' he said. 'We did well. The boys are still hard-out. They're busy on a three-million-dollar home not due to be finished 'til November.'

He was trying to knock his own house into shape, had torn up the floorboards and lowered the ceiling. He touched the new ceiling. 'What d'you reckon – bit bright?' He'd bought very white ten-millimetre ply for $15 a sheet. 'The house was rat-infested,' he said, and pointed to a black rubbish bag in the kitchen. 'Full of droppings. When I pulled down the ceiling, paper and nests came spilling out. The smell! Took days to get rid of it.'

He had no family, was on his own. Moving to Mercer marked a return to farming in the district where he was born. 'I'm excited about it but it's not been the greatest of seasons to kick off, and I'm just praying it's not going to get cold.' He was thinking about his thousand ewes.

Peter Black, whom he'd known since school, called in to see if he needed a hand. Black, a drain-laying contractor, employed eight people. 'Mercer's good,' he said. What did he like about it? 'It's quiet. And it's got the rowing club. All my kids have rowed for Mercer.'

Paul started up an electric saw. Peter shouted, 'Mercer used to have an IGA, a Four Square, a butcher shop. Twenty-six truck and trailers used to be based here. They'd take sand to Hamilton and Auckland when they dredged the river.' What did he make of the modern Mercer Food Junction Service Centre? All day, every day, traffic on the State Highway One Waikato Expressway turns on to an off-ramp, crosses an overbridge and stops for gas, for coffee, for the familiar happy stench of McDonald's. Peter said, 'I never go there.' The history of Mercer was still on his mind. 'Go and see Terry Carr,' he said. 'Lived here all his life. Retired now. Fit as a trout. He's down the road, waiting for his dog to die.'

The houses of Mercer nestle in a foothill above the river. Terry was at home with his wife Dorrie. She said, 'It's not a very happy home today.' She looked at Terry. He met her eye, then put his hands in his pockets and sat down in the dining room next to the brightly painted kitchen.

Dorrie put on the kettle. The sky had turned darker; midday had the pall of five p.m. Terry said, 'Just buried the dog.' What was its name? Terry said, 'Lucky.' And then he brightened. 'He was lucky to be alive! Lived like a king. Never slept in his kennel. He'd back in and decide it wasn't for him. He always slept in the shed. But he was going blind and deaf and… We took him to the vet this morning.' Back home, Terry had put on his gumboots and got to work with a shovel in the front garden in the rain. 'That's where he is now, old Lucky.'

The sudden absence of his fourteen-year-old border collie made the house feel empty. 'I guess I'll move now,' Terry said. 'The dog was the stumbling block. He would have hated it.' He meant Pukekohe, ten minutes' drive north, where Dorrie had lived while Terry stayed in the family home, waiting for Lucky to die. 'The new house had nowhere for him to run around. It's one of those places where you can hand a cup of tea through the window to the person next door.'

Dorrie said, 'No, it isn't.' She admitted their home in Mercer was on a larger section, which included a vast magnolia tree. 'It's not in great shape,' Dorrie said, 'because someone's not looking after it.'

She looked at Terry. They both smiled. She said she was seventy. Terry said, 'I'm seventy-seven. No, seventy-eight?' Dorrie said, 'Think again. You're seventy-six.' Terry said, 'You're the boss.' They shared another fond and private smile.

They had lived apart for two and a half years. Dorrie stayed over on Saturday nights, after a round of golf at nearby Te Kauwhata. The rest of the time Terry looked after himself, cooked his own meals. 'Spuds and vegies. Sausages. Steak once in a while.' Dorrie smiled again. 'Bachelor's heaven.'

Did he shop at the service centre? 'No.' He gave a brief history lesson. There used to be shipping on the river. There used to be railway station tearooms (they inspired poet Rex Fairburn's quality pun 'The squalid tea of Mercer is not strained'). There used to be a wine bottling plant. There also used to be a tennis court: it was on their property, abandoned now, netless. They had laid the court in 1971 for their two kids, as well as everyone in Mercer, to enjoy. 'We ran Housie down the pub to pay for it,' Dorrie said. There used to be a pub.

Soon, too, Terry would be part of Mercer's past. Pukekohe had a doctor and a supermarket: 'We're just waiting for a Farmers, then we'll have everything we need.' Terry looked out the kitchen window towards the front garden with its freshly dug grave. He said, 'I've got no excuse now.'

A big blue roadside sign decorated with a knife and fork beckons motorists to the Mercer Food Junction Service Centre. 'We get, like, 250 customers on a slow shift,' said the bleary youth behind the counter at Mobil Oil. How many on a busy shift? The thought made him drop the bags under his eyes; they fell halfway down his face. He said, 'Unimaginable.'

The unimaginable numbers, streaming in from the four-lane expressway, flicking cigarette butts in the car park, yawning in the forecourt, busting for a piddle inside the service centre mall on the banks of the slow, broad Waikato River. There were five tenants: McDonald's; an ice-cream parlour; a food court with a choice of Country Chicken or Indian curry; an Esquires Coffee House next to a Pokeno Bacon Café. For children, entertainment options were limited to a small carousel with three luridly painted ponies sniffing each other's bottoms, and another coin-operated ride with a notice in Chinese above a notice with an incredible English translation: DON'T SPLIT AND FOR PROFESSIONAL ONLY.

Inside the mall, filling their faces, were the tourists, the families, the lovers, the hungry and muttering teenage hordes. Also, the truck drivers and the duck shooters, and the drag racers on their way to the nearby tracks at Meremere and Hampton Downs. Everyone was on their way to somewhere else: like all departure lounges, the service centre could be anywhere. It felt like nowhere.

Even stranger, the town was neither here nor there: it had been pushed aside when the State Highway One bypass was built in 1992. The new expressway separated the houses from the river. The shops closed down and up went the service centre, like some sort of squat, brightly lit robot. It became the central fact of Mercer's existence, reducing the rest of the town to a bystander. Does the centre belong to Mercer, or does Mercer belong to the centre?

North lie Pukekohe and the Bombay Hills, the fresh air and open countryside of the Franklin district, with winter crops in the long brown fields and signs advertising a possum shoot. South is the Waikato, potent with the forces of Taupiri Mountain and Tūrangawaewae Marae. In between, in the middle of this grassy and riverine nowhere, is cramped, damp Mercer, dissected and disassembled by a motorway. It was always a transport hub: it used to be a shipping town, a railway town. But it also used to be a town.

By the river, where welcome swallows skimmed the water's surface and goldfinches rustled in the tops of willows, the rugby clubrooms were abandoned, the H of the rugby posts bent out of the shape. At the Mercer Reserve, steps led to a flagpole draped in thick moss. On a side street in the shadow of the service centre was a compelling and eccentric war memorial, a statue of a First World War soldier on top of a gun turret rescued from British gunship HMS *Pioneer*, which had blasted at Māori in the land wars.

Opposite the memorial was something alive and thriving: the famous Mercer Cheese Shop, recognised in over 30 national awards as producing New Zealand's best cheese. Dutch cheesemaker Albert Alferink opened the shop in 1982. It used to be the butcher store. It's now a destination for gourmets. Life, too, was good on the river. Just before dusk on Friday afternoon, three teams of rowers emerged from the rowing club on the western side of the bank and set off towards the sunset. They followed the tide, flowing north.

After dark, life was played out in great high spirits at the Last Post Tavern, a small friendly bar with room for a pool table and a wood burner. The jukebox played The Drifters and Bruce Springsteen very loudly. There were about a dozen drinkers in on a Friday night. Friday night is always a happy ending to the working week – or, for that matter, the non-working week. I got drinking with a bunch of unemployed men who drove in from nearby Meremere. I went to Meremere the next day. It had a dairy surrounded by barbed wire, and an abandoned dementia unit, painted turquoise. On the balance of things, I preferred Mercer.

I took my glass out on to the Last Post's smoking deck. Dennis Dunbar lit up. His hair had turned white and his face bright pink. He said he had come to Mercer twelve years earlier. He'd been living in Pukekohe, on a lifestyle block he'd agreed to buy from a friend. The friend's marriage broke up and the man's lawyer kept phoning to demand he settle the deal. The lawyer was a woman. 'I told her, "Listen. I only deal with men." She had a right go at me. I thought, fuck this. I'm off.' I saw a house for sale in Mercer. Drove up and couldn't see a fucking thing, the mist was so thick, but it had a two-car garage, big enough for my Indie racing car, and I thought, right. The day I moved in the sun was shining and I could see straight out to the Coromandel ranges, the Waikato Heads and Mount Pirongia. No, true! Best views in New Zealand! And what I always remember is I looked over and saw this hawk. It fucking winked at me. Winked, the bugger. I could not believe it. I was set.'

Hawks circled, and possibly winked, over Mercer all that wet Friday. On Sunday, the place surrendered to something else Dennis had mentioned. Amazing white Waikato fog rolled down the river, sat low on the swamps, and rubbed up against pine trees in the hills. It disappeared at the touch of rain, waited until the rain cleared, and then rolled back in. Strange to think of it descending through the ages, before the Māori and then after Mercer was settled, the town named after Captain Henry Mercer, shot through the head and killed at the battle of Rangiriri in 1863, descending when the railway line from Auckland reached Mercer in 1875, and in the winter of 1970, when Harvey and Jeanette Crewe were murdered.

Mist descended on Sunday morning, when Des Thomas was asked for his age and replied with a startling kind of arithmetic: 'I was eighteen when Arthur was arrested, so that makes me fifty-eight.' The younger brother of Arthur Allan Thomas, he lives across the river in Pukekawa, on the road where the Crewes were killed in their home.

He was in his work shed in 1979 when the phone rang with the news that Arthur had been granted a pardon. 'It was Dad. He said, "Muldoon's going to release Arthur today." My wife Kay – my wife at the time – was getting the mail. I ran down to tell her.' That night, Arthur spent his first night of freedom at Des's house after nine years of prison but couldn't sleep. 'He came screaming in here,' said Des, sitting at the kitchen table. 'Kay had made him up a bed with flannelette sheets. He just couldn't believe how soft they felt.'

Talk of that night made the house feel like a kind of heritage site. The narrow hallway, the kitchen window looking out on to a field of onions – Des's house acted as the culmination of a story that began the night of June 17, 1970, a night about which only minor facts remain established. Jeanette Crewe had cooked peas and flounder for dinner. She'd bought the fish earlier that week in nearby Meremere. She dusted it in flour and pan-fried it. She and her husband Harvey watched TV – *Peyton Place* played at 9.37 p.m. Harvey sat in an armchair. Jeanette knitted. Their brains were blown out by a .22. Five days later police were called to the house. The Crewes' daughter Rochelle, eighteen months old, was found standing up in her cot. She had soiled nappies. Her parents were missing. Justice Robert Taylor would later set the scene in his introduction to the 1980 report of the Royal Commission: 'A bizarre story of a bloodstained house, empty but for a weeping infant.'

The Crewe murders remain the most famous in New Zealand history, and the most resonant. Something about them continues to touch a New Zealand nerve. Strangely, it's not because of the people. No one ever talks about Harvey or Jeanette Crewe. There's sympathy for Rochelle, the 'weeping infant', who has grown up not knowing who killed her parents. There's sympathy, too, for neighbouring farmer Arthur Allan Thomas, who was stitched up by the cops and sentenced to life imprisonment.

More than the cast, though, the murders have stayed in the national consciousness because of their setting: a double killing, at night, in rain and wind in the middle of winter, on a farm near Pukekawa, population 600. On the day he was murdered Harvey Crewe worked on the drains on his farm, went to a stock sale in Bombay, and inspected a bull in Glen Murray. Thomas's alibi was cow no. 4 – it was crook, in a sling in a tractor shed, and Thomas was busy calving it. There were ten sheep in the Crewes' paddock. A wheelbarrow was a kind of getaway vehicle: police believed it was used to transport Harvey Crewe's body out of the house – across the thick carpet, past the china cabinet, the tea wagon, the writing bureau.

The search for the bodies was carried out in heavy Mercer fog. They were found a month apart in the Waikato River. Both had surfaced only because of freak flooding and a tidal surge. Jeanette was discovered by whitebaiters in an area known as Devil's Elbow. She was wrapped in bedclothes that were tied with wire. 'I'm convinced in my own mind that she was raped,' police inspector Bruce Hutton told the author David Yallop. She had been shot in the side of her head; it seemed to have happened when she was lying on the carpet with the left side of her face to the floor. There was an untouched flounder on the round dining table. There were blood drag marks. Jeanette had dropped seven stitches of her knitting. One of the needles was bent. There was blood in a saucepan in the sink.

Arthur Allan Thomas came from a family of ten, was a country music fan, and especially liked Johnny Cash. His motive, police said, was sexual jealousy. They flushed out niggling irrelevant details. At a farewell party for a colleague in a topdressing firm in Dargaville, Thomas had bought someone's 'prized collection' of pubic hairs. He had entertained fellow workers by playing secretly taped 'love talk' that had taken place with a girlfriend in his car one night in Maramarua. Then the police got relevant: according to the Royal Commission, they planted evidence.

In his book *Beyond Reasonable Doubt* Yallop writes of Thomas: 'His state of mind on hearing announced a verdict he knew to be wrong must have been one of unspeakable anguish.' His family campaigned for his release. In memory of his jailed son, Arthur's father created a weird sculpture by his letterbox on Mercer Ferry Road, using car axles and other replicas of court evidence. Investigative journalist Pat Booth got interested; later, so did Yallop, who wrote to the prime minister, Rob Muldoon, asking for Thomas to be pardoned.

Thomas had been arrested on November 11, 1970; he was released on December 17, 1979. To evade journalists, he slipped into Des's house.

Justice Taylor ordered compensation of $1,096,450.35. The sum included a payment to Des of $5,420 for expenses. But it never actually ended for Des on that night when Arthur arrived at his front door a free man. He continued to badger the police and ask who killed the Crewes. He said, 'I've been pointing the finger at this joker here whom I think did it.' It was strange to hear him say the man's name out loud. It was like being told a terrible secret.

He brought out a document he'd typed up. It was a criminal profile of his suspect, who still lived in the district. Des had an archive of documents. They included an unanswered letter to Rochelle Crewe and a letter to Ross Meurant, a former policeman who had worked on the Thomas case. Des wrote, 'Jeanette had teeth smashed out of her jaw, they were both shot in their own house, bundled up, weighted, and thrown into the Waikato River like farm animals.'

It was 40 years after the killings, 30 years since Justice Taylor's report – the case had become Des's life's work. 'People say, "Oh, it's wonderful you're doing this for your brother." It's nothing to do with my brother. I'm talking about an unsolved double murder.' Sir Bob Jones, who urged Muldoon to consider the Thomas case, attended the retrial and thought the charges were a travesty. His verdict on Arthur was, 'A prize bunny.'

Des Thomas, though, was quick-witted and watchful. He had led a life on the edges of his obsession. He drank at the Last Post most Thursday nights. He delivered natural bore water from his property ('I've just had a real busy three months because of the drought') and sold firewood. He had a gorgeous girlfriend, whom he introduced as Blondie. She said, 'I've had to live with it. It's Des's thing. My feeling is the killer is someone no one has ever thought of.'

Mercer was the love song of Caesar Roose. When Roose founded a shipping company he became the town's chief employer and benevolent tsar. Everyone owed something to him. In 1921 he transported Princess Te Puea and her people from Mangatāwhiri to the new Tūrangawaewae Marae. A young Arthur Allan Thomas worked as a boilermaker in his shipyards.

Roose followed the river, building cargo vessels and luxury launches, and dredges to tickle treasure from the riverbed: the finest sand in New

Zealand was Mercer sand. He bought trucks and trailers. He owned a timber mill, a quarry, a coal mine. For about 40 years Mercer was in its pomp. Roose sold the business – the new owners soon gave up on shipping – and died in 1967. His name lives on: the bridge from Mercer to Pukekawa is called the Caesar Roose.

'Look what I've found,' Caesar Roose's daughter Jeanette Thomas said at her marvellous home in Pukekawa. She presented a pair of mounted silver scissors, their jaws wide open. She had snipped the ribbon with them to open the bridge in 1972. She said, 'Te Puea's second husband told me once, "Your father kept Mercer from slipping into the water."' At 76, Jeanette was the curator of her father's achievements; she spoke of nothing else at 'Rio Vista', the house she shared with her husband Bill. Earlier that day Des Thomas had said, 'Say hi to Uncle Bill and Auntie Jeanette when you see them.'

Bill sat in an armchair with a rug over his knees. A big, rangy man, he got up to give a guided tour of the house – the lovely cedar panelling, the balcony that looked over the river. Out the front was a giant cactus. We stood in darkness on the balcony and I asked about the terrible years when Arthur Thomas was in prison. He said that his brother, Arthur's father, had never stopped fighting. 'Strongest man I ever knew.' Then he talked about breaking in the farm. 'Two drums of 2,4,5-T every year to spray the gorse.' There were gunshots in the dusk. *Wise's New Zealand Index*, 1945 edition, said of Mercer, 'Good duck and swan shooting.' Jeanette on Mercer: 'It was always known as the three Rs: river, railroad and Roose.'

A very jolly and beautifully spoken woman, she had driven from St Heliers in Auckland, where she was helping look after her grandchildren, for the interview. There was a vast oil painting of her family on the wall – Bill and Jeanette and their six healthy and wealthy children, posed on hay bales. The walls also included heroic photos of the Roose shipyards and the Roose fleet. She brought out a photo of the kauri house on Tuoro Island in Mercer, where her father was born. Willows and silt have since covered the channel, and the island is now part of the west bank of the Waikato River. The house was destroyed by fire in the 1960s.

The house in the picture bore a striking resemblance to one in a deceased estate advertised for sale opposite the Mercer Cheese Shop. Jeanette flung her hands up to her face in horror. 'Oh!' she said. 'The cheek of those people! It's not the same house at all, of course, but they used a photo of Dad's home to advertise it. I went straight down there to hear an apology. I thought, I can't have this. The whole thing was that he was born on an island and needed to do everything by boat. That's why he knew so much about the river. To have people think his house was in town! I was so furious I decided to buy it.' She bought the house? 'Well, you see, they'd started the auction when I got there.'

She made a vague reference to turning the house into a Caesar Roose museum. But two fabulous exhibits have been open to the public for the past 30 years: the old rusted and beached dredge and old rusted and beached launch on the banks of the river between Mercer and Meremere. Both had belonged to her father. Both are familiar to motorists and train passengers travelling beside the river. Both are reminders of that fond subject: What Mercer used to be.

Now, disassembled by the motorway and bullied by the service centre, the town was a vacuum. Inevitably something had rushed to fill it in the distinctive shape of Joe Heta. Joe lived on the former Mercer reserve beside the river. It looked as though he had set up a commune – there were three buildings on the bare unfenced property, including the old Mercer Town Hall, raised and trucked to this forlorn spot – but apart from several dogs, including two white bichon frisé, he was alone on that Sunday afternoon in the mist, a lithe, nimble man of uncertain age, wearing a poncho, a hunting belt, a warm pair of pants, and boots. He had lightly tattooed hands, a nose ring and approximately four teeth.

He was infamous for his protest in December 2008 against the launch of a 1.5-million-dollar tourist houseboat, *Discovery 1*, at Mercer. He said the owners had failed to consult his iwi, Ngāti Naho. Joe and 'several accomplices', according to the *Waikato Times*, pitched a tent on the riverbank directly in front of the boat's path. This caused great embarrassment to Tainui elders, who were on hand to bless the boat. The owners waited until the tent was packed up, and launched *Discovery 1* a few days later.

Drinkers at the Last Post said, 'Watch him. He's full of bullshit.' But he had charm, humour, eloquence, and possibly even a point. On the tremendously pompous website of the Ngāti Naho Iwi Development Trust Board, where he is referred to as 'hereditary chief, by right of whakapapa and forum votes', he lists the trust's aims and objectives. They include honourable intentions – 'To assist whānau in hardship … To encourage education' – but also: 'To apply for funds … To seek, accept and receive any donations.' Joe refused to be interviewed or photographed. His visitors, he said, needed to have a complete understanding of Māori history in Mercer, or Te Paina, as Māori called the place. He said he had come from a tangi and needed silence to restore his soul. His soul seemed to be flexible, because he then said he would talk for money.

About 30 or 40 minutes passed in this manner. He was good company, but it was so cold standing outside on his peculiar estate, even though the fog had rolled away. He said, 'What's the time?' It was getting on to two. He said, 'The fog'll come back at half-past four.' He was right. It was so thick that the only way of seeing the river was to stand at its edge. As soon as you took a step backwards, it had gone.

# 13 WINTON
## THE GOODNESS OF SWEDES

G raeme Ingils advertised himself as the strangest man in the Southland town of Winton, pop. 2,700. He had painted enormous and very angry signs on the front and side of his battered wooden house. They made for interesting reading in the otherwise perfectly normal country town. Here, near the bottom of New Zealand, a 20-minute drive to the last petrol station in the South Seas, was anarchy and a lot of paint. I walked across the road from my room in the Paramount Motel to speak to the author.

A head poked around the corner of his house and shouted, 'Shut up!' His two lanky English pointers barked at the high metal front gate. The head disappeared, the dogs kept barking, and then Graeme emerged from the front door. He was small and hairy and his eyes weren't right. I shouted, 'I'm interested in the signs!' A smile showed through his close grey beard.

He opened the door of one of seven car wrecks that didn't keep down the weeds in his yard, and ordered the dogs inside. They lay down on the back seat. He said, 'Shut up!' They stopped barking. He approached the gate, folded his arms and said, 'Well, I had a head injury in 1986.' This signalled the beginning of an ancient mariner's tale. Before he got any further I said, 'Are we going to stand here and talk at the gate, or do you think I could come in?' He apologised for his manners and opened the gate. It was tied together with rope. Graeme had the look of a man who was falling apart at the seams.

The wealth of Winton gloated beyond the front and back of his rotting house. His hopelessly overgrown backyard looked over the yards of the town's biggest employer, the sawmill, which smoked day and night, while the greatest prosperity sailed past his front gates – Fonterra milk tankers, their precious cargo sloshing back and forth, pouring money all over Southland.

Graeme had nothing. He was on a sickness benefit. We sat down by the front steps. 'I can't invite you inside,' he said. 'It's filthy.' The front steps were filthy. Graeme was filthy. Two dead motor mowers, one on top of the other, were heaped in a corner of the filthy porch.

The city of Invercargill was only 30 kilometres south on State Highway 96. Guests at the Paramount Motel were just across the road, reading terrible novels and smoking in the sunshine outside their rooms. It all felt a long way away; it was like looking back at childhood.

I was in shadows. Graeme relented and said, 'Okay, come inside.' I wished I hadn't insisted.

The air was fresh and clean at Winton's most famous addition to New Zealand history, the cemetery, where a headstone marks the death of Minnie Dean. The only woman to be hanged in New Zealand lived at 'The Larches' at the north end of town. The bodies of two children and a child's skeleton were discovered on her 22-acre property after police dug up a freshly laid flower bed. Dean, the so-called 'baby farmer' who took in illegitimate children for a fee, was hanged on the morning of Monday, August 12, 1895, at Invercargill gaol. She had woken at four and requested her last meal: a nice hot cup of tea.

The Press Association reported: 'Hundreds of people assembled outside the gaol, and stopped three hours without breakfast. ... During the execution, a boy fell from the roof of a building on to the ground, a distance of 30 feet, fracturing his skull.' Dean was hanged at eight. Her body travelled by train to Winton. Her husband Charles – 'feckless and dull of intellect' a typically balanced report described him – picked her up on his horse and dray. On the way home he stopped in at Top Pub for a drink.

It was only 40 years earlier that axemen had hacked Winton out of the bush and the town had attracted its first settlers – from Limerick in Ireland, and from Edinburgh, Ballantrae, and somewhere called Portchullen in Scotland. A turn-of-the-century photo on the wall at Winton's Middle Pub – the other two pubs are Top Pub and Bottom Pub – shows the dirt track of the main street and a lot of tree stumps. It looks depressing. In reality it was probably even more depressing. Headline 1908: OLD AGE PENSIONER BURNED TO DEATH. 'The Larches' had burned down, unnoticed, in the night. The next morning the charred remains of Charles Dean's body were raked from the – as a misprint had it – 'smocking ruins'.

Winton grew, slowly. Rhubarb grew, quickly, in mounds of fowl manure. Sheep and cattle arrived. The Allen family arrived, including the brother of the last living survivor of the Battle of Waterloo. Tinned meat and tongues were exported to Britain from Winton's Boiling-down Works. Wells were dug; children were told to beware playing anywhere near them, and given an incentive – the devil, their parents said, lived down the well. It became a local custom for schoolboys to jump on Minnie Dean's unmarked grave.

One…two…three…four Fonterra tankers drove by Graeme Ingils' house in less than an hour on a warm Friday afternoon in early autumn, when the town clock, which also gave the temperature, read 26 degrees.

It wasn't 26 degrees. It was more like 17 or 18. Gillian McFarlane really did grit her teeth. In her Country Manners gift shop on Winton's main street she sold silver spoons to a customer, and continued expressing her outrage at the incorrect temperature. She said it was a scandal. Last November, when the Tour of Southland cycle race came to Winton, the temperature on the town clock had made the wild claim that it was minus four degrees. 'TV1 and TV3 were here,' she said. 'It's a very bad look.'

She had agitated for it to be fixed but no one wanted to know, including Rotary, which had donated the digital clock and temperature gauge. 'Rotary like to donate, then abandon. Bunch of wallies.'

At least it was an improvement on the old town clock. The time on that had been wrong. Actually, it had been right but only twice a day, and just for a minute. Gillian said, 'It was 20 past ten in Winton for 27 years.' Permanent morning or everlasting night? Was there a difference in those 27 static years? Winton, going about its sheepy business at the bottom of the South Island, with fat trout jumping in the Oreti River and flat, swamp-drained fields stuffed with New Zealand's best swedes.

Then came the revolution. Margaret Kane at the Paramount Motel said it happened overnight. That was how it felt when the first wave of North Island farmers arrived in the mid 1990s and began converting sheep farms to dairy. Cheap wool and lamb chops made way for the lucrative swirl of cow milk. Southland was now the fastest-growing region for milk output, with an increase of 50 percent in the past five years.

Old traditions remained. Winton was about to host the Bride of the Year contest. A frost arrived that morning; Margaret Kane said, 'You don't have a swede 'til you've had a frost.' I said, 'What did you say?' I had heard her the first time but I wanted to hear her say it again, for the sound and the certainty of it. She said, 'You don't have a swede 'til you've had a frost.' I asked her about the virtues of swedes. She said, 'They're animal feed but kids like 'em raw. They taste like apples. Or turnips.'

As ever, shearing gangs were in town for the season. They included Megan Thomas, 20, from Balclutha, and Debbie Clarke, 45, of Winton. Debbie poured a bottle of Tui into her teacup. We were sitting in the beer garden of Middle Pub at noon. 'Fonterra have a good thing going, but… nah, sheep'll come back,' said Megan. 'There's still shearing work around.'

New practices thrived. There was only one empty shop on the main street, which was an elegant destination for Saturday shoppers from Invercargill, Gore and Queenstown. Winton is a pretty town. There are mauve rhododendrons, horse chestnut trees, and sunflowers that grow to terrific heights. Crime is rare and usually petty; there had been a run of diesel thefts, senior sergeant Richard McPhail said, and last year thieves from Christchurch targeted jet skis. They were caught in the cemetery after they'd got stoned and slept it off by the gravestones. You can get a big feed at the burger bar, which does the Winton Stop Over for $9.90 – double beef, double cheese, double pineapple. There are jewellery and fashion stores, beauty treatments, an expensive restaurant.

I asked Gillian McFarlane to name the most popular item in her gift store. She pointed to a pot of Scullys Lavender Sleep Aid. 'When they asked me to sell it I said, "It's a load of hogwash." My father was a doctor, you see. They said, "Well, take a dozen free of charge." A woman came in the next day and asked about it. I said, "Madam, it's up to you if you want to buy it, but I'm telling you it's pure bunkum." Well, I sold out by the end of the week, re-ordered it, the same thing happened, re-ordered it. I generally sell two or three pots every day.'

I liked the thought of Winton enjoying a sound sleep, and I liked Gillian. I liked her archaic language – 'hogwash', 'bunkum'. I liked her frantic impulsive manner. She said, 'I was put out on the streets at a very early age by my parents to help save Manapōuri.' Was it nature or nurture that made her so… loud? She had a kind of American confidence. She had been born in Invercargill, and travelled to London, then New York, where she met her husband Marc. I would have felt disappointed if he was merely a Mark because so much about Gillian's life spelled the word 'different'. I heard that word quite a few times in Winton. It was the worst thing they could say about someone.

They grimaced when they named the local arsonist who, they suspected, had burned down the museum last year; he was, they said, 'a dipstick'. They shrugged when they described the new dairy farmers as 'North Island knob heads'. But they narrowed their eyes when they said: 'He's different.' They meant Graeme Ingils, the outsider with the signs and the dogs. They also said it of Gavin Bell, proprietor and editor of the town's excellent newspaper *The Winton Record* – he was new to Winton, had come from Matamata in the North Island in 1994. Asked about Gillian, they said, 'She's different.'

The antagonism was less to do with her agitations about the temperature reading than her famous and quite radical overhaul of Winton's Open Day. Open Day is held every year on a Sunday and attracts visitors from Southland; there are stalls, music, floral displays. Most amazing of all, the shops are open. According to Gillian, though, 'It'd waned. I spent my time apologising to people from Queenstown who came expecting an event. I began to think, what do we do here that's special?' And then one day last year she had an epiphany. She was driving home on a gravel road when she suddenly braked hard. She'd seen Fonterra's slogan on a letterbox: IT STARTS HERE. 'I thought, It's the grass! It's always about the grass, and what we turn it into!'

The light bulb in her head illuminated the idea that dairying produces ice cream. She pushed – and pushed and pushed – the Winton Business Association and Winton Area Promotions, and Winton's Open Day thus became Winton's Ice-Cream Sunday Festival. There were ice-cream stalls, weird and wonderful ice-cream flavours, ice-cream art. Gillian said, 'It was terrific. It created a dynamic and was the biggest open day ever. Shopkeepers were rushed off their feet.' Gavin Bell at *The Winton Record* said, 'It was... o-*kay*.' And Chub McHugh, chair of Winton District Council, said: 'It was... good. But there's room for improvement.'

Only the taxman called him John; everyone else acknowledged Chub as Winton's unofficial mayor. The wide range of his endeavours – past president of Lions, the rugby club, the bowling club; trustee of this, trustee of that – suggested he performed the work of many men. Chub was also the size of many men. You could say he was Winton's focal point. More than its politician-in-chief, he was its host, a role he also performed as a publican. Chub had taken over the Middle Pub nineteen years earlier, on May 19. A man wearing a cap walked in. Chub said, 'Gidday, Jock.'

Everyone knew Chub and spoke of him with respect and affection. He knew everyone, and everything that went on. I mentioned the exotic presence of Filipino men standing around on the main street. He said they started arriving three or four years ago to work on dairy farms; the wives ran a support centre and had set up their own credit union and insurance. 'I've actually got one of them working for me. They're great employees. You tell them what to do and they'll do it.'

Other new families from South Africa, England and Zimbabwe had led to a rise in Winton School's roll from 160 to 241. Gillian said, 'About three years ago my husband came home and said, "I just saw a black person. Really black!" I said, "So?" He said, "Isn't it wonderful."'

I saw a Frenchman. 'I milks the cows,' he said. Not all of them – there were a record 418,337 dairy cows in Southland province last season, outnumbering people four to one. He gave a possibly Gallic sigh when he said he worked 60 hours a week for ten dollars an hour after tax. But wealth was elsewhere. On a recent weekend, Gillian had counted five four-wheel-drive Porsches in Winton.

I was more excited when she said Graeme Ingils had come to see her that day. I said, 'You know Graeme?' Yes, she said, they'd met a few times. I received this information as very good news. He'd told me he didn't talk to anyone in Winton. By the time I'd left his appalling house, shaken at what I had seen inside, I was in despair that his life must be just about entirely insufferable.

The two signs on the side of his house read ACC SUX and REINZ SUX. If these beefs against the Accident Compensation Corporation and the Real Estate Industry of New Zealand were general, then the two signs on the front of the house were specific. They targeted a Labour Party MP and a National Party MP: DAMIEN O'CONNOR IS CORRUPT and PHIL HEATLEY IS A CROOK.

With the dogs in the back seat of a Nissan, a Kingswood, two Subarus and other wrecks in the long grass, a blackberry bush coiled over the back fence, and Fonterra tankers, silver streaks, driving past on a warm Friday afternoon, Graeme had begun his tale.

A tree had fallen on him in the bush. He was living in Nelson. He went on accident compensation. Then he won $50,000 on Instant Kiwi and bought a three-hectare lifestyle block in Motueka. 'Beautiful it was. Sun in the morning. It looked over d'Urville Island.'

He lived on it with his partner, Christine, in a house bus. He dug a well, made plans to plant olive trees. 'But I was getting sicker and sicker. They couldn't figure out what was wrong with me. They said, "Post-concussion syndrome." They said, "There's something wrong with you up here."' He tapped his head. 'But it felt like I was wasting away inside. It got to the point where I said to Christine, "I'm no good to you. Let's just sell up. You need your own life."'

I had the feeling his narrative was about to hinge on a fatal decision. He duly provided it. He said he couldn't find a buyer so he called in at the electoral office of Damien O'Connor. The next morning a member of O'Connor's staff turned up with a buyer 'but I woke up so ill I could hardly walk. I was having one of my episodes. I said, "I can't talk to you." They said, "Is there anything we can do for you?" I said, "You can shoot me." Okay. Now, what do you think they should have done?'

I said, 'Told you they'd come back when you were feeling better.' He looked stunned. It was the wrong answer. 'No,' he said. 'They should have got me some medical help.'

He returned to his story. They – O'Connor and his people – took advantage of a sick man. He sold up. Christine left. 'Someone said, "You can get a house in Nightcaps for $10,000." I was so sick I didn't even think what the hell I'd do when I got there. I just thought, I can afford that.'

Nightcaps is a small coal-mining town near Winton. The real estate salesman, he said, lied to him. 'I got sucked in. Again.' Life was dreadful there. He moved to Winton. 'But I'm not living anywhere,' he said. 'I just exist.'

That was the long and the short of it. 'Imagine how angry I am. I should never have sold in Motueka. I can't get over losing Christine and losing my property. Look where I am now!' He waved a hand at the house. It was a dump, a shabby wooden box – if it looked haunted, then Graeme was its ghost. The signs, he said, were 'my way of poking something back at them'. Why had he also targeted National MP Phil Heatley? 'Oh well,' he said. 'They're all crooks.' As for the car wrecks, he used to work as a panel beater and had bought the wrecks with the intention of fixing them up and selling them. 'But that all turned to custard. My health just got worse.'

In October 2008, though, he discovered the true cause. 'I was suffering from vitamin D deficiency. I've probably had it all my life. If the soil in the garden's no good, your plant won't be any good. I was a sick plant. I've been taking pills since finding out, and I'm just about back on track. Two weeks ago I started feeling really good.'

Thank god. He frankly admitted he thought of his situation as hopeless – 60 years old, apparently friendless, no prospect of work – but on the plus side his health was returning. He said he'd started taking long walks. I thought, maybe things aren't so bad for Graeme. But then he invited me inside the house.

The air was fresh and clean at the farm of Todd and Fleur Anderson. The couple ran sheep and cows. Todd's passion was genetics. 'I just love breeding animals,' he said. He had broken the world record three times, paying $13,200, then $15,500, then $16,000 for Southdown rams. He always bought his rams from Chris Medlicott, a legendary stud breeder in Waimate, Canterbury.

Chris and his wife Shelley were visiting the Andersons. Freshly picked roses stood in a vase. The house was tasteful and immaculate, despite the presence of Todd and Fleur's three young kids. Todd came from Invercargill; Fleur had worked in human relations at TVNZ and Sky City in Auckland. 'We love Winton,' she said. She had taken her eldest and youngest children to the town's maternity centre for five nights of antenatal care. 'It's beautiful there. Just beautiful.' Todd spoke fluently about farming – 'protein production, you can call it. That's exactly what it is really' – but I was dying for him to show me his latest acquisition, a Southdown ram he had bought from Chris Medlicott for $13,000 at the Canterbury A&P Association's Stud Ram and Ewe Fair in January.

The ram was in a pen with six ewes. Todd grabbed hold of him. 'He's just all power,' he said. 'Sheer power. He's exceptionally balanced. Good top line; it flows all the way to the shoulders. He doesn't look very big.

That's the secret to a good Southdown: they don't look big, but they weigh… I saw him as a lamb. He was an excellent lamb. All power, early maturing.'

Todd claimed, 'We've had vegetarians eat Southdown meat.' Well, it was entirely permissible to stare at the ram's compact, well-muscled hindquarters and imagine the delicious rib-eye cuts he would father. He had a name: Tasvic 308, an abbreviation of Tasmania and Victoria. Friends of Chris Medlicott's father who lived in those places had given Chris his first Southdown ewe when he was fifteen, a thank-you for his family's hospitality. The gift led to his Southdown stud farm in the Hook district near Waimate.

In 2005, when he sold Todd Anderson a ram for $16,000 – still the world record – he said in an interview with *The Press*, 'I want to breed one better than him. … You always have to aim high. I have yet to breed the perfect sheep.' And now perhaps he had. I asked Todd which was his best-ever Southdown ram. He grabbed hold of Tasvic 308 again and said, 'I think this is it. This is the most excited I've been in a long time.'

His excitement was contagious. It was a genuinely thrilling experience to witness sheepy perfection in the flesh, but after I left and came back to town to gnaw on a Winton Stop Over, I ran into Graeme Ingils. The joy I'd felt drained away. Every time I saw Graeme, I was reminded of his home and contents.

He had taken to walking, a lot, several times a day. I ran into him every time I returned to my motel. His perambulations were no doubt just something to do, but also for the exhilaration of feeling alive and well. It was the most exercise he'd taken in years.

Well, he needed a good airing. The stench and abominable filth inside his house had hit me like a shock. The sitting room wasn't a sitting room. There was nowhere to sit. It was piled to the ceiling with axles, fenders, tyres. It didn't make any sense; it was like a house that had been turned inside-out. A scrap metal yard had become the interior of his home. It wasn't a home, it was a prolonged nervous breakdown.

The kitchen wasn't a kitchen. It was a pond of grime. Every room was dark. All the curtains were drawn. The coatings of dust were thick as toast. There was the smell of damp and the stink of dog; the two scents added up a stench that was high and very bad. He searched for a photo of himself before he was sick. I stood in the hallway as he dragged a suitcase out from under his bed. The bedroom was, vaguely, a bedroom. It had a bed, a TV, a closet. It was dark and it stank. There was no way I was going to ask to see the toilet.

I felt dizzy, short of breath, but it was not my own health I was concerned about. I imagined the poor hairy devil living in this foul hovel day after day, obsessing about his vitamin D, bitter and monomaniacal, behind closed doors and shut windows and drawn curtains, moving among the junk and the rust. What was it he'd said on the front steps: 'I'm not living anywhere. I just exist.' I couldn't wait to leave. I'd felt afraid – for him, and of him. Also, I began to hate him. He felt something much worse: he was ashamed.

Well, he had every right to feel ashamed about what he'd allowed himself to sink to in his disgusting house. He refused to shoulder the blame. He saw himself as a victim, pushed around, sucked in, left for dead. But the strangest thing about Graeme – for all his physical weakness, his emotional collapse, his insane decor – was that he was completely sane.

He listened. He had a sense of humour. He was generous. He had good manners. He had friends too, if you counted Gillian McFarlane, and he also referred to a 'mate' who visited from nearby Ōtautau. And despite his insistence that he was a kind of hermit, there he was, out and about on the streets of quiet pretty Winton, getting some air and exercise, scarfed up as a cold wind blew in from the south. Maybe the town would reach out and save him. Maybe he would reach out and save himself. He looked good for his age, and he had beautiful blue eyes.

# 14 TANGIMOANA
## LAMENT OF THE OCEAN

You couldn't hear yourself cough in Sanson. All the world and his wife gunned its engines through that dot on the map of the North Island at the intersection of State Highway One and State Highway Three. It was like a delta town, small and quivering on the banks where two great roaring rivers met, but there was nothing watery about it. The dry, biscuity flatlands of the Manawatū Plains stretched out as far as the eye could see. There wasn't much to see. The only thing that rose above the line of the horizon was exhaust smoke burning from cars and rigs and horse floats about to pass through Sanson, pop. 450.

The motel's striking colour scheme – white with red trim – gleamed in the bright summer light, and put you in mind of the Red Cross. A caravan park at the back of the property was a retirement home for John Field, 74, a big man with a big red nose and a body as brown as a chestnut. He sat outside his caravan wearing only a small pair of shorts. 'The ex-missus is in Havelock North and I've got two children somewhere in London. So I'm happy.'

He had set up a portable TV on a picnic table and was watching Trackside. 'I don't gamble,' he said, 'but if I was I'd be making a lot of money.' How much money? 'Well, I predicted the winners of a quinella in Wairoa yesterday. Five dollars would've got me two hundred and twenty.' Betting was a luxury. He stuck to the necessities. There was an eighteen-can carton of Double Brown at his feet, and a loaf of bread and a pair of pliers on the picnic table.

At the petrol station, Peter White from Bulls was inside paying for gas. His large beard looked as coarse as horsehair. He'd graffitied his own car. A theme had emerged: POLICE SUCKS. ACC SUCKS. RUTH SUCKS. The headlines drew a crowd – me and a teenage kid. I observed, 'A lot of things suck.' The kid nodded, and said, 'Apparently.' I asked, 'Why d'you think Ruth sucks?' He said, 'Be a girlfriend who dumped his arse. He's all bitter and shit.'

The kid was wrong about the girlfriend and right about the psychological state. Ruth, Peter said, was Ruth Dyson, a former ACC minister. It was under her watch that the department had wronged him.

Peter ranted about his ancient grievances for a while and then drove away. Everyone drove away at Sanson. That was the point of the place. The few who remained gathered after dark at the Sanson Club, a private bar set up in a classroom of the former primary school. John at the caravan park claimed the school closed down because it was beneath the flight path of the nearby Ōhakea air base.

Sanson's theme was noise. Automobile traffic, air traffic – such volume for a dot on the map. It inspired a quest for peace and quiet. Half an hour away, out west, was the peace and quiet of beach settlement Tangimoana.

The road to Tangimoana led past low fields of crops. It led past Ōhakea, where a black RNZAF helicopter fluttered and flapped like a lovely black moth, and indulged in a lengthy exercise that had something to do with lowering a rope. There was an amusing AA sign that claimed: OHAKEA DOMAIN. It pointed to an abandoned swimming pool painted eggshell blue. The fields glowed golden in the sun. There was the Clydesdale Memorial Hall, stucco and nailed shut. Everywhere, there were white cabbage butterflies, great clusters filling their boots and scoffing the light green roadside, falling as thick as snow.

And there, at the end of the line, was Tangimoana, pop. 290. It was sandy and there weren't many streets. It smelled of pine needles and sea salt. A ginger cat stretched itself on a white windowsill; an old man stretched himself on a bicycle. There was one guest staying at the caravan park, an old divorcée with pleading eyes. There was one telephone box outside the town's one store, the Country Shoppe, which had closed down.

A river-mouth town, a fishing village. The tide was unusually low that afternoon. It surprised the skipper of an aluminium boat tauntingly named *No Worries*. He'd got a good catch of gurnard, crossed the bar back into Tangimoana, but as the tide streamed out the motor wouldn't catch, and the boat had to be roped and pulled back through mud to the boat ramp.

The light in the sky began to pale. The sand was sketched with driftwood, great crates of the stuff, lying white and sun-bleached, as smooth as bone. It was a classic west coast beach, with big rollers crashing on the shore and gouging out the dark sand. A family of three parked at the boat ramp. A little boy leaped out of the car, and immediately kicked and chased a rugby ball. His mother wore a T-shirt that read TWATZ UP DARTS. The surf's muffled collapse, the warmth of the sun, *No Worries*... I drank in the sight of bar-tailed godwits legging it through the low tide and happily dozed off, resting my head on the sand.

A brief history of Tangimoana, part one:

March 15, 1965: A swordfish is washed ashore on the beach.

July 13, 1987: The decomposed body of a nineteen-year-old Massey University student is found in the dunes. It has been there for several weeks. 'No suspicious circumstances,' say police.

August 16, 1990: The decomposed body of a 30-year-old man from Bulls is found in the dunes. It has been there for four months. 'No suspicious circumstances,' say police.

October 25, 1993: Clothed in a bra, jeans and socks, the body of teenager Michelle Dermer is found in a Tangimoana swamp, eight weeks after she was last seen leaving a friend's house to walk 100 metres to her home. 'Suspicious circumstances,' say police.

They interview several persons of interest, even her brother Jason, who is in prison serving a life sentence for killing a student and burying the body in a shallow grave in Lindis Pass. The cause of his sister's death is ruled accidental.

January 13, 2010: A pilot whale is washed ashore on the beach.

The chronicle of death on the beach was courtesy of Ron Gardner, 81, the first person I talked to in Tangimoana. He was walking along the pavement. That sentence needs completing: he was walking along the pavement by himself. His wife Joan had died six months ago. 'I'm just on my own now,' he said. 'The neighbours keep an eye on me. I got a pushbike. I try to keep fit.'

He was fit as a fiddle, slim, with a good straight back and working man's hands, but he was lonely. In fact, his heart was broken. He lived life as a full-time widower. How was he coping? He said, 'Not very good.'

We walked back around the corner to his house. 'There's Joan,' he said. He pointed to a photo of her on the card prepared for her funeral. There were photos of Ron's two brothers. 'They're both dead now. That one had his own fishing trawler. He picked up survivors off the *Wahine* in it.'

Ron and Joan had raised their family in Wellington. When Ron retired, he bought a caravan. 'We went all over the place.' Where to? 'Well, we got as far as Foxton.' He heard about a section further up the coast at Tangimoana and bought it that same day. There were two houses on it: a yellow stucco bach, which his son's family sometimes stayed in, and his own modern home. He'd stacked firewood for winter. The contents of his fridge were milk, butter, eggs, three bottles of beer, and an enormous jar of mayonnaise.

He found Joan's scrapbook of news clippings about Tangimoana. A friend had started it and later passed it on to Joan, who kept it up to date by snipping the few stories about Tangimoana from *The Dominion* and *Manawatu Evening Standard*. As well as reports about decomposing bodies, there were a lot of stories about the building that had made Tangimoana famous.

The US spy station had opened on August 18, 1982. Ron's scrapbook contained numerous newspaper stories quoting government officials denying it was a US spy station. The denials kept coming, even after 1984, when peace campaigner Owen Wilkes revealed it was a US spy station. That same year *Listener* journalist David Young wrote, 'It has a high-frequency, direction-finding (HF-DF) antenna array, which acts like a giant vacuum cleaner, identifying and sucking up radio communications traffic within 3,000 kilometres.'

No it hasn't, responded government officials, somehow keeping a straight face. It was an X-file played out as pure farce. For years, the worst-kept secret in New Zealand was the existence and operation of a US spy station, its sophisticated HF-DF antennae array on non-stop listening alert in the unlikely seaside village of Tangimoana.

The Americans had chosen the site in Tangimoana because of its obscure location on government land, and also because its iron-sand base offered a low 'noise floor'. The spies could listen in on top-secret yap in perfectly silent conditions. They, too, had come to Tangimoana for the peace and quiet.

Good for them. Was it good for Tangimoana? Intelligence-gathering among the quiet iron sands, electronic interceptions as rabbits bred exactly like rabbits outside the tall barbed wire fence…

'I was fortunate enough to speak to an old-timer who had a hand in rigging the antenna,' wrote a correspondent to the website *Mysterious New Zealand*. 'One particularly high-gain array (the curtain type – looks like a giant spider web) they were installing began throwing riggers around by zapping them with RF energy. This was being picked up from the HF transmitter site at Hīmatangi 30-odd kilometres away. …Talk about free power eh.'

But what else was released? What paranoias and manias were conducted through the fields of static? What psychic voltage moved in the air? What's the frequency, Kenneth? It can't have been any good. The point of the US spy station was harm. What did it do to Tangimoana, population allegedly 290?

There was a story missing from Ron and Joan's scrapbook. 'What's that?' he asked, smiling. I said, 'The vigilantes.' He said, 'Oh. Them. Well.

A bad business.' He'd stopped smiling. 'Leave me out of it.' He put on the kettle for a cup of tea in the spotless kitchen. The radio played the Elton John and Kiki Dee duet 'Don't Go Breaking My Heart'.

She was in her garage in Tangimoana on Friday afternoon building a trailer. She looked like she knew what she was doing. She knew what she doing. 'My background is building. I was with Fletchers. I did project management construction.' She was 41, with bright sparkling eyes and short curly hair just beginning to grey, wearing work boots and an old pair of jeans loose around her slim hips, and her bare arms in her T-shirt were black with grease. She was the infamous Tracy Thomsen, up on charges of kidnapping and threatening to kill.

Tracy was with her husband Marcus, 37, an engineer and tractor driver up on the same charges. I interviewed them in the front yard and Tracy did most of the talking. Marcus bowed his head and seemed reluctant to be there.

Tracy said, 'The whole thing stuffed us. Emotionally for me, I couldn't handle it. Emotional fucking wreck.'

I said, 'Did you go on medication?'

She said, 'Nah, I went on alcohol – alcohol-induced comas sometimes. That's the only way I knew how to cope with it and get to sleep so my mind wouldn't be going all the time. I was a very angry, bitter person so I made it my mission to get that family out of town. Come hell or high water. And they ended up moving out of town. Yep. I thought, well, this isn't going to be all in vain.'

I said, 'How did you achieve that?'

She said, 'They had all the windows in their house smashed in the middle of winter. They had no water. No vehicles – they had their motorbikes stolen from outside their house while they were in bed, and taken down the river and burned out. Just made sure their life here was hell. Yep.'

Her bitter little satisfaction didn't seem to do her much good. 'The whole thing blew my whole life apart,' she said. 'Lost my business. Police took away my liquor licence and firearms licence.' Then she said in a quieter voice, 'Me and Marcus split up for a few months.' He'd returned only that day. Her face crumpled and she made a tremendous effort to fight back the tears. She lost the fight.

I turned to Marcus and said, 'How does it sit with you that you now have a criminal record?'

He said, 'Yeah, nah, it's good. I'm not ashamed of what I done at all. It's good to walk around and know that I done the right thing.'

'What would you have changed?'

'Not told anyone. I wouldn't have told anyone and gone by myself so no one would have known.'

'And done what?'

He laughed.

I said, 'Beaten the shit out of him?'

'Ahhh, yep. Probably. Yep.'

'But you'd have been done for assault.'

'No, because no one would of known. And no one would of been any the wiser.'

'But he'd have probably reported it to the cops.'

'Well,' Marcus said, 'he probably wouldn't be here to report it.'

I really wasn't sure whether 'here' meant Tangimoana or whether it meant alive. Marcus said, 'If you were going to do it by yourself, then no one would know. If he's just walking around in the middle of the night, and no one knows he's there, and no one knows you're there... But the way we did it was just... looking back at it, it was just stupid.'

A brief history of Tangimoana, part two:

Tracy and Marcus Thomsen, their close friend Kieran Grice, and two other men were arrested on September 2, 2007 for what they did that Sunday night in Tangimoana to 16-year-old Jonathan Blair. The police found him in a bruised and bloody mess, with his wrists and ankles bound by cable ties. The charges included kidnapping, assault, intent to injure, and threatening to kill. The accused were looking at prison. They pleaded not guilty. They said they acted on the advice of police when they restrained Blair.

Yes, they said, they wanted to run Blair out of town, because they believed he was the culprit behind a wave of petty crimes.

No, they said, they didn't threaten that they were going to bury him in the forest.

Yes, they said, they used physical force to take him out of the house.

No, they said, they didn't beat him up.

Their actions were reduced to one exciting word that looked so good on banner headlines: VIGILANTES.

The whole drama dragged through the courts for three years and three trials – two were declared mistrials – until some charges were dropped, Tracy, Marcus and Kieran pleaded guilty to other charges, and were each given sentences requiring them to perform community work.

It seemed like a light sentence, but they were adamant they shouldn't have been up on anything in the first place. The court case had changed their lives for the worse. They felt victimised, sensationalised as 'vigilantes', and now they had to pay back crippling legal fees. They all said they'd never done anything wrong, that they'd tried to do the right thing.

What was the moral of the story? Marcus said, 'Don't get caught.'

Tracy said, 'Don't do what a police officer tells you to do.'

They took some satisfaction in the irony that only person in the whole drama who went to prison was Jonathan Blair. He was sentenced to eight months for a range of petty offences, including a burglary he had committed the night before he was due to give evidence against Tracy, Marcus and Kieran. He'd been caught in a derelict building intending to steal copper wire. After being granted bail, he had popped into another courtroom down the corridor, and taken the witness stand to tell his story of the night he was set on by vigilantes.

Tracy said, 'The paper made it like these big strong adults beat the living shit out of this poor little kid.'

I said, 'Wasn't that the case?'

'No,' she said. 'I wish it was.'

'What about threatening to kill him?'

'Nah, fuck off. We wanted to run him out of town, definitely. We said, "You've got to leave town. Just stay away." Definitely we said that.'

She described Blair as a big kid with peroxide hair and FUCK THE POLICE tattooed on his knuckles. He had come to live with his aunt and uncle in Tangimoana and suddenly there was a spate of crimes. 'Lawnmowers getting taken, a couple of houses broken into. I heard a story that Ross down the road caught him taking whitebait out of an old guy's whitebaiting bucket.'

Then, she said, her shop was broken into and burgled. What got taken? 'Cigarettes and lollies.' She suspected Blair. She went to see him at his aunt and uncle's house. 'The only smokes they ever bought from me were Longbeach 40s because they're the cheapest, but the uncle, the aunt and Jonathan were all smoking different kinds. One was John Brandon, one was Winfield Red. I forget what the other one was.' I was impressed she remembered two of the brands. In any case, the family denied any wrongdoing. Tracy called the police, who came out to the shop several days after the burglary, said there wasn't anything they could do, and left.

Around that time the shop was graffitied with the words BITCH, SLUT and WHORE. Then Tracy came across Blair and a teenage girl loitering outside the shop at one-thirty in the morning. Blair was carrying an iron bar. He took off. She called the police, who came out that night with a warrant for his arrest. They left empty-handed. Blair had moved out of his uncle's house. People heard that the uncle had got drunk, given his nephew a thrashing, and thrown him out. No one knew where he was staying. He'd gone to ground in a river-mouth town with a population of 290.

Then, she said, 'It all went out of control, really.'

So, Sunday night in Tangimoana, September 2, 2007: the crash of the Tasman Sea, mosquitoes breeding in the backwash of water behind the camping ground, creepy eavesdroppings at the American spy base hidden behind trees. Tracy, Marcus and their son drove to Palmerston North to watch *The Simpsons Movie*. It was Father's Day. They drove home, and got to bed at eight-thirty.

'So then,' said Tracy, 'we got woken up by Kieran. He's in the volunteer fire brigade and they'd got put on standby because Jonathan Blair had threatened to burn down the shop and a house. He'd beaten up someone that day, a young guy at university, and been driving around town all day like a lunatic in a silver Honda, and he was still hiding from the police, and we got word he was hiding out at this girl's place.'

Tracy spoke to a policewoman in nearby Feilding. 'I says, "Are we just supposed to sit around and wait for him to burn something down before you'll come out and do anything?"

'She says, "Have you got an idea where he is?"

'I says, "Yes."

'She says, "Well, if you can get a group of people together and detain him, and then give us a call, we'll come straight out."

'I says, "How are we supposed to detain him?"

'And she says, "You can use reasonable force."

'I says, "Well, what's reasonable force?"

'She says, "You're not allowed to beat him up. If you beat him up, we'll know."

'I says, "All right, expect a phone call soon then."

'So we went around there. I said, "You guys go around the edge and I'll go to the door." I thought me being smaller, being female, I might be able to keep him calm. Ha! Good intentions.

'I went to the door and knocked. It was a sliding door. I stepped back and the guy who owned the house pulled back the curtain. I told them we'd come to restrain Jonathan until the cops arrived, and he says, "Jonathan, it's for you."

'He comes to the door and grunts, "Yeah?" I tell him we've come to restrain him for the cops. He looks around sideways and sees the guys.

'I says, "You're not getting away this time." He steps back and I grab him, put one hand on his shoulder and the other on his arm. I put my head down and I'm holding on for dear life. I didn't know what else to do so I just held on to him. I get dragged inside the house and yell out to Marcus for help. Marcus comes in and grabs him, puts his arm behind his back, picks him up in a bear hug, carries him outside and throws him off the deck on to the grass.'

Marcus entered the narrative. 'Yeah, nah, we fell off the end of the deck. I couldn't see. It was dark.'

Tracy continued, 'The other guys came around and held him down too. I was still inside the house and they says, "Why are you doing this?" I says, "He's threatened to burn down the shop. We just want the police to come and get him." I says, "Call the police." They says, "Don't worry about that, we're gonna call the police straightaway."

'So everything was all calm inside, not a problem. The guys were sitting on him outside, and I just sat on the edge of the deck and waited for the police to come. He was yelling and screaming and crying, "Let me go, let me go. I promise I won't do anything again." And "Hey, just let me go and I'll be good, we'll have a few beers and we'll go out fishing." Fishing!

'So this went on for three-quarters of an hour. Because he's kicking and punching and the guys are trying to hold him down on the ground, Kieran came up with the idea of getting cable ties. He ran back home – I remember he had his moccasins on – to get some ties, and he came back and he ties his ankles together and his hands behind his back.

'Two of the guys pick him up and put him in the middle of the driveway. Jonathan's just sitting on his lonesome on the gravel driveway. He's got a bit of blood on him and his shirt's a bit mangled 'cos his nose hit the kitchen bench when Marcus struggled with him.

'So the police turn up and the first thing they do, they come running straight over to him and yell out, "Who did this? Who did this?" And Kieran goes, "I did, sir. I did." And the cops go straightaway, "Arrest him! Arrest him for kidnapping!" No questions, no nothing. Bang. Decision made. Done.'

How much of Tracy's story was true? In court, crown lawyers said the family hiding Blair were terrified, and frantically called the cops out to the house to prevent the teenager being murdered. Tracy claimed they looked on blithely as the kid got hogtied and said, 'Not a problem.' The three trials, the policewoman in Feilding 'covering her arse', as Tracy put it, the expense, the enormous stress, the rancid coleslaw and mayo sandwiches for lunch in the court cells, Marcus leaving her... Just about the least of it was the taint of that exciting word 'vigilante'. Was it even a taint? 'Yeah, well if that's what it takes when the police don't do their job,' said Tracy, 'then whatever. Maybe there need to be a few more in little communities around New Zealand.'

In 2005 I reported on a peculiar drama in the West Coast town of Blackball, when a butcher and a sickly lunatic persuaded a convicted paedophile to pack up and leave. Graham Wootton had bought a house in town. The police told the school, the school told the parents. Pat Kennedy, 61, the town's butcher, and his friend Geoff Strong knocked on Wootton's door. They said, 'You probably know a paedophile has moved into town. Are you that person?'

He would neither confirm nor deny. It wasn't the most brilliant answer in the world. When they knocked on his door, they didn't know if Wootton was the man they wanted. Five other families had recently moved into Blackball and fingers were pointed at every new face, but Wootton's witless reply gave away his identity.

His visitors told him he wasn't welcome. Wootton said, 'Do you expect me to just pack up and leave?' Yes, they said. So he did, that day, with his wife, a deaf mute. The couple had already left when a local man and sickness beneficiary Alan Gurden, 38, set up a vigil across the road from Wootton's house to discourage him from returning.

Blackball, pop. 360, content to mind its own business, was suddenly the hub of vigilantes and vigils. While Gurden and friends camped outside Wootton's house in tents, others brought scones, cakes and sausages, did the dishes, and provided firewood to burn in a 40-gallon drum. There was crazy talk of tailing the furniture truck when it came to empty Wootton's house.

Possibly even less sanely, the town's visiting vicar agreed to perform an exorcism on the house. The previous owner had been a woman described as a grumpy old bitch, who chopped down a stand of attractive oak trees. Before that there had been a woman who spent a lot of time in the pub to get away from her violent husband. Before that there was a man who topped himself. Maybe the exorcism wasn't such a bad idea. The walls crawled with years of misery.

I arrived in Blackball on a Friday afternoon in late autumn. I walked down the main street until it was completely dark, as black as the coal that built the town. I turned along a side street and saw a couple sitting on deckchairs in their front yard. They had lit a small wood fire and there was a pot of something cooking on the logs. I stood and spied on them, hypnotised by the beautiful flames, and thought, They look like the luckiest people in the world.

This was almost certainly sentimental nonsense, but the town was so pretty, with its willows and rowanberries, its drowsy and delicious smell of burning coal from every chimney.

Not quite every chimney. Wootton's house of misery already looked as sealed as a tomb. I snooped in the letterbox. There was an unopened letter from the Ministry of Justice. I snooped in the garage. There was a flyer on the floor advertising children's karaoke. A woman and her two daughters, aged nine and eleven, offered to 'host your party … we love to sing, and are available to hire for birthday parties or any special occasion'. I also found a sheet of paper containing a handwritten lyric Wootton had copied from the song 'Honky Tonk Angels'. Second verse: 'I didn't know God made honky tonk angels / I might have known you'd never make a wife.'

A paedophile who played and sang country music, was married to a deaf mute, and bought a home in a small cold town before being slung out on his arse – his life had turned into a country music dirge.

Mist covered the hills, and trailed Grey River, Blackwater Creek and Moonlight Creek. The willows wore red, the oaks yellow. Above the men's toilet in the pub there was a sign that read HOG SWAMP and a poster advertising local boxer Eric Briggs, 'the West Coast Tattooed Man', who ran a lawnmowing business. I was shown what sphagnum moss looks like by a guy who wandered into swamps and harvested the stuff with a pitchfork.

There were lovely elms, and thick flax bushes, and wide clumps of bamboo growing out of the marshy soil. Everything was coated by the thin black smoke and delicious aroma of burning coal – famously, Blackball is the birthplace of the Labour Party, which took place following the 1908 coal miners' strike. Trucks from nearby Roa Mine trundled through town, carrying bags of coal dust bound for Japan.

Wootton lived in Blackball for three weeks until his abrupt eviction. He walked into Gina Howton's general store one day with his wife. Gina asked what had brought them to Blackball. He said he had heard the shop was for sale. 'You heard wrong,' said Gina, but he was very insistent. She said, 'How would you run a store with a deaf wife?' He said, 'Oh, but she's very clever.' He said he was a hairdresser. 'He was clean-cut,' Gina said, 'looked like he had money. And his wife presented well. She had extremely alert eyes.'

Our conversation was interrupted when two customers walked in. It was half past three in the afternoon and they were in happy drunken spirits. 'I feel like a rum and raisin ice cream between beers,' said one of the men, who flaunted a mullet.

Around the corner, vigil organiser Alan Gurden was at his house bus, packing up to leave. He said he needed to get away for a week. That was a good idea. I wished the townspeople had got rid of him instead of Wootton. He was in bad health, physically and mentally; his hands shook, he was on the verge of tears, he couldn't think straight.

He said he suffered from 1080 poisoning. He suffered from something. He was on an invalid's benefit, got migraines and couldn't remember dates. He had painted deranged sentences on his house bus: DEAD CARCASSES FLOATING IN THE WATER! and THEY LIE AND LIE AND LAUGH WHILE YOU DIE! The angry ravings dated from his protest against 1080 drops. 'I issued a challenge to Helen

Clark and Grey District Council. I said they were terrorist saboteurs.'

We sat underneath a cabbage tree while his black pig, Rainbow, snuffled in its pen. In helping to get rid of the paedophile from Blackball and hold the government and the Corrections Department to account, his motives were pure, he said. 'They're from moral correctness. It's a personal crusade.'

And then he said, 'How many criminal convictions do you think I have? I'll tell you – none. There was one time when I was spoken to by the police. My wife and I nearly split up in... This is where my brain lets me down. We were living in a house in a valley with no power, the water was frozen solid in the tank, we had to get water from the creek, and we had an argument. She was very stressed. She phoned the police and said her husband tried to take away her son. So there was that one time.'

There were mutterings in the pub on Friday night about 'hippie bigots'. I liked that term but it missed the essential point about Gurden: he was nuts.

I ran into Geoff Strong at the pub. 'This is our town,' he said. 'This is where we live. This is our castle.' He had fond memories of a group of locals in the mid 1980s who called themselves the Blackball Pipe Band. A dozen or so 'transient punk people' had moved into town 'so the Pipe Band got bits of pipe and went through them like a dose of salts. All the punks fucked off'.

I got away from Strong and relaxed over a beer with Mike O'Donnell, 37, a former Greymouth punk known as Rotten. In case he forgets his nickname, it's tattooed on his chest. Rotten was an easy-going guy. 'Blackball has its moments,' he said. 'We've just had the Easter fair.'

The annual pub crawl was coming up. Participants would don gloves and kneepads, and crawl across the road between Blackball's three pubs. Various games and tests of character were planned; previous challenges had included a seven a.m. dip in the town pool, coal-shovelling competitions, and a game where you drank a pint of beer, ate a bowl of dry Weet-Bix, then blew up a balloon until it burst.

The fun and games, the beautiful colours of autumn, the photos of Michael Joseph Savage behind the bar, the black-faced sheep dozing in backyards, the abandoned glasshouses covered in blackberry and rowanberry, the thick mist and the still air and the quiet days and nights – it must be a lovely place to live. The house where a paedophile hairdresser and country singer lived with his deaf mute wife went on the market for $145,000.

Blackball and Tangimoana: both were out west, isolated, bogan, gothic. So was Pātea in Taranaki, where another saga of summary justice played out in 2010. What happened in Pātea was even more elemental than Tangimoana: its central narrative was the pursuit of food.

Two fisheries officers drove to the banks of the Pātea River and seized illegal fishing nets. They told the Hāwera District Court that Pātea man Darryl Hutton – whom they identified as six foot four, with a large build and a full beard – yelled at them and said, 'If you try to take the nets, you're fucking dead.' He also advised the officers, 'This is my town, my river. We do what we want. You can take the law and fuck off.'

He made a gun sign with his hands, pointed to both officers, and said, 'Kapow, kapow, kapow.' He also said, 'If you ever come back here again you're dead, you won't be leaving here alive.'

The officers then happened to notice six other men beginning to walk towards them in a line. One wore a balaclava and had a pit bull straining on the end of a chain. They also noticed that Hutton had a wooden club tucked down the back of his gumboot.

Another detail that caught their attention was that people had gathered outside every surrounding house. The people stood there and watched. No one called the police.

Meanwhile, the officers' car was stuck in the mud.

One of the officers said, 'I thought if we made it home in an ambulance we'd be doing pretty well.' The other said, 'It was like something out of a bad western.' He had been in threatening situations before but 'this was the closest I thought I was to dying.'

The stand-off lasted about 30 minutes until the cops arrived, tempers calmed, and the people outside every surrounding house went back inside.

In court, Hutton pleaded not guilty to two charges of threatening to cause grievous bodily harm, and wittily remarked that the club was tucked down the back of his gumboot because he'd put it there after attending a kapa haka session.

The judge sentenced him to 200 hours' community service and warned that the next time he threatened assault he'd send him to prison. He sent him to prison in 2011 for six months after Hutton admitted hitting his girlfriend in the face. *Taranaki Daily News*: 'Judge Roberts noted Hutton's early guilty plea but also noted his previous convictions for assault, assault on a female, rape, breach of parole, and threatening to kill.'

Hutton was bad news. Alan Gurden, the henchman of Blackball, was fucked up. But Kieran Grice of Tangimoana was the nicest vigilante you could ever meet.

Small, witty, impulsive, Kieran was a romantic, someone who felt moved by life. He was also bogan incarnate, with his tattoos of Angus Young ('I'm mad on AC/DC. Favouritest band in the world') and black T-shirt tucked into black jeans. He'd just come off working fourteen days straight, welding in the Wellington railyards, when I met him on Friday night at Tangimoana Boating Club. He needed a drink. He said he had to pace himself for his stepdaughter's 21st the next night. He wasn't pacing himself. It didn't look as though anyone was. The club, a members-only bar around the corner from the campground, was enjoying a brisk trade, which is also to say that just about everyone was completely off their faces.

I arranged to meet Kieran at his house the next morning. I got there at about ten and met his partner Brenda, her daughter Nikita, and Nikita's boyfriend, Michael McKay. They were in the kitchen cooking up strips of fresh venison. Michael said, 'Go well with one of these.' He opened the fridge and took out some beers. 'Can't hurt,' said Kieran. We went outside and sat around a picnic table in a kind of garden grotto, fringed with native ferns he'd rescued from earthworks in the bush.

I was surprised he hadn't suggested we drink in his shed. He loved his shed, which was as enormous as an aircraft. It was his second home, possibly his first. His house was just somewhere to crash, and cook up strips of venison. He said, 'I lock the shed but I never lock the house.' He'd set up a bar, and the shed also contained his motorbikes and chainsaws. He talked about his love of machinery and then he said, 'I really wanted Brenda to buy me a bulldozer for Christmas. I found one that was nice and it was only $30,000, but nah.'

He was fervent about the bulldozer, crazy about Brenda. He said he met her in a pub when she was eighteen and he was eight. 'She was playing pool and I fell in love with her. I said, "I'm going to marry her."

'Time went past, she got married and had two kids, and then I came along and said, "Brenda, you're the one I want." I was with someone else, but when I saw Brenda again I thought, oh, cool. I wanted her. I had my mind set. Now I just got to convince her to buy me a bulldozer.'

He talked about his welding work, how he set himself to the task and went for it. 'I'm known as GC at work. The initials don't stand for Jesus Christ. They stand for Grumpy Cunt.' I'd met his mum at the Boating Club the previous night and she'd told me Kieran was dyslexic. He said, 'I was held back in form two for a year, I was so hopeless at reading and writing. I went to high school for nine months. When I turned fifteen – boom, I was out of there and straight away got a job.'

Michael McKay poked his head around the corner and asked, 'More beers, boys?' He threw a couple of bottles our way. I said to Kieran, 'So. The night in question.'

'I suppose I was the ringleader,' he said. 'I was the one who rallied everyone together. I said, "I've had a gutsful. Let's go grab the little bugger."

'Me and a mate next door had been working on cars in the shed – oil changes and servicing, that sort of thing. We went to the boat club for a couple of beers and that's when I got the phone call from the fire chief saying, "You're on standby." He'd heard the little bugger was threatening to burn the shop down.

'I went around to see Tracy, and Marcus and said, "Jump in the wagon." I'd heard through the grapevine where the little bugger was hiding.

'We grabbed him and he's crying and pleading, "Let me go, let me go" and lashing about continuously. Wouldn't sit still. I thought, how do we restrain him? And then I thought, shit, I know – cable ties.'

What gave him that idea?

'You know, like on *Police Ten 7*.'

Sunday night in Tangimoana, and an AC/DC fan suddenly inspired by a reality TV show to grab some cable ties from his garage and use them to hogtie a kid squealing on the lawn.

'And then,' he continued, 'the police turn up. I thought they were gonna say, "Rightio, that's all good. You can go home now and we'll contact you if we need to." But no, suddenly we're the bad guys.'

There was something missing in his narrative, a crucial detail unaccounted for. 'I understand,' I said, 'that when you raced home to get the cable ties, you were wearing slippers. Why was that?'

'I normally wear slippers to the club,' he said.

Nikita's 21st birthday party went off. There were drunk, affectionate speeches. I talked to an astronomer wearing a sombrero. Michael McKay wore what appeared to be a scarf but was actually an ingenious beer-holder – there were pouches at either end. Kieran was legless, his heart near bursting with how proud he was of Nikita. Nikita was there with her very cute child.

I talked to a guy who said his licence plate read GDNYM8. I asked him to translate. 'Good on ya, mate.' He'd got it in honour of the line on the Speights' TV commercial. Marcus was there. Tracy wasn't. The previous night at the boating club she had got tanked on gin and screamed at him, 'Go back to your fat teenage whore!' She fled and he ran after her, his work boots crunching on the gravel. 'Let her go,' voices shouted from the bar.

Grant McDowall was there. I'd met him earlier when he was in his backyard, hosing down his boat. He'd just come back from fishing and had three enormous albacore tuna in a white bucket. He was with his son, Aaron, sixteen, who has Down Syndrome. 'Only his second time out at sea but he was good as gold, eh Aaron?' Aaron gave a thumbs-up.

We went inside. 'I'll just put some music on for the boy. He loves Irish music, Scottish music. Drinking songs.' Aaron sat back, listened, and drank Diet Coke.

Grant worked for the fire service. He'd been living in Palmerston North but his marriage had broken up. 'There wasn't anyone else. We just got sick of pissing each other off. We parted on good terms. I was at a bit of loss as to where to go and I thought, where have I gone where I was happy? I'd always liked fishing in Tangimoana so I looked for a house here under $100,000. That was all I could afford. I found this for $82,000. The grass was up to your neck but no worries.'

He'd built the shed with Kieran, Marcus and Tracy. 'The skills among us are pretty awesome,' he said. 'Marcus is a top, top engineer. Kieran would have to be one of the most sought-after welders in the whole of the Manawatū. And Tracy – well, it was really Tracy who built that shed. It was all her that did it. Her idea, her know-how.'

I mentioned that a woman at the boating club had told me Tangimoana was full of lonely people – ex-husbands, ex-wives, widows. 'Yeah, I suppose so,' Grant said, and off the top of his head he named five people who lived by themselves. Then he described the weather. 'We get horrific westerly storms, very strong winds.'

He said it was time he made Aaron his lunch. 'He loves his sausages. He's always hounding me to put them on for him, eh Aaron? You all right there, mate?' Aaron looked over at his dad and gave a thumbs-up.

Hell was over the fence. Grant lived next door to Willie Seabrook, 54. There was a face lurking somewhere behind Willie's beard, and a human being floating somewhere within the 30 litres of beer he said he drank on average every week. His house stank of damp and dog. The furniture was chewed down to the slats. There were old stuffed toys inside a glass cabinet. 'My youngest has some kind of brain disorder. I don't know what they fuckin' call it – motor neuron or something. His skull never grew. He's normal, he just can't read or write.'

There was a massive hole in the ceiling: I smelled a rat. There were cob-webs and stains decorating the wallpaper, a hot-water bottle on the floor. He was married once. 'The old girl left me.'

Every time I came back to Tangimoana I picked up a whiff of the boozy fug drifting from Willie's dog-eaten, rat-nibbled, bachelor shack. It followed me down the street on Saturday afternoon, when a tough bastard with wraparound dark glasses, a goatee and a shaved head swung his hips along the pavement, his pit-bull terrier straining at the leash and squinting its pink heartless eyes.

At the boating club on Sunday afternoon, there were drinkers arguably less damaged than Willie. Conversation turned to a sixteen-year-old girl in town. 'Rooted her,' lied an elderly man with a face so red with alcohol it was nearly black. 'Didja? Good on yer, boy,' said the fire chief.

No one said anything for a while. Elbows bent back glasses. A woman said, 'I used to laugh so much here that it hurt. Not like that anymore.' The fire chief said, 'I'm thinking of doing something about that.' He refused to comment any further. He looked as though he'd last made someone laugh in about 1712.

A jeep came to a squealing halt in the car park. The driver, a woman with flared nostrils, slammed the door shut and bounded through a cloud of dust. She talked very fast; her swollen eyeballs were as big as her head; she ground her teeth and bounded to the bar for a drink. The elderly man swayed on his heels and said, 'Rooted her.' The fire chief said, 'Didja? Good on yer, boy.'

Earlier that day I had been invited in for a cup of tea by a man who had just finished mowing his front lawn. 'Ron told me about you,' he said; he'd been talking with Ron Gardner, the lonely widower. He looked both ways down the street before he opened the gate. 'I don't want them knowing you were here,' he said. 'I knew the boy they beat up. A bad bugger. But the way they did it was just wrong. It was a police job but they grabbed him and give him a bloody hiding. They threatened him they were gonna cut his head off and bury him in the forest.'

He was raving. 'They're baddies. Druggies. Always boozing up and drugging up. Kieran used to be quite a nice guy until he got tangled up with the Thomsens. Tracy's a good worker, I'll give her that. It's the best thing about her. But nah.' He screwed up his face. 'She's bad news.'

He bagged the fire chief. I didn't mind that. I did mind when he bagged a friend of Kieran's whom I'd met at the twenty-first. He was a decent gentle guy who'd suffered a terrible accident working at the Port of Tauranga. He got whacked with a crane, had sixteen screws put in his back and now couldn't have children. He was married. He and his wife were saving to pay for in vitro fertilisation. 'I just want a family and to be able to work.' Could he work? 'I can do maybe four hours a day before the pain makes it unbearable and I gotta lie down.'

He wasn't exactly getting a lot of sympathy from the man who made me a very weak cup of tea – he skimped on the tea leaves and poured less than a teaspoon of milk. He said, 'I know who you should talk to.' He made a phone call. I was given an address. I walked around the corner in the peace and quiet of a weekend afternoon in Tangimoana and was met by a woman lurking at her front gate. She looked right, she looked left, and then said, 'Okay. You can come in.'

We sat in the backyard by a hedge, but first she checked with her husband that their neighbours were away. He said they were. 'Good,' she said. 'We can talk here.' But, just in case, she lowered her voice, and sometimes she whispered, and now and then she hissed.

While she talked about how much she loathed Tracy Thomsen, and described how Tracy had, apparently, managed to profoundly damage Tangimoana, I started thinking about the US spy station. I had visited it earlier that day. The woman hissed, 'She's nearly ruined this town but most people won't speak out because they know what'd happen.' What'd happen? 'A brick in the window. Or there was one lady – they pumped raw sewage on to her paddock.'

Just before Tangimoana there was a turn-off that led to the spy station. The station was a modest office compound, white, only one level, surrounded by barbed wire and a sign that read DEFENCE AREA.

NO ADMISSION EXCEPT ON BUSINESSES. It didn't advise that trespassers would merely be prosecuted; they would be DETAINED AND SEARCHED.

'We don't want her here,' my hostess said, as her husband ferried out two glasses of iced water. 'She's overstayed her welcome.' Gordon McDowall, the fireman from Palmerston North, had told me Tracy had 'done shitloads for the community'. He'd mentioned her volunteer work on the reserve committee. But my hostess said, 'She stood over people to get on to the reserve committee. It's a need for power and control.'

The spy station was next to a heap of sawed-down trees.

'Over the years people have discovered what she's really like.'

There were two cars and a motorbike inside the compound.

'All the riff-raff come here because there's no policing.'

The New Zealand flag flicked and flapped.

'We won't associate with the boating club or the volunteer fire brigade. They're all her drinking buddies. You'll see them loading up their boats with crates of beer.'

The spy station looked like a demented bunker. The wind got up. It shrieked through the pine forest on the other side of the road. I looked at the forest and thought about Phil Cowan, a 26-year-old dope dealer who disappeared in Wellington on March 25, 2001. His silver Nissan was found dumped in Bulls with traces of his blood inside. The car's ignition barrel had been tampered with, and the passenger door interfered with. By September, police had decided Cowan had been murdered and his body disposed of. In 2003 three men were accused of the murder but discharged after the judge stopped their trial. Cowan's parents believe their son is buried somewhere in the Tangimoana forest.

The hissing on the summer lawn: 'She told everyone how she'd told the kid they were going to take him to the forest and kill him. She was laughing about it, saying he was so scared that he literally shit his pants.'

It was a really hot afternoon. I needed that glass of water. I sat there sweating, and leaning forward to catch what my hostess was saying as she lowered her voice for fear of being overheard, and I started thinking, what the fuck is this? It was absurd to be hiding in the corner of a backyard in bright, sea-salty Tangimoana. It felt less like an interview than an undercover assignation.

She kept apologising. 'I know what I must sound like.' No, no, I said, thinking that she sounded malicious, petty, vengeful, bitter. Well, she said, I was asking about Tangimoana and so I may as well hear it straight. 'It's the truth behind the scenes.'

She said if I didn't believe her she could arrange for me to meet other people to hear their views, but I cringed at the prospect of another clandestine appointment. I wanted out. I wanted away from Tangimoana. It was lovely, friendly and beachy, also oppressive, pissed, plain weird and just going about its business. Perhaps it only seemed as though it were intent on minding everyone else's business. It felt smaller each time I visited, as though its few streets were creeping closer together. And each time it felt more infected by the US spy station, by the crackle and pop of static, by the white noise and the intercepted broadcasts, and the pursuit and accumulation of state secrets.

Enough. It inspired a quest for civilisation. Half an hour away, quivering on the banks of State Highways One and Three, was Sanson. Every time I returned there it felt as though I were journeying towards higher ground, could breathe easier.

One afternoon I went for a walk. I suspected I was the first person to go walking in Sanson since about 1712. I turned the corner from the motel and walked along the side of State Highway Three as traffic shot past. I headed for the rugby ground. I liked the look of it. It had an old wooden stand at one end, with a corrugated iron roof. I climbed up the stand and sat down in one of the rows. It was nice sitting there looking down on to an empty field, the H of the rugby posts. I turned around and saw a sentence graffitied along one of the back rows. It read: LET'S ALL BE HUMAN BEINGS.

# 15 MOSGIEL
## LOOKING FOR TROUBLE

I t was out there in the dark night, crime, covert and creeping, up to no good in the small Otago town, with its Scottish street names and splendid rhododendrons, or fanned out on surrounding Taieri Plain, that flat lonely expanse of long country roads with windbreak walls of solid hedge. To the untrained eye, there was nothing to worry about. You might think Mosgiel's population of 10,000 were safe in their beds. You might even misconstrue the town as desperately boring. But all you had to do was wait. Mosgiel would reveal its secrets.

'Okay,' said Malcolm Macleod. 'This is what we've been talking about.' He was behind the wheel of a snug four-door-drive Toyota Ipsum emblazoned with the legend 'Mosgiel–Taieri Community Patrol'. The writing made it resemble a police vehicle but the occupants were citizens. It was just after eleven on a cold evening. The windows of the car were open so the inhabitants could listen for signs of trouble or distress.

Malcolm had pulled up behind a factory in an industrial estate on the outskirts of the town, pop. 10,000. Allister Green, sitting in the passenger seat, shone a high-beam torch on a factory door. Malcolm said, 'See how the white undercoat of the door frame is showing through? It makes it look as though the door is slightly open. That's a classic example of what we were saying earlier about using our eyes.'

But the door wasn't open. Saturday night and Mosgiel slumbered on. Nothing was happening.

The community patrol drove around from ten p.m. until two a.m. every Friday and Saturday night, always as a pair, one driving, the other shining a torch, both staying alert, focussed and, hardest of all, serious. Allister had an agile build and thinning hair; he worked in IT. Malcolm was overweight and short of breath; he supplied equipment to treat sleep apnoea. They were men of middle age, decent citizens, husbands, fathers – a dad's army. They wore fluorescent vests. Neither was likely to panic and squawk, 'Don't panic!' There wasn't the opportunity.

The patrol car crawled along a residential street. 'See, there's a hazard,' Malcolm said. He shone his torch on a dumpster bin on the pavement. 'Someone not watching where they were going could do themselves an injury.' On the pavement? 'There are no street lights,' Allister said.

They drove around the corner. There were still no street lights, nor lights in any of the houses. 'Just to make you feel safer,' Malcolm said, 'I'll lock the doors.'

It was a few days before Guy Fawkes Day; a sky rocket fizzed up into the night air. Allister and Malcolm identified the launch pad at Memorial Park. There were two adults, three small kids and a teenage couple holding hands. The powdery remains of fireworks lay on the grass. 'Hopefully they'll pick it up when they're finished,' Malcolm said. The patrol car crawled on.

They knew about the man who spent weekends in a lock-up he rented at the industrial estate. He lived in Ōamaru and came to Mosgiel on weekends; he put a sleeping bag on the floor and made meals on a gas cooker. 'There's another guy lives there,' Allister said. 'He feeds 50 or 60 feral cats.'

Mosgiel by night, the alleyways, the deserted lots, the back streets – Allister and Malcolm made excellent tour guides. There was an astonishing voyeurism, an officially sanctioned nosiness. Allister said, 'You start to find sly ways of observing people without being watched.' Malcolm said, 'We find all sorts of nooks and crannies.'

The car crawled along at 30 kilometres an hour. It turned off the main street, Gordon Road, and crept behind a pharmacy. Malcolm said, 'This is just a typical alley. We'll do a wee scout. This is where you sometimes see pissed young kids fornicating, all sorts of things.'

But no one was fornicating. Saturday night and Mosgiel slept on. Nothing was happening.

'It's amazing what you can hear just driving slowly along with the windows down,' Malcolm said. 'You might hear broken glass, or you might hear nothing.'

He drove into the grounds of Taieri College. Allister said, 'We check on doors and windows. A couple of weeks ago I saw a light on in the school gym. I thought, that's a bit strange, and called it in to the police.' Had there been anything amiss? 'No.'

Later, on a deserted side road near a sawmill, Malcolm said, 'The police tell us a sexo frequently comes here.' A sexo? 'That's what the police call sex offenders.' How did the sexo offend? 'He parks up at night and pretends he's listening to the radio, but he could be masturbating, looking at a video, reading dirty books.' Interesting. What crime was being committed? 'At the end of the day,' Malcolm said, 'a sexo is a sexo.'

But no one was wanking. At 11.21 there were rabbits at the electricity sub-station. At 11.49, in the nearby village of Outram, a hedgehog crossed the road. At 11.56 Allister said, 'It'll all kick off in four minutes. I've seen it happen before. Nothing, all quiet, and then with a click of the fingers' – he clicked his fingers – 'all hell breaks loose on the stroke of midnight.'

On the stroke of midnight, the patrol car pulled off the road and along the dirt track leading to Outram Glen, a popular swimming hole in the Taieri River – and out of the darkness, suddenly, illuminated by the car's headlights, was a gang of 40 or 50 teenagers.

Something was happening.

In Mosgiel in broad daylight the most common signs of life were approaching death – old people, squadrons of them, their mobility scooters whispering along Gordon Road. Mosgiel could lay claim to the biggest concentration of rest homes and retirement villages in New Zealand. The inmates formed ten percent of the population – an estimated 800 people and 300 staff. There were Brooklands, Mossbrae, Birchleigh and Glendale. Holy Cross College had townhouses for retired priests. In the very clean, very quiet, very spooky retirement village of Chatsford, Isabella Divers, 94, sat on a deckchair in her garage with a packet of Toffee Pops in her lap – she was waiting for a lift to visit her nephew in hospital. On her cardigan a badge advised I AM VISUALLY IMPAIRED, but she was in fit and dandy spirits. She said, 'I have a tot of whisky every night. That helps.'

The grandest rest home of all was Maran-Atha, a magnificent pile built in 1900 on Gordon Road as Dr Allan's residence and surgery, and reopened in 1959 as a rest home by the Open Brethren. Clarence Pringle, 91, said, 'They take us to church in Dunedin on Sundays.' Bill Leslie, 85, said, 'And they drove us to the Waihola Tavern the day after it burned down to see what was left.' What was left? 'There was a team of horses out front.'

Bill was a big lad. He sat out on the front porch in shirtsleeves and talked about his days of farming – dairy, then cattle. He said, 'I had a head operation. I'd bought a horse off Robinson – he was a great one at the rodeo, could ride anything. The horse was as rough as they make them. One day he set off the calves on a stampede. They came at the horse full belt and tipped his front foot. I went head over heels. Sconed me out.

'Then I had a clot problem. I got put in the hospital in Dunedin. I phoned the manager at Maran-Atha and said, "What do I have to do to get in?" It wasn't easy. Someone turned up for an interview and said, "A strong healthy man like you, wanting to be put in a rest home?" They said, "The people I worry about are the taxpayers." I said, "I used to be one of those."

'They couldn't make out why I specified this place, but it was because of my sister. She had polio at eleven, and had a room here for fourteen years. I'm in that room now. An old fella who was in there fell out of bed and ended up dying. They said, "You can have his room if you want it." I said, "I'm not going to let that go by."

In the dining room at lunch, Bill reached over to a sideboard and picked up a handbell. He rang it to announce grace. The men sat at their tables, the women at another; beef stew was served, with potatoes, broccoli, peas and carrots. The staff were tremendously nice and cheerful. 'Would you like me to push your chair in closer, Olive?' 'Here you are, Emily. Does the beef need cutting?' Residents are served breakfast in bed at seven a.m.; most go back to sleep for a while. There was morning and afternoon tea, Housie, indoor bowls, craft and God.

After lunch, Lawson Adam, 80, sat in his high-ceilinged upstairs room. It was bathed in sunlight. He had trouble talking; he had no trouble playing a hymn on his Hammond organ. There was an open packet of blackballs on the couch, and toothpaste, a toothbrush and Johnson's Baby Powder beside the washbasin. Lawson brought out a family album. He had written about his childhood on the family farm in Otokia, about his brothers and sisters, about a world of hope and suffering: 'Katy was the first born. She was a lovely child but was tragically drowned. Second came Peggy, who as a toddler ingested some barley grass, causing death. The outcome of the next pregnancy was a stillborn boy.'

Maran-Atha was full of lively spirits and kindness and good company. There was another kind of rest home in Mosgiel, independent, lonelier, outdoors – the caravan park. It was on a rural edge of the town, with room for twelve berths.

Len, 71, had lived there for eight years. 'I was a grocer in Dunedin,' he said. 'I came to Mosgiel for a lady. It didn't work out. We were dance partners and I can't dance anymore.' His lungs had packed up. 'A month ago I collapsed in a heap at the RSA. Legs just went under me.' He was trying to cut down on smoking to two a day; he had fashioned an ashtray from a Marmite jar half-filled with black water.

Retired driver Tom Bell had lived at the caravan park for fourteen years. He kept a tidy ship. The bed was made, the dishes stacked. He said, 'Mosgiel's got everything you want. You wouldn't catch me living in another town in New Zealand. No – no way. Great scenery. The only thing you can't see is the damned sea and who wants to see that?'

But then he said, 'I'm off soon. Drive down to Invercargill, then right up the West Coast, over to Picton, and jump on the ferry and go all over the North Island.' An epic road trip. 'You got it. And then,' he said, 'I think I'll be due for the box.'

Saturday night's patrol had begun at Allister's house in a new subdivision of faux mansions on the foothills of Saddle Hill. All of Mosgiel rests beneath the sensual hump of Saddle Hill, named by Captain Cook from on board the *Endeavour* on November 26, 1770: 'In the country was an elevated saddle hill, whose summit appeared above the clouds. From this hill, the land fell in a gentle slope… Empty then and emptied now – the theme of Mosgiel's modern economic history is collapse, with the closures of Fortex freezing works (900 jobs), the famous Mosgiel woollen mill (140 jobs), and in 2008 the Fisher & Paykel dishwasher assembly plant (400 jobs).

But the town soldiers on, very 1950s with Andy's Milk Bar, Knox's Milk Bar and Monte Carlo Milk Bar, very 21st century with Perreaux Industries, which makes and exports amplifiers to 30 countries. Paper Plus and The Warehouse set up premises in 2009; McDonald's wants in.

The streets are full of horse floats. Baghdad Note, the grey gelding that won the 1970 Melbourne Cup, was trained at Mosgiel's charming Wingatui racetrack. There are a lot of oak trees and peeling gum trees. Poverty always finds somewhere to go; the wrong side of the tracks is a kind of slum hidden away on Sinclair Road, where converted air force barracks have gone to rack and ruin, windows are smashed or boarded up, and car wrecks rust in front yards.

The Mosgiel–Taieri Community Patrol doesn't go there. It doesn't go any place where its patrol car might get boxed in. 'And they don't confront,' said Bill Feather, who serves on the local community board that gave $9,000 to start the patrol. 'They report anything suspicious to the police and get in a safe position.'

Bill was born and bred in Mosgiel, like his parents before him. He said, 'My grandmother came here from Rangiora. I lost my grandfather in the first war, in… Linda?' Linda, his wife, sat in the kitchen with a cup of tea and a really good-looking ham and tomato sandwich. She called out, '1915.' She was about to dress up and drive to Dunedin for a meeting of the Methodist Women's Fellowship.

There was a photograph in the hallway of the couple smiling in the gleaming sunshine of Hamilton Island on Great Barrier Reef. Bill worked at Fisher & Paykel all his working life; the Hamilton Island trip was a present from the firm, to commemorate 40 years' service. He was enjoying his retirement. 'We're blessed living in this street,' he said. 'The council mows the grass once a week.'

But he was aware of the danger beyond his driveway. It came as close as the driveway itself. 'Civil disobedience is the main thing, the nuisance value of people walking the streets late at night and knocking over letterboxes.'

He talked about the patrol's formation, inspired by a public meeting held by Tubby Hopkins, vicar's warden at Saint Peters Anglican church in Caversham, Dunedin, and national deputy chairman of Community Patrols of New Zealand. 'People said it was a good idea but nothing ever got done. I was always waiting,' Bill said, 'for someone to take charge.'

Allister Green took charge. He said, 'Bill promoted the idea that I was the new champion. I had a lot of drive. I wanted a safer community. I was always reading about needless petty crimes by school kids.' What kind of needless petty crimes? He said, 'Gangs of kids kicking in letterboxes.'

But there was also the arrival in Mosgiel of the barbarian hordes known throughout New Zealand as boy racers. They came on Friday nights, Allister said. They'd leave Dunedin at midnight and do a circuit across the Taieri Plain to Allenton and Outram, and thence to Mosgiel – to Dukes Road, right in front of the deserted Fisher & Paykel factory. There were a hundred, maybe two hundred, of them. 'They didn't know what to make of us at first. Then they got peeved and more intimidating. I've heard that next time they see us they'll try and tip the car over.'

The patrol has 43 members drawn from the citizenry. Malcolm arrived at Allister's house. Malcolm liked to talk. He talked about his sleep apnoea business and his unlikely sideline, hiring out exercycles. 'I've got a hundred thousand dollars' worth in stock.'

Then he gave a kind of resumé. 'I was the first male student in New Zealand to do homecraft. I'm a chef by trade. I knocked off school the day I turned sixteen and began an apprenticeship at a bakehouse in Dunedin the next day. … I opened my own restaurant. … I worked for DB as a hitman. If one of their pubs needed sorting out I'd go in and do it. I started getting quite a few threats. I couldn't go into certain pubs for a drink.

'I worked at a lodge in Blenheim. My flair was doing buffet sculptures… I went to Australia and worked for Ansett; I jumped into a can there. The trouble with me is I give it a big nudge and then burn out.'

It was getting on to ten. Malcolm and Allister drove to the police station. They entered through the back door, pulled up chairs in the kitchen, and looked at the report from the previous night's patrol. Alistair said, 'They did 93 ks. We can get up to 120.' Nothing had happened. Malcolm said, 'It's not all beer and skittles. We do a lot of stuff in the background.' Mosgiel constable Nayland Smith was in the control room, sighing as he shuffled through boring paperwork. He'd worked in Auckland once. 'It's great being home,' he said, 'but I miss the action.'

The community patrol was ready for the night's rounds. Malcolm opened up the boot of the patrol car. It contained traffic cones, a First Aid kit, towels, gloves, wipes, and rolls of toilet paper. Malcolm said, 'You just don't know if you'll need it.' They put on their fluorescent vests, and drove into the dark Mosgiel night, towards something happening at midnight, at Outram Glen.

On Saturday morning in Outram, Geoff Woodcock said, 'I'm continually shocked at how beautiful the Taieri is.' He had moved to Mosgiel five years earlier with his wife Melanie. They had now sold their house there and rented in Outram, a village of 200 households. 'It's a real boom time here for young families. You do hear about people coming down from Auckland to live here.' Miriam said, 'Who?' Geoff said, 'That girl Tracey looks like an Aucklander.' Miriam said, 'What makes you say that?' Geoff said, 'She wears make-up.'

He works from home as an IT consultant. 'Work is for rainy days and nights. If it's a beautiful day we go to the beach. We were at Sandfly Bay last week; the kids played a game between three seals.' They have four kids, Jacob, seven, Keziah, five, Gabby, three, and Tim, one.

Geoff was lean, youthful and smart, and had seen a vision come to life: he had built Mosgiel's playground. 'It was a quality-of-life issue,' he said. 'There was just nowhere to take your kids. The existing park was a set of squeaky swings and an old fort.' The playground is a spectacular achievement, large, exciting, gleaming with new equipment; attractive families come from as far away as Milton – an hour's drive – to bring their kids and make a day of it. The playground cost $750,000. Geoff chaired a local trust and worked hard to raise the funds. This included finding another $30,000 to top up the council's $85,000 for a toilet.

Geoff said, 'The toilet! Oh, God. Where do I start? Okay. There were lots of kids urinating in bushes. We pushed eighteen months for a toilet but the council offered us something really horrible, square and boxy, just ugly. And impractical – one of the trust members had once been locked in one just like it. We had world-class playground equipment in the park, so we put in another $30,000 and they gave us what we wanted.

'It was well worth the wait. The toilets are exceptional. It's a Nova Loo; I first saw them in Albert Town near Wānaka and really liked them. They're curvaceous, modern, spacious.'

Toilets were an unusual subject to inspire such a passionate speech but Geoff was a man of strong convictions. He made another speech. 'We looked at lots of catalogues of playground equipment. A lot of them were neutered and sedated. It was that PC, risk-averse thing, cotton-wooling.

'All the safety compliances these days with playgrounds – something's been lost along the way. We spent $30,000 on soft-fall surfacing. It does your head in! A playground should have a mix of danger and risk. If kids can't hurt themselves, there's something wrong. Adrenalin is fun. Pain is good. Pain,' he said, 'is a teacher.'

'Pain,' said Larry Williamson, 'is a switch.' Larry was an amazing sight. At 48, moustached and long-legged, dressed in cowboy boots, cowboy hat, and tight Wrangler denim, he stood as trim and straight as a board. The thought occurred that he might be a mean son of a bitch, but he was another kind of character – a good ol' boy. He tipped his hat to women.

He drained his beer and wiped his moustache. 'Mine,' he said, pointing to the rifles and pistols displayed on the wall of the Silverstream Steakhouse and Bar. 'Them too,' he said, pointing at two beautiful saddles – his prizes as the New Zealand Rodeo Cowboys Association champion saddle bronc rider in 2001 and 2008. He won the last saddle as the oldest bronc rider in New Zealand. 'I've broken everything there is to break,' he said. Pain, the switch: 'You turn it off for eight seconds.'

He meant the eight seconds of adrenalin, skill and madness on top of a bronc. 'It takes 30 or 40 rides for you to remember the whole eight seconds. The first few times you might remember only the first second. It's all about timing, rhythm and balance. And breathing: you can get away with not breathing for the first two or three seconds, but then – bang! – you're on the ground. I try to breathe the whole time.'

He spoke in a deep slow drawl. He talked about rodeo life: the travelling, the rooms above pubs, the hopelessness of maintaining a marriage. He had competed professionally in America, Canada and Australia. He now worked as a farrier. It seemed likely he spent a fair bit of his time at the Silverstream Steakhouse and Bar.

The pub was off the beaten track in North Taieri, at the back of Mosgiel, on its lonesome with a wide open space, a log fire, Fender guitars on the wall, and a stage for live country music. The publican lived next door in a caravan. 'Marriage fell over,' Ken Reeves said. There were slices of burnt toast in the sink. He'd filled a Marmite jar with cigarette butts. 'Back when I was farming in Winton I'd go to the pub three or four times a year. Now it's every night.'

He had a happy red face and a beer in his hand. It was getting on to lunchtime. He said, 'I'll show you around next door.' He led the way over grass and dust to the pub. By the back door a rubbish bag had split open. 'Bloody dogs getting in the rubbish again,' he said. He had taken out a lease on the neighbouring bowling club. He pointed to a field out the back. 'I've got plans to turn that into our own private rodeo.'

Ken, too, was a good ol' boy. 'We attract good solid country people,' he said, and poured himself a beer. He ran a hell of a good pub. It was big and very friendly. It was the kind of pub where you wanted to stay all day, maybe gaze at the play of sunlight and shadow on Saddle Hill, listen to the music of travelling and broken homes, and stay 'til closing time – it was the kind of pub that celebrated freedom.

Saturday midnight at Outram Glen, a gang of teenagers picked out by headlights: they had escaped Mosgiel's desperate boredom to have a party on a riverbank. Malcolm and Allister's presence was unwelcome, a drag. The men weren't police; they were self-elected party poopers of middle age. Three pretty girls in short skirts walked by. 'All right, girls?' Malcolm asked. 'Yeah,' they said, and kept walking.

Mosgiel, with its lovely lines of poplars and bees in the azaleas, its cupcake of the day at the Aurora Café and a tray of four dozen farm eggs in the back seat of a gorgeous wood-panelled, olive-green Pinto Squire parked on Gordon Road; horsey, fresh-aired Mosgiel, cradled beneath Saddle Hill, happily dangling twelve kilometres from urban Dunedin… but crimes do occur. Last year a man armed with a machete ran off with $400 from the Mini Mart, and another villain was arrested after climbing through the roof of the ANZ bank and attempting to cut open an ATM. He was seventy-one.

Malcolm and Allister were driving away from Outram Glen and towards the Mosgiel police station for a cup of tea when their police radio relayed an update from Dunedin. There had been a report of youths kicking in a letterbox: 'One is wearing a tartan top.' A tartan terror on the loose in Dunedin. 'It's all happening,' Allister said, 'in the wrong town.'

# 16 WĀNAKA
## THE STORIES OF OTHERS

The alarm clock rang at five-thirty in my room in the Manuka Crescent Motel and I got out of bed like a shot. Something amazing was waiting outside but the light of dawn would chase it from view. I turned off the electric blanket, switched on the bedside lamp, put a jersey and a pair of pants over my pyjamas, and ate breakfast standing up in the kitchen – the Manuka Crescent prides itself on serving guests two slices of bread and a single-serve box of Skippy Cornflakes. I blew on my cup of coffee made from a 1.5-gram sachet of Premium Freeze Dried Robert Harris Swiss Gold ('an aromatic smooth golden roast with delicious nutty cocoa notes') as though it were a hot coal. I was out of the room by 5.43, creeping and crunching over the driveway gravel towards the pavement, where I looked for Venus.

Martin Unwin had told us it would be visible in the eastern sky. This was during his speech about the planets. He always asked for permission to stand up and address the class. I always said yes. I wondered if he was a genius. Martin had once designed an underwater lighting system in a fish farm to prevent salmon from maturing too early, but that seemed the least of his talents.

He was 59 and surrounded by a beard. He bounced on the balls of his feet when he walked. One day, he came back late from lunch because he had walked up Mount Iron. He was a tramper and a white-water rafter.

He lived in Christchurch and was about to start commuting to the back of beyond at the end of the line on the West Coast – his wife was to become sole-charge teacher in Haast.

Martin worked for the National Institute of Water and Atmospheric Research, and volunteered as a spokesperson for the Canterbury Astronomical Society. One day he brought in a telescope so we could stare at the sun. It trembled, and his filters made it look red. His speech about the planets was to advise the class about a rare opportunity to see Venus, Mercury, Mars and Jupiter. The planets, he said, would be visible in the hour before sunrise all that week.

I asked him at morning tea one day about his slight stutter. He said it was bad when he was young. Did he think it was physiological or psychological? He said it always got worse when his sister was around. I said I hoped he might write about that one day because I liked the way his mind worked, and was curious to read how he would write about his own life. One day he brought in an old photograph and wrote:

It's just two wooden Ministry of Works' huts in a bare field. The black and white photograph of the infant Lauder atmospheric research station in 1960 is faded, but sharp and clear. The empty spaces behind emphasise the isolation, the distant mountains suggest the scale.

People came. Gordon and Rima Keys arrived with their young family in 1963, after five years in Samoa and Rima's native Rarotonga. Next winter, hoar frost filled wire-netting fences, and snow lay for three weeks. Now long retired, they look towards Lauder from their home above Alexandra. They will never leave.

Alan and Colleen Cresswell, then in their early twenties, arrived from Christchurch in December 1964. At his job interview, Allan stepped from the Alexandra airport into Blossom Festival week. 'It's lovely,' he told Colleen. 'Lots of trees, orchards, gardens – everything is so green.' Driving across a brown Maniototo midsummer they approached their new home with mounting apprehension – where did this landscape come from? Colleen gathered schist slabs to build a rock garden. One day she added some translucent pink rocks from the next-door field to her pile. A few days later the puzzled farmer called by to ask why she wanted his salt licks. They came for two years, stayed for twelve.

Others fell in love with the land immediately. Nineteen-year-old Ruth Stillwell and her husband came from Northland to work on a station near St Bathans, from where she later joined Lauder as a part-time typist and librarian. Driving north from Alexandra into a painted land of open valleys and linear ranges she was excited. She thought, I'm going to the mountains.

The land defined our horizons, measured our days, and embraced our senses. From our family living room, we saw morning light on the Dunstan Mountains. We saw the distant Hawkduns shimmer in the midday sun, and the soft amber glow of evening light settling on the Raggedy Range. Two sharp, craggy hills framed our southern sky. At night we listened from our beds to the roar of nor'westers ripping through a narrow defile in the North Dunstans. We watched summer thunderstorms turn afternoon skies from blue to black, and felt the chill on winter nights as hard starlight hammered down through freezing air. We smelt wild thyme under our feet as we explored the hills, and drank smoky tea brewed in a battered billy on riverside picnic fires kindled with dry willow. We lived there for ten years, and for a lifetime…

Wānaka is stupendous on the eye, a tourist mecca with papery willows and poplars in autumnal orange, an alpine lake, mountains waiting for snow – it was already so cold the lake smoked. The town's retail and hospitality precinct was tastefully laid out facing the lake. It didn't do McDonald's or KFC; it did curries, interesting beers, merino jumpers. There were a lot of old people. But it was a party town, too, and every night happy groups of 20-somethings wrapped in scarves and woolly hats headed into town. Teen-somethings did other stuff. From the police file in *Wanaka Sun*: 'Police called to disorder at an Aeolus Place party. A fourteen- and fifteen-year-old were detained in an intoxicated state, many also affected by the use of the party drug Kronic.'

The sun looked red and trembling through a filter, but exposed in a clear blue sky it didn't have any warmth in it at all, and lay about like a white inert lump. The mountains were bare and dark and enormous. They took up half of the sky. The rest of the sky was just as bare. It didn't budge all that week. It looked as hard as marble, and as fixed as the mountains. It didn't allow anything resembling cloud or wind. I arrived on Monday, which looked the same as Tuesday, Wednesday, Thursday, Friday, Saturday, Sunday. Good. All I want from the world is for it to stay the same.

As a creature of severe habit, I value old habits, but I'm constantly on the lookout for new ones. Not only was Wānaka the same thing over and over, it presented new opportunities to do the same thing over and over. The same breakfast – toast, cornflakes, 1.5-gram sachet of Premium Freeze Dried Robert Harris Swiss Gold – in my room at the Manuka Crescent. The same ten-minute walk in bright sunshine every frosty morning to Mount Aspiring College. The same view of enormous mountains and smoking lake and blank sky.

On the corner there was a wild strawberry tree growing out of a bank. The soft red fruit fell on to the pavement. I picked up a berry one morning and held it in my open palm. I was walking to school with painter Jane Zusters. She said, 'Look at the way it forms shadows.' I wondered how small it would have looked in her palm, because she had such big paws.

The same classroom, Room 12, in a prefab block beside the soccer field, the same intolerable heat blazing from the radiators, and the same windows being opened to let in fresh mountain air. And the same students, arriving in scarves, hats and coats.

On the first day of class I asked them to interview each other. Beth McArthur wrote: 'Former cartographer Jan Kelly of Wānaka says, "Retirement is a misnomer. I work very hard." The 66-year-old writes poetry, the inspiration for which comes from the beauty all around. … Jan's interest in natural history is brought to life in the lizard garden she has at home.'

Jan wrote: 'Beth McArthur of Alexandra is attending a writing course so she can write her memoirs. Having been a typesetter, she now at age 66 has a small computing business doing desktop publishing. "I am adjusting to being a widow," she said. "I've had a very tragic two years. My husband fell off our rock. He always said that no one would fall off the rock." He was a merino classer, she said, very fit, very active; he called himself "the old blind guesser" because classing wool is by feel. His accident changed both their lives in an instant. "It took only a minute. Everything is different now."'

Beth moved heavily. Lonely, she sat in the front row. Jan, clever and thin, worried about people and sat in the back row. Everyone sat at the same desks every day. The teacher's desk was jammed into a corner.

I'd appeared at the college a few years earlier, one of six writers touring schools, libraries and town halls on a road trip arranged by the New Zealand Book Council, and remembered it as a plain and faintly depressing holding cell – the usual New Zealand high school, the familiar prefabricated misery. It was strange to return and see it given over entirely to adults. They were jolly and polite. They grunted when they bent over above the drinking taps, and squeezed their wide hips past doors marked BOYS and GIRLS. Watching them chat about woodblocks and watercolours as they nibbled on digestive biscuits and poured thermos tea in the playgrounds, it was as though they had liberated the college, civilised it. They'd also aged it. It was like a retirement home with netball courts.

The Upper Clutha Community Arts Council has staged the Autumn Art School in Wānaka for over 20 years. My role was to teach adult writing classes for a week. I loved every second of it, beginning with the first seconds when I walked from the motel to the school. The ten-minute amble felt as if I were being pulled in by the tide. It was the force of an acquired new habit, and the decision to get up before dawn on Sunday and find a vantage point to observe the planets turned into an opportunity to do the same thing I'd been doing all that week for one last time. After breakfast I walked from the motel to the school. There was the wild strawberry tree, *Arbutus unedo*, with its soft red fruit on the pavement in the glow of a street light. There was the high line of the mountains, forming a darker tone than the black of night. There was the steaming, freezing lake. There was the school. I looked at it with longing, already nostalgic for the days and the lessons, already missing my sixteen students.

Richard Howarth had an open face: you could easily read on it the pleasure he took in wine and vintage cars. He was 57, lived in Wellington, kept a holiday apartment in Wānaka, and had recently accepted a generous financial package from his law firm. Don McDonald was nimble, and looked at life with an amused sideways glance. He was 71, lived in Picton, and had returned from a cycling tour across America with his second wife, Val.

Brian Miller talked fast and muttered even faster. He was always on the move, restless, searching, loyal – he visited David Bain in prison to show his support. He was 63, lived in Dunedin, and had no real need for a writing course – he was a pro. As a publisher and an author, he specialised in science textbooks, memoirs, and local histories such as his lively book about Macandrew Bay on Otago Peninsula.

Macandrew Bay School was presented with a surplus air raid siren after the war. The school committee viewed the new arrival, then could not resist taking it outside and winding it up on a still moonless night. After a few seconds of wailing, followed by the howling of all the neighbourhood dogs and lights going on all around the bay, the siren was tucked into the basement, never to be used again.

Tough little blades of grass stubbled the hard surface of Lisemore Park opposite the school, where I walked each lunchtime and ate the caterer's delicious sandwiches. It was another new habit. I observed it with my usual bovine obedience – wandering into stands of pine trees, then wandering out and following a concrete path that curled up and over small hills and valleys. It made a nice break from the sound of my voice talking all morning in classroom twelve. I thought about how to keep the students occupied and possibly entertained in the afternoon. I thought about them all the time.

Jane Bloomfield, 45, blonde, sexy, with hooded eyelids, commuted from Queenstown, where she wrote about the adventures of Lily Max, a character she'd developed in her novels for young adults. Diane Wales was arch and witty, with a kind of moneyed nonchalance about her. She dressed well, and wrote, 'After a life on the edges of remote airstrips, Sally Middleton, 70, now divides her time between painting and gardening, and caring for her elderly husband.' Sally was small and industrious, a talented portrait artist. She wrote, 'Diane Wales, now 74, was a young school teacher in Christchurch and married to her first husband when they produced three sons, who now live in London, the Cayman Islands and Auckland. Diane lives in Dunedin. She says about coming up to the week-long Autumn Art School, 'I had to set up an incredibly complicated system to look after my 84-year-old husband.' I thought about their ailing aged husbands.

Sarah Ballard, 61, was tall and willowy, a chatterbox, apparently nearly blind. She grew up in Manchester, and wanted to come to some kind of terms with her father, a doctor and an alcoholic, whom she remembered staggering up the stairs while her mother implored him to just die. Her eyesight was so bad that when she wrote at her desk she lowered her head barely more than an inch above the page. It always looked as though she'd dropped dead. This was my first teaching job and I didn't want to lose anyone, but Sarah was wonderfully and exuberantly alive. I heard talk in the town that she had a beautiful singing voice. One day I asked if she would stand in front of the class and sing a folk ballad. My excuse was that it would demonstrate another way of telling a story. I just wanted to hear her sing. It was true what they said about her in town. I looked at Sarah as her voice soared around the classroom, and turned my head and wept.

There were a lot of tears in classroom twelve. I invited the painting teacher in the next-door classroom to come in and answer questions about her life. Gala Kirke talked about growing up in communist Slovakia. She talked about leaving for New Zealand after the Velvet Revolution. She talked about her paintings – art critic T.J. McNamara once identified her as 'a rising star' – and about how she seldom had time to paint since becoming a parent, and a teacher at Christchurch Girls' High School.

She said she hadn't talked about the earthquake before. When it struck she was tipped down a flight of stairs but didn't think about that: she was desperately frightened for her two little boys. It took her and her husband two hours to drive 15 kilometres across the shattered city to their children's playcentre. The memory of those two hours of fear rushed at her, ambushed her, as she sat in front of sixteen students in classroom twelve. She said they'd sold their house, were leaving Christchurch. She didn't care all that much where they were going to live: the point was that it wouldn't be in Christchurch.

Two days later I invited an ex-footballer to come in and answer questions about his life. There was a public notice in the school grounds advising that Richard Johnson would be holding a training clinic during the holidays. I heard shouts and laughter, and looked over to the fields, where I saw Johnson with eight or nine kids.

He talked about leaving Australia at fifteen to pursue his dream of being a professional football player in the English Premier League. He lived the dream. He played for Watford. He scored a cracking goal against Manchester United. But then he picked up a bad injury, and drifted, falling back down to a club in Australia. He was hoping for a transfer to Malaysia. It fell through and he got drunk, then drove, and when the cops tried to pull him over he did a runner… He was looking at maybe six months in jail.

His voice slowed down. He looked at the floor. The shadow of his former self crept into classroom twelve. Johnson closed his eyes, took in a mouthful of air, and puffed it out. He said the judge gave him a break. He now lived at Jack's Point in Queenstown with his wife and son.

The Slovakian painter about to escape, the nobbled Australian soccer player back on his feet – the makeshift press centre in classroom twelve at Mount Aspiring College wasn't fussy about where it got its pound of tears. One day they came from Robyn Bardas. Red-haired, 45, opinionated and Australian, Robyn lived in Hāwea Flat. She told the class she wanted to write about and come to some kind of terms with, her parents, but she also wanted to find a way, ultimately, to write about, and possibly come to a semblance of some kind of terms with, the death of one of her children. It happened eight years ago. She swayed on her feet: it was happening again.

Then there was the day senior constable Mike Johnston was going to come in but had to cancel – he was telling a Queenstown family that their son was dead. Trainee pilot Marcus Hoogvliet, 21, had died with instructor Graham Stott, 31, when their Robinson 22 helicopter crashed in strong winds in Mount Aspiring National Park. A ground and aerial search by 20 volunteers helped recover evidence from the wreckage at the head of Arawhata River. Most of the machine was in a ravine. 'It was a difficult thing to see if you weren't on top of it,' Johnston told reporters.

The moon, shaped like a bracket and white as ice, was softly sinking towards a black line of some nearby hump. To its left and down a bit was Venus, bright and obvious. Two other planets were to the right and down a bit. It was exhilarating to witness the planets in the night sky, just before dawn, in the cold autumn air of a mountain town – I walked past the school and up the road to the reservoir, where I sat and rested, stargazing.

Mercury, Jupiter, Mars – one of them was missing behind cloud. Cloud! That clean, immaculate sky, as scrubbed as a sink, had finally budged. The first light of dawn began to smudge the sky. It was too early to return to my room at the Manuka Crescent. I had too much air in my lungs, I needed to keep going, somewhere, so I set off towards the nearby hump beneath the moon, and walked on the side of the highway towards Cromwell and Queenstown. I looked up: I could see the moon, Venus, and now only one of the other three planets.

All I had on were the pyjamas beneath the clothes I stood up in. I was free, floating through an empty stretch of road, clinging on to my last few hours in Wānaka. I thought about Toni Cathie, 68, who played bridge and tennis, and wrote with a delicate touch and fine wit. I thought about Prue Kane, red-haired, a quarter of an inch short of six foot tall, at 30 the youngest in class, who wrote amusingly about returning to live in Wānaka after her OE. Family friends gasped and clutched at their throats when Prue told them she was still unmarried. They'd ask, 'What's wrong with you?'

Jeanette Emmerson, 63, small and pale, from a high-country farm in the Lindis Pass, was related to someone famous: her daughter Anna had won the 2009 World Wool Record Challenge Cup for producing the world's finest bale of merino. The cup was presented at a function in the Italian Embassy in Paris; there were 200 people, and a five-course meal at which the waiters wore uniforms. Anna, Jeanette wrote, was born on New Year's Eve in 1975, grew up 'non-conformist and antagonistic', outdoorsy, a deerstalker who once spent a solitary winter in a cabin on an island in the middle of a frozen lake in Alaska, then came back to New Zealand, bought a block of land, built her own woolshed and farmed a thousand merinos. The fleeces in her award-winning bale were shorn from a mob of 450 wethers.

Mylrea Bell, 55, mother of two boys, tutor in business consultancy, wrote a comic and entertaining memoir about her pig. Caroline Harker, 46, a former documentary maker who came to Wānaka for love, composed a memoir about her dinner.

I was quite happy to eat Alice. I expected to be a bit squeamish about it. After all, we were friends.

A year ago the farmer went away and left me in charge of our herd of nineteen cows. They were calving. I had to go up the hill every morning, check they were okay, and count them.

The first day I counted eleven calves and nineteen cows. The next day I counted eleven calves but only eighteen cows. I found number nineteen alone on the other side of the hill. She seemed to be in labour. I left her to it.

The following morning she didn't look too comfortable. She was still standing up but the calf's head was hanging out the back of her. I managed to get up close by walking very slowly and crooning softly. I like the way some animals let you near them when they need help.

I rubbed her back for a while, working my way down towards the calf. I could see a leg was half out too, and I reached out to stroke the calf.

It was cold. Cold enough for me to be sure it was dead.

The cow looked over her shoulder at me with big droopy cow eyes.

'That's a shame, Alice,' I said. I don't know why I chose that moment to give her a name.

I patted her gently and then grasped the calf's hoof. I put my foot up on Alice's rump, lent backwards, and pulled as hard as I could. Alice groaned and staggered as she tried to push the calf out but it didn't move far.

We tried again a couple more times but the calf seemed to be stuck.

'Looks like I'll have to call the vet, Alice,' I said, as I rubbed her back all the way up to her ears. 'We'll get it out soon. Just hang on.'

It was five hours before the vet came. I took her up the hill and we found Alice lying on the ground, moaning. The vet said I should have called her earlier. The calf could have been dead inside her for days. Now Alice was really sick. The dead calf was swelling up inside her.

The vet got down to business. She pushed her whole arm up inside the cow trying to find the other hoof, but she couldn't find it, so she got out her scalpel and cut the calf's head off.

Next, she reached in again and found the other hoof, tied a chain around both hooves, and winched out the headless calf.

I didn't watch. I sat on the ground stroking Alice's cheeks and humming softly. The vet said Alice would probably die. If a cow doesn't get up, she said, it dies.

For the next three days Alice lay on the ground. When I visited her she would try to get up but her back legs didn't work. I gave her water in a bucket and some hay, but nothing changed.

The next day the farmer came home. He got out his gun and headed up the hill. I didn't go. I tried to keep busy with a few chores.

He came back with a smile on his face. Alice was standing up.

After that she got better by the day. At first she couldn't stand for long, then she walked with a horrible limp, one hoof dragging on the ground behind her.

One day she was back with the herd, and we knew she was going to be fine. Every time I saw Alice I called hello, but as time went by she ignored me. Eventually she stopped limping.

The vet said Alice was damaged inside and would never be able to have a calf. Alice had a good spring. Lots of hay. Plenty of new grass. Warm sunny days. But the time to put the bull out with the cows was approaching and Alice had nowhere to go.

One day, while the cows were eating their hay, the farmer got his gun out again. The bullet went in right between her eyes. Her legs slowly folded underneath her. The other cows watched her for a while and then turned their attention back to the fresh hay.

Alice's life was short but it was mainly pretty good. When she came home wrapped up in beautiful parcels labelled fillet steak and roast beef and ribs, it felt like eating her was the best thing to do.

The hump beneath the moon got closer and closer as I walked along the verge of the highway. I came to a stile, and a sign that announced the hump was, in fact, Mount Iron. I climbed the stile and set off to conquer it. I fancied the idea of being the first person to climb to the summit that morning.

I had barely got as high as the first foothill when I saw a retired couple walking down. 'Morning, Steve,' they said. How did they know my name? Who were they, and what were they doing up so goddamned early? They must have climbed Mount Iron in the dark. I pondered the questions and saw another retired couple walking down. 'Morning, Steve,' they said.

Five days in Wānaka and I was already part of the furniture. Four more early-bird trampers trotted down the mountain with cheerful first-person salutations. I recognised a man and two women from various morning and afternoon teas at Mount Aspiring College. It felt good to belong. It was a wonderful tramp, steep and unbelievably scenic – I walked into and then above a soft thick carpet of woolly fog that moved through the valley in a lovely white twist. Lake Hāwea lay beneath it. I trudged onward, past rosehip and rowan berries, thistle and thorn, the plants holding with a tight white-knuckled grip on to the hard rock of Mount Iron. I came to a bald spur. A sign said DANGER.

I thought about Beth McArthur, lonely and sighing in the front of the class, daring to write about becoming a widow.

We didn't put our names down for what happened. My husband fell off our rock. It's a ten-metre schist rock on top of which we had our home built 40 years ago. He always said, 'No one will ever fall off the rock.' But he did. Just like that.

It was a warm summer evening. I remember the date, of course. November 3, 2008. Just an ordinary Monday.

After our evening meal we planned to drive the fourteen kilometres to our ten-acre block at Springvale to tend our peonies but Dick decided to stay at home and watch TV. A night off. I said, 'Well I'm going out to weed that garden in front of my office.'

Dick wandered out the front door during the ads. 'How's it going, young Beth?' he asked.

'Good.' I replied. 'I'm just going to pop over the rock and cut down that seedling elm.'

'I'll do it for you,' he said. I gave him the secateurs and he descended the couple of metres to the small tree, then returned saying, 'I'll need the loppers.' On his way down he lost his footing and fell. It was a free fall. He fell feet first, arms outstretched. It was 7.30 p.m.

I made a 111 call. 'Ambulance, fire, police?' the operator asked. 'Ambulance,' I screamed.

I thought people might think I pushed him. Nobody will ever want to buy our property. Why did I say I was going to get the seedling elm?

My God, this isn't real. It should have been me who fell. This isn't fair. It's not right.

As I hurried down the hill to find Dick, Lynette next door called from her balcony. 'Is everything all right?' 'No,' I screamed and breathlessly continued on down the hill.

By the time I got to Centennial Park the ambulance was screaming round the corner from the opposite direction.

'Help! Get me up. Help!' Words from Dick. He was alive. Thank God. I was still about 30 metres away.

The ambulance officer told me to stay back and sit down. I was still holding our home telephone. It was now out of range. I borrowed the paramedic's phone.

'Bridget. Dick has fallen off the rock,' I said. 'Is it bad?' our youngest daughter asked. 'Yes,' I replied.

I felt a hand on my shoulder. It was a policeman.

The paramedic directed me to the far corner of the park to show the fire brigade to the accident site. Malcolm Macpherson pulled up. 'I'll direct the fire brigade,' he said. His wife, a doctor, was at the bottom of the rock helping with Dick.

Under the tree, on the grass, Bridget and I huddled together. The fire brigade got to work. Soon, two lines of men with arms outstretched were bearing my husband from man to man, gently, carefully, and finally through the open doors of the ambulance.

'How many brothers and sisters do you have?' Joy Watson from Victim Support asked Bridget in the corridor of Dunstan Hospital.

'Three,' she said.

'Ring them right now.'

I felt I'd been cut in half. I wanted to cuddle Dick but wasn't allowed that close to him. The emergency staff were working on him. Life-saving measures. A nurse cut off his shirt. I never did like that shirt.

At last I was allowed to talk to him. I kissed him. 'My arms are tingling,' he said. 'Something strange is happening.'

The team from Dunedin Public Hospital arrived in the rescue helicopter.

We walked out to go home to shower and pack for what lay ahead. Sue and Malcolm Macpherson took me. The ambulance doors were gaping wide open. 'Where's Dick?' I asked. 'He's in the helicopter,' Sue replied.

Bridget drove. We were almost in Milton, which is one and a half hours from Alexandra. Bridget broke the silence. 'We haven't said a word since we left.' I replied, 'What is there to say?'

The puffing and hissing sounds from the oxygen equipment indicated that Dick was still alive. Dots blinked across the heart monitor and the oxygen saturation recorder was in place, along with a drip.

It was about three a.m. Linda was awake to greet us. 'He's broken his neck,' I said.

Bridget and I went to bed in Linda's spare queen-size bed. We cuddled each other and cried. Bridget slept for about an hour. I couldn't sleep. The pillows were damp with our tears.

The next morning at the intensive care unit at Dunedin Hospital a consultant and a medical registrar took Bridget and me into a room. The official diagnosis was delivered. Dick was C5 tetraplegic. Complete. He would never walk again.

They said Dick would be transferred to the Christchurch intensive care unit as soon as a plane or helicopter became available. Wrapped and strapped in red blankets and silver survival sheets for the flight, Dick looked like a giant Christmas cracker.

By the time I puffed my way to the summit of Mount Iron it was mid-morning, bluish, windy, cold. A sign informed climbers of the mountain's geological history – it was formed by glaciers, was once a thousand feet beneath ice. There were views of the mountain ranges, Fog Peak, Black Peak, Shark Tooth – and Rob Roy, which was covered with snow all that week.

There were views of the past. I'd come to know the ranges and valleys in travels with my father. He lived his final years in another of the 'cold lakes', Tekapo, and later in Fairlie. I'd visit. We'd take road trips, stay in motels. We'd go to Wānaka. We'd go through the Lindis Pass.

In 2003 I wrote about our last trip together:

A great many things were going on in the middle of the South Island
two weekends ago. In Ōmarama on Saturday night – no doubt you heard
about this on the news – it rained at three a.m.

That was at the end of a warm crisp day in winter, not a cloud in the
sky, and hardly another car on the road. Out of the wind, poplars still
held their autumn blaze. You could see that most vividly on the shores
of Lake Benmore, and beside the Benmore Dam, where a father and son
were fishing next to the No Fishing sign.

I was on a road trip with my dad: another father and son spending
time together in the middle of the South Island. We went indoors to see
fish. The pub in Kimbell has a 43-pound salmon, caught by L. Rooney
in 1970, mounted on a wall. It's above the jukebox ('The Man Who
Shot Liberty Valance', 'Rocky Mountain High'), and next to a gallery of
photographs marking great days in the history of the McKenzie Collie
Dog Club, established in 1891; in 1950, at the club's jubilee trials, vice-
president Roy Rapley appeared in a kilt.

Next door to the pub – there are two doors in Kimbell – is Lloyd
Harwood's Silverstream Gallery. Lloyd draws portraits. 'You should be
able to see the eyelashes really well,' he promises clients. He also paints,
although he is colour-blind. Much of his gallery is devoted to landscapes
of Randall Froude, 'the Monet of the South Pacific', whose paintings have
generated over eleven million dollars in sales – they have hung in Japan,
Australia, England and the US. Where does the artist currently reside?
'Over there,' said Lloyd, and pointed through a window to a house on
the other side of Kimbell Creek, behind a row of cottonwood trees.

All the pretty towns: Geraldine, where you can buy your best investment
in the middle of the South Island, a hand-knitted woollen hat; Waimate,
which gives its name to Oligosoma waimatense, the endangered scree
skink; Twizel, which is illuminated at night by an electric light sculpture
– 43 flashing sequences, imported from Japan – on top of a power pole.
So much space, such abundance. The vital statistics of the middle of

the South Island included 900 hectares of onions, 4,000 of potatoes, 7.7 million head of sheep and 505,000 of beef cattle.

But crime has run rampant. In Fairlie a sheep was shot in the leg; police suspect the sniper fired from Mt Gay Road. A mobile sheep yard was stolen in Albury. Thieves also made off with firewood, filched from the open sheds of two elderly women in Twizel, and went to a lot of trouble to nick the stainless steel circular map from the layby at Mount Michael. Good people continue to do good things. John Campbell has been re-elected as pipe major of the Mackenzie Highland Pipe Band. Caroline Bay had just hosted the thirty-seventh national square dance convention, and the South Canterbury Cat Fanciers Club is about to hold its thirty-eighth championship show. And you could go to Kurow, where the butcher is famous for his smoked and pickled tongue, or shop in Ashburton, where Kitchen Kapers sells a frightening range of plates in the shapes and patterns of cabbages.

It rained in Ōmarama on Saturday night. That was a surprise: the night was clear as glass. Sunday morning was damp, cold, grey. The only warmth to be had was the bonfire lit by the new owner of the Aruhuri Motel. It was his first weekend in business and he was burning a lot of old cardboard boxes, and about to throw a harmonica into the flames.

All fires are mesmerising, especially so on a winter's day in a small friendly town. A slide in the children's playground was set in a mound of dirt. Outside the police station, a policeman's cap was placed on top of a tree trunk with the sign DO NOT FEED THE POLICEMAN. Scraps of burnt cardboard floated above the motel.

'Look,' I said to my father, and we stood together watching the cardboard fly through the air like burned birds, on a morning in the middle of the South Island, in winter, before snowfall.

# 17 GREYMOUTH
## THE PIKE RIVER MINE DISASTER

The most unforgettable film in New Zealand history is the CCTV silent movie recorded at the Pike River coal mine on a Friday afternoon in early summer when the lives of Conrad Adams, Malcolm Campbell, Glen Cruse, Allan Dixon, Zen Drew, Christopher Duggan, Joseph Dunbar, John Hale, Daniel Herk, David Hoggart, Richard Holling, Andrew Hurren, Koos Jonker, William Joynson, Riki Keane, Terry Kitchin, Samuel Mackie, Francis Marden, Michael Monk, Stuart Mudge, Kane Nieper, Peter O'Neill, Milton Osborne, Brendon Palmer, Ben Rockhouse, Peter Rodger, Blair Sims, Joshua Ufer and Keith Valli came to an end in darkness, underground.

The following winter, on another Friday, with snow on top of the Paparoa Range, a bunch of flowers rotted in a wire-mesh gate that served as a roadblock in front of Pike – no one bothered to add the word River, it was only ever the flat and joyless monosyllabic Pike.

The route to Pike crossed Big River Bridge and followed Logburn Road towards the mountains. It was big, dark country. The fields were dug up like furrows in a drainage technique called humping and hollowing. A road sign carried an illustration of a weka and the command DOGS PROHIBITED. Signs festooned the roadblock gate: ENTRY BY APPOINTMENT ONLY; IN AN EMERGENCY DIAL 555; DO NOT LITTER. A bunch of red plastic flowers wrapped in cellophane had been placed on the side of the road. In smudged ink, a card read RIP BRENDON FLY TRUE LOV YOU ALL WAYS MINDY.

Families of the 29 men were given a private screening of the film. It was later shown at a press conference. The longest version, available on YouTube, is two minutes and 31 seconds.

The chief coroner ruled on what no one could know and said the men died on November 19 'either at the immediate time of the large explosion that occurred in the mine or a very short time thereafter'. He worked on 'the available evidence'. But the bodies weren't available. They remained in a tomb of granite and coal.

The mine exploded on November 19 at 3.44 in the afternoon. An emergency was declared at 5.51. Six days later, at 2.37 p.m. on Wednesday, a second explosion ripped through the mine and all hope was lost.

The CCTV camera was fixed to the left of what looks like the opening of a cave. The static image on November 19 shows an arch cut through grey and solid rock. The ground is wet and puddly, with tyre treadmarks heading into the cave, and there are scaffolding pipes and a metal roof. The sunlight is very bright. It burns on a stand of West Coast native bush – beech forest, ribbony, mossy, unlike native bush anywhere else in New Zealand. It has a sweeter smell, the light is darker. Pike was set deep in forest, beyond the White Knight Bridge.

'Oh God, it's so beautiful there, honestly,' said Cath Monk. Her husband Bernie said, 'The water's so clear, and it's running over granite stone, and there are ferns growing everywhere.' It was Friday night at Greymouth's handsome Paroa Hotel, purchased in 1955 by Ham and Corrie Monk. Their sons, Bernie and Winston, now manage it together. Bernie's son Alan was behind the bar. There was a framed photograph of Alan's younger brother Michael on a small table by the door. It showed a good-looking guy with an open face. The portrait made it seem he was guest of honour; a visitor wondered aloud if it was his birthday. Michael worked at Pike. He was building an underground dam.

Talk of the scenery at Pike reminded Cath to fetch something. She came back with a large rock. 'Granite,' she said. 'One of the guys gave it to me. It's from out of the mine.' She said they went to Pike on Christmas Day. 'It's a beautiful place but it's so far away. You just can't go and visit. We want him home with us.'

The two-minute 31-second film opens with a faint movement: what looks like a strip of rag, fixed to the inside wall of the cave, stops blowing into the mine and flops down, inert. This is the beginning of the end, the moment the methane gas explodes about two and a half kilometres inside the mine.

'Concussion ... thermal injuries ... acute hypoxia ... The men would have died within three to five minutes of the explosion,' the coroner said.

'I was here working when it went off. I heard it,' said Gina Howton, who ran the general store in nearby Blackball. 'It was like that first clap of thunder in a storm. I thought, no one will come out of that alive.' Some of the men were customers. 'A couple of guys who worked there said, "It's gonna blow. Not if, but when." That's what they said.'

The next week transformed quiet Blackball into a madhouse. 'Hours and hours of helicopters going back and forth, people coming in all the time and breaking down. Everyone popped in: families, police, the media, the rescue guys. I hate to say it but tragedy is good for business. It's true. It was like that with the paedophile too.'

The paedophile of Blackball, made to leave town and never come back, as recorded in chapter 14. Gina and her husband Paul had lived in Blackball for two years when that went down; they had moved down from Auckland. 'Paul always says when we go back, "It's good coming back to New Zealand."' Did she miss Auckland? 'Probably Briscoes is the only thing.'

At the pub, drinkers lined the bar, played pool, wore black jeans. There used to be a friendly little guy who called himself Rotten and boarded upstairs. Word was that he had shifted to Greymouth to board upstairs at the Royal. It was true. He was in his room that Saturday night. It had a single bed and a hand basin. It cost $140 a week. Rotten said, 'I want to move on and up. Get a girlfriend. But I'm a hobo. That's the truth of it.'

Downstairs at the bar, a hot fire blazed in a very old fireplace. 'Look at the brickwork,' he said. 'These are primo fuckin' bricks, mate.' Rotten was hairy, wore black jeans, said the last job he had was knocking down and replacing a boiler at the Kotere meat works.

The drink made him sentimental. 'My mother touched my face, and said, "Get it together." I had a mohawk then. I said, "But I have got it together. I've got a girlfriend." My mother died the next day. I went to the house and my stepbrother said, "She's passed away." I said, "Where to?" It took me three days before it clicked. I just could not believe it. I was doing an engineering course in Stillwater. The students formed a guard of honour for me with screwdrivers and spanners, any tool you can name.'

The publican approached Rotten and had a word in his ear. 'I do odd jobs around the place,' Rotten said, and returned a few minutes later with a bucket of coal. He threw a shovel into the inferno. It sparked and made a noise like a wave crashing on shingle. Rotten touched the brickwork with his fingers. They felt like art. He said, 'Primo fuckin' bricks.'

It was so cold outside it boxed your ears and ripped tears from your eyes. The night was loud with the smashing Tasman Sea. Inside, there were good times for families at the packed Bonzai Pizza Parlour, good times for happy drunks at the sing-song Revingtons Hotel, good times for cool people upstairs at the funky Franks Café. In the morning the famous wind known as The Barber cut through town on the back of the Grey River, heading seaward, its freezing cold and piercing blade attended by a tail of white mist.

The best place in town for a good breakfast was ABC Quick Lunch. The day warmed up, softened the air, and allowed Greymouth's familiar woozy scent to rise up: the scent of coal.

In the CCTV footage outside the coal mine, the rag fixed to the wall is actually a piece of plastic tape attached to a rib bolt. It was referred to as such by associate professor David Cliff of Queensland University's minerals industry safety and health centre. Cliff's name was regularly in the media in the days immediately following the Pike explosion. He explained what was happening inside the mine. He said that temperatures may have soared higher than 1,200 degrees centigrade when the fireball exploded.

He also explained the significance of the plastic tape. It usually inclines towards the mine, following the flow of air, he said. But it flops down at the very beginning of the two-minute-31-second film because a shock wave has been set off: the mine has exploded.

'The guys in the tunnel would have felt the shock wave and all the entrained dust etc, but the air would still have been breathable. … That may be some glimmer of hope.'

Pike production manager Steve Ellis also held out hope. He told the royal commission he believed some of the men had survived the first blast, that they could have taken refuge near a compressed airline, or been sheltered by mining equipment. Rescue teams were put on standby. They remained on standby. The weekend was a long agony of nothing happening.

Nothing continued to happen on the Monday. 'At the moment we are in rescue mode,' Trevor Watts, general manager of New Zealand Mines Rescue, said in response to a suggestion the miners may have come to harm. The front-page story on that day's *Greymouth Evening Star* read: 'It could be teatime before the first rescue bid at the Pike River mine even gets under way, distraught families of the 29 missing men were told this morning. However, after three out of four air tests proved clear, there was hope the rescue effort could enter the mine around noon…'

When the plastic tape flops down and just hangs there, the image on the CCTV film stays exactly as it is for the next minute and 36 seconds. The light doesn't change. There's an orange sunspot on the inside wall of the mine entrance. The plastic tape doesn't budge.

The weather that Friday was lovely, clear as a bell. Christmas was only five weeks away. Summer on the Coast, swimming, fishing, beer, family – the afternoon felt ripe with promise. It was a day that felt very good to be alive on the Coast, that strange and magnetic republic. Of all the republics within New Zealand, the Coast is the most devout, makes the strongest claims for independence. Half the time it doesn't bother calling itself West – it's never heard of West, there's only one Coast. On one side of the Southern Alps, New Zealanders; on the other side, Coasters, a distinct race, isolated, constantly asserting they're staunch, but actually deeply afraid and for good reason. The Coast – underground, at sea, in bush – has a long history as a death trap. There is more pain and trauma here than anywhere else in New Zealand. Nineteen dead at the Brunner mine in 1896, nine at Dobson in 1926, nineteen at Strongman in 1967 – the dates of mining disasters run deep.

The men at Pike ranged in age from seventeen to sixty-four. The youngest, Joseph Dunbar, was on his first day at the mine. His father told journalists he hadn't seen his son in eight years, didn't know he was living in Greymouth, didn't know he'd become a miner. He said, 'Why was my wee boy in there?'

Wayne Abelson said, 'Those bastards running Pike should have been thrown in jail right from the very beginning. They flaunted the rules. Pike was never safe. They offered me a job. I told them there was no fucking way I'm working in a single-exit mine with that amount of methane in it.'

He was 53, very large, and worked as a coal miner at Spring Creek. On Sunday afternoon he was in his house in Greymouth overlooking the sea. The front deck had just been built. It didn't have any furniture on it. Two large women sat on the bare boards and smoked in the chill wind in silence, and then came inside and folded towels in the living room in silence. The odour of the house was thick with dog. The TV was tuned to the crime investigation channel on Sky: Wayne had been watching *World's Toughest Cops*. A large teenage boy walked into the kitchen, put his head in the fridge, and walked out. Wayne said he used to work as a fisherman. 'There's always a wave with your name on it. You've just got to dodge it. It's no good doing a boring job.' There was a large wild pig in a cage in the backyard. Wayne said, 'Hello, Boris!'

In the low-income suburb of Blaketown, where no trees grew and the wind clawed at house paint, three adults and one child were in the possible presence of God inside a little old white stucco church. Pastors

Alan and Claire Holley were with their young daughter, and a woman who waved her hands in the air. They belonged to The River, an Assembly of God sect. 'We formed only four years ago,' Alan said. 'Greymouth is spiritually cautious but we believe people will come to trust us as we prove we're stayers.' A congregation of one had to be described as a low turnout. 'I'd prefer it was bigger, yes.' How much bigger? 'I was expecting another three people today.' He worked as an electrician at the Kotere meat works. Did he know anyone there called Rotten? 'No,' said Pastor Holley.

At the Grey River bar, the swell pitched a fishing boat up on an alarmingly high wave as it somehow made it out to sea in one piece. A crowd of five drove to the wharf to watch. Boats crossing the bar have long counted as one of Greymouth's most exhilarating spectator sports.

A criminal defence lawyer was about to head back to the office and prepare for an upcoming rape trial; he talked about defending three generations of the same family, the grandfather, father and son, who were all unemployed.

Jerry Fulford, a tall man with a very full beard, said as waves assaulted the wharf, 'Physically, the Coast is amazing. But people's attitudes are depressing. All they can do is rape things. Coal. Gold. It's an extractive mentality. I don't call them coal mines; I say the people have coal minds.' He worked as a stonemason and builder. 'They call me the working hippie.'

The tide collapsed on to the black shore, sick and foaming. It was a day to stay indoors. Joe Gillman looked into the fire and said, 'When someone dies, a piece of you dies.' His house was known to everyone on the Coast. It had an eye-catching sign out the front that read WELCOME TO ALL THOSE WHO WISH ME WELL. EVERYONE ELSE CAN GO TO HELL.

Joe was in some sort of agony. There were framed photos of beautiful women on the wall of his house. Perhaps the most striking one wore her dark hair long and was on the back of a motorbike. 'I met her at Jackson's Bay wharf. I was 55, she was 22. I thought, what would she see in me? But she was there again the next day. She died at 32 of breast cancer.'

Out the front of Joe's house a smaller sign read NO HIGH VIZ CLOTHING PAST THIS POINT. Why did he object to high-visibility clothing? Anger roused him, brought him out of his agony. He said, 'A meter man came the other day dressed in high-vis. Who the hell did he think he was? A bloody meter man! It's gone too far.'

Hurt, eccentric, intense Greymouth, pop. 9,000, with its rich, tingling scent of coal. A freight train gave a tender hoot as it trundled into town on Friday afternoon, pulling six carriages of timber from the sawmill at Stillwater. I made my way to Grey District Council to interview the mayor, Tony Kokshoorn.

A frisky sort of rooster, chatty and bright-eyed, Kokshoorn gave interview after interview during the crisis at Pike. He said, 'This place is never far from a news bulletin. It's normally a struggle type of story – a flood, a mining disaster. I'm writing a book at the moment. Here's half of it.' He handed over a fat lump of manuscript, *The Golden Grey: Westland's 150th Anniversary*. 'It's going to be 400 pages!' He flipped to sad pictures of the 1967 Strongman mining disaster and said, 'It's going to be up to date. It'll have Pike in it.'

He had been at his weekend bach putting in a lounge suite when he heard ambulances whirr past. Then the phone rang: the police. 'I said to the wife, "It's blown its top." She said, "What has?" I said, "The bloody mine – it's blown its fucking top!"

'I was one of the first to get up there. It was still light, about six or seven o'clock. The search and rescue guys were ready to go in. "Koko" – that's what they call me – "Koko," they said, "we're ready." I said, "Yeah, I hope you're going in shortly." But there was a terrible air of inevitability about it. We all knew in some way.'

He sat behind his desk wearing black dress pants and a purple shirt. There was a selection of ties on a yellow plastic coat hanger in the corner. He laced his fingers together and said, 'Greymouth is a town that's weighted down by this huge disaster.'

Then he leapt up from his chair. 'All the media who came – it was like a city. It was incredible. For weeks! Just this huge attention.' He hefted a giant scrapbook on to his desk. It was stuffed with press clippings about Pike. 'Just look at this – goes on forever. There's bloody more of them over on the shelf,' he said, his eyes shining. He pointed at a stack of scrapbooks. 'Eight of them, all chocka. I'm never far away from the news media, don't you worry about that! I reckon I'd go unchallenged in New Zealand for press coverage. What d'ya reckon? Hey, look at this one.'

He had flipped to a story about an opinion poll that listed him as the tenth most trusted man in New Zealand. He laughed and said, 'Bloody old Koko, eh. Not bad for a kid from Ruru. I'll tell you what, I'd rather be a big fish in a small pond. I've no interest in looking beyond the Coast. I fight for the Coast.

'I lobbied hard for Pike to open. We know it will open again. We're on the cusp of a mineral boom, and that will be led by coal and then gold. China and India are screaming for what we've got. The Paparoas – they're chocka with coke and coal. There's six to ten billion dollars' worth in there. This is Greymouth,' said the mayor. 'This is a coal town, and we're proud of it.'


This is Notown. Fred Nyberg, 76, warmed the teapot on the coal range in his one-room hut. He cut open a tin of condensed milk. His hut in this ghost town in beech forest half an hour inland from Greymouth was off the power grid. He ran his seven-inch black and white Rhapsody TV from a twelve-volt car battery.

Serene, gentle, wise, Fred was living a West Coast pastoral. Outside his window there was one fantail, one hawk. Further along the road, there was a historic cemetery and the end of the road. 'I get Māori hens wanting to come in here,' he said. 'wekas. I'll see them once in a while, always on a morning of little dew.'

Fred's immaculate hair was combed into a kind of quiff. He was elegant in a cardigan and brown nylon pants. Notown – so-called because a surveyor viewed the tents hurriedly pegged out during the 1860s' gold rush and commented, 'It looks like no town at all' – thrived until the turn of the century, and was deserted by about 1920.

'I had it to myself when I first came here,' Fred said. He'd lived in Notown for 25 years. He bought the hut for a hundred dollars. The shower was next to the food cupboards; the bed, coal range, and a Formica table and two chairs were in the other room. He laid a cloth over the television. There was an umbrella in the outhouse.

He poured the tea and said, 'I'm an avid reader; if the weather kicks up, I can read six bloody books in a week. I cook well. I eat good tucker. I make sure I eat my vegies every night, and always do me a good meat stew every Sunday. One day I'll have to surrender to old age. But I love doing what I'm doing. I love panning.'

On the wall of the hut: a calendar from Morris and Watson Precious Metal Refiners. Outside the front door: gold. Had he made any money? 'Let's say I'm comfortable,' he said. 'Nothing can hurt me. But I'm not greedy. It's a hobby, you could say. I just love the sheer joy of doing it.'

He talked about the creeks, about using a pump and an old cradle. There was a light in his eyes. The light was golden. Fred warmed both hands around his teacup and said, 'When you're out there panning you don't feel like you have blood running in your veins. You feel like you have something beautiful running through you. It's a feeling of peace. It's a great feeling. A great feeling.'

The one minute and 36 seconds when nothing apparently happens on the CCTV film – when the light doesn't change, when nothing moves, including the all-important piece of plastic tape – ought to be boring. It isn't: it's terrifying. David Cliff described what was going on inside the mine: 'The explosion pressure wave would have reflected like a billiard ball off the walls and could have passed multiple times in differing directions throughout the mine – much like making a break at snooker where the balls hit the cushions multiple times.'

Two men survived. Daniel Rockhouse was knocked off his feet, lost consciousness, and regained it about 20 minutes later. 'I was just freaking out,' he told the royal commission. 'I then closed my eyes and thought that was it. I thought I was dead and was screaming, "Please don't do this." I don't know if I was talking to God or something. I was just freaking out. I was screaming, "Is there anyone out there? Help. Help. Help." But no one answered me.' He got to his feet, found a workmate, Russell Smith, unconscious and dragged him on a long walk through the mine to safety.

The royal commission was held in four stages and met at the district court. The premises were formerly a supermarket. In the aisles of justice on a Friday morning, thirteen family members of the 29 men sat in four rows of reserved seats and maintained their vigil as a man from the Department of Conservation gave evidence. He talked about dealing with the Pike mining company before the explosion. When he asked to see their emergency response plan, he had to advise the company that a number of names and phone numbers were out of date.

Bernie Monk was in court. As spokesman for the Pike families, he made it his business to attend every day. He took it all in. There were allegations about the mining company's slack attitude towards safety issues. There were criticisms of the police. There were allegations of hopeless mismanagement at the rescue scene. The mine manager considered using a fishing rod to lower a gas monitoring device down the ventilation shaft; St John Ambulance Service suggested lowering a stomach pump to suck up air samples; Mines Rescue lowered a radio and a lamp in a bucket.

Control room operator Daniel Duggan, who lost his brother Chris in the disaster, tried to contact the men immediately after the explosion. His voice over the intercom echoed in the mine: 'Anyone underground? Anyone?'

A seismic listening device was attached to the tunnel entrance. It would relay any tapping by miners to indicate they were alive.

A defence force robot was sent down the mine. It was battery-powered, operated with four cameras and carried a thousand metres of fibre optic cable; when it arrived at Pike, it was accompanied by a team from the Explosive Ordnance Disposal Squadron. It got a little way into the mine, got wet and conked out. Tony Kokshoorn said, 'Why the hell didn't it have a bit of Glad Wrap over it?'

Inside the mine there was Stuart Mudge, 31, described by his dad Stephen Rose as 'fit, very strong and very healthy'. Rose told reporters, 'When the explosion happened Stuart was probably driving a very valuable piece of machinery. Working with that machinery and those guys is the pinnacle of his working career.'

There was Francis Marden of Barrytown, described by his wife Lauryn as a family man, an artist, a potter – 'I am wearing a piece of jewellery he handcrafted. He was a great gardener who had an affinity with the birds, communicating with them, I think, because of his gentle nature.' She told the *Greymouth Star*, 'He hated every day of it [mining] … only did it to pay the bills. He could ride a horse, shoot a gun, he has built us two houses from the ground up. …

'Francis was anything but a miner. Some stories have said he loved going to the pub with his mates. He never went to the pub. He was too tired when he got home to go anywhere. He's never set foot in the pub.'

There was Terry Kitchin. His partner Tara Kennedy told the royal commission she held out hope he'd survived the first blast. 'I was going home every day and telling my three kids that Daddy would be home in time for their birthdays,' she said. They'd made Welcome Home cards for him.

There was Zen Drew. His father Laurie Drew sat in the royal commission with a tattoo of an enormous spider – possibly a tarantula, but it didn't seem the right time to ask – covering the top of his skull.

There was Michael Monk. The day of his memorial service was also his birthday. 'Michael,' sighed Bernie Monk. 'Well, Michael at 23 was very motivated. He had a lovely girlfriend, Gemma, and you could tell the way things were going to go with those two. He'd bought a section for $165,000 overlooking the sea for the two of them to build on. But anyway in a split second it's all over.'

He sighed again. 'He was very quiet as a boy. He hardly said boo. Then he spent a year overseas and travelled around Europe when he was seventeen, eighteen, and that's when he came out of his shell. That's right, isn't it?'

Cath Monk said, 'No, he came out of his shell before that, when he was made a prefect at St Bede's.'

Bernie was thinking about something else. 'Let's get the men out. It's all I think about. The way I feel about the royal commission is, let the police prosecute those who should be prosecuted, and just scrap the commission and spend the money on getting the guys out.'

He talked about meeting the prime minister at the public memorial service for the 29 men. He called him 'Keys'. He said, 'I said to Keys, "Don't think you can give me a flash memorial and bring all those dingoes in to shake my hand and then walk off."'

'We've saved the mine from being sealed off twice. We've had bullshit after bullshit.'

Cath said there had been Pike families in that night, eating dinner at the hotel: the families met every Wednesday at the Holy Trinity Church. She talked about the night of November 19. 'We were going to have a pot-luck dinner at our house: a lady from work was leaving. I rang Michael to put the chicken on. Of course he never answered.'

She put her hand on Bernie's hand. She said, 'I never read any papers or saw the TV news all that time we were waiting because they might have said he wasn't alive. You had to believe he was alive, didn't you?'

She gripped Bernie's hand, put her other hand to her face, bowed her head. 'But anyway in a split second it's all over.'

Friday night at the Paroa Hotel in the republic of agony with no end in sight. The recovery of 29 men from a toxic underground mine remains indefinitely postponed.

What happens after one minute and 36 seconds of the most unforgettable film in New Zealand history is that all hell breaks loose. It really does: it's not a metaphor. Hell breaks loose from the Pike mine and shows itself. For one minute and 33 seconds, the underground pressure wave travels two and a half kilometres through the black mine, killing all or some of the 29 men ('concussion … thermal injuries … acute hypoxia') who were at their jobs on a Friday afternoon in early summer. The piece of plastic tape – that seemingly innocuous rag attached to a rib bolt on the inside wall of the cave opening – anticipates the explosion. It stirs suddenly, and swings towards the tunnel, only for a moment, and then swings back with even greater speed in the opposite direction. Hell is on its tail.

Hell arrives. A white flash fills the screen, a dazzling shaft of light that bursts again, and again, and again, dancing. It is stone dust, ripped off the sides of the tunnel. The blast lasts for 45 seconds. Throughout the crisis of the next six days, the mine will often be referred to as 'the barrel of a gun'. The film is the gun firing, but it looks more like a volcanic eruption from a crater tipped on its side, ejecting white-hot lava.

The blast goes on and on. The violence is all the worse for being on a silent movie: you have to imagine the noise. The scaffolding shakes, the roof wobbles; dark objects spit from the tunnel; a sheet of metal tied to the inside of the cave is flung forward, and bangs against the walls – it's a speed sign, advising vehicles the limit is 25 kilometres per hour, in which case the explosion is breaking the law.

The force, finally, is spent. There's one last white flash: the stone dust travels through the open air, hits the stand of native bush, and the impact lights up the screen. The trees shake, and then settle. For the last six seconds of the film, the plastic tape reverts to normal – it follows air into the mine. Once more it's a lovely afternoon, sunny and calm.

The weather was like that three weeks later when the public memorial was held at Greymouth's picturesque Omoto Racecourse beneath the Paparoa Range. An estimated 11,000 people attended. There were courtesy buses from Blackball, Dobson, Paroa and Karoro. Some people came by boat. There were picnic rugs, sun hats, chillibins. The service ended with the national anthem. The loudest cheers were for a haka by the Blaketown Rugby Club. Families of the 29 men placed ferns on 29 tables. Personal items were added – a surfboard, a cricket bat, ski boots, a cloth with Egyptian patterns. The mourners were piped out by bagpipes. A little boy held on to balloons on a string. He let them go and the bright colours rose against the tender green of beech forest that surrounded the racecourse. He looked up and waved, and said, 'Bye-bye, Daddy.'

# 18 COLLINGWOOD
## LENNY, DENNY, BUTTONS AND TINK

Buttons was there. Gorsey was there, Brighty was there, Tink was there. In short, everyone was there. It was Friday night. The wood burner was roaring. Len, long-haired, 60, was in top form, talking rapidly about gold, milk, good bastards he had known, and how the thing about Collingwood was that it was a one-pub town.

Mate, he said, we don't stuff up in this town. Mate, he said, I've never once witnessed a single punch. In Tākaka, he said, there were factions, and the town had two pubs. Well, three, he said, including the one for dope smokers.

Collingwood Tavern was about to host the annual pig-hunt prize-giving – $150 for heaviest boar and $50 for longest tusks, children's prizes of $20 for heaviest hare and heaviest goat. The fat of the land was soon to be dragged out of the hills of Golden Bay, that amazing Eden at the top of the South Island, up and over the marble and rock of Tākaka Hill. The central fact of life in Collingwood, pop. 250, was Tākaka Hill. The rest of New Zealand lay over it.

On one side was Aorere River, radiant with trout, whitebait, gold; on the other side was the Tasman Sea. When the tide was in, it licked the shore. When the tide was out, it went way, way out, leaving a parched mudflat as far as the eye could see. One of New Zealand's most extraordinary postcards shows Collingwood at low tide. It looks like a nuclear-testing site in Nevada. The sky is light blue. The photographer stands on a low hill; there is a dirt track in the foreground, then a cabbage tree, then the red roofs of nine low buildings on either side of the main street. Then, the mudflats, bare as a desert. In the distance, Farewell Spit. It looks like the loneliest town in the world, deserted and beautiful, the end.

It was supposed to be the end of the world that weekend. May 21 was the doomsday predicted and widely publicised by a California radio preacher, Howard Camping, who had spooked the superstitious Christians of Samoa when he erected doomsday billboards in Apia in March. News of the apocalypse travelled to Collingwood as a joke, something to laugh at on Friday night in the tavern, where Len and Buttons and their mates drank from a long, thin, sensuously designed glass holding three litres of beer. They called it The Barmaid. The Barmaid cost $30. Steak pies cost five dollars, and the bar also sold Panatella cigars.

Mate, Len said, you should have been here when I had my sixtieth. Mate, he said, I had a rock 'n' roll band, a pig on a stick. Mate, I had this place honking. There were riotous photos on the wall.

Buttons was about Len's age, maybe older, with suspiciously jet-black hair. It looked like a toupee. It wasn't a toupee. His mother had jet-black hair and she was ninety. Buttons drank his beer and talked about fishing. You should try smoked stingray, he said. Some people say it tastes like bacon. What people? Well, he said, I do.

Len drove a Fonterra milk tanker, a rigid truck and trailer carrying 25,000 litres. It didn't interest him. Nah, he said, I'm into classic Ducatis. Got a 1928 Ford Sports Coupé. Where? In the shed. I'm a shed man. He was also a gold man. He'd found some good nuggets over the years. You want to talk to this fella fossicking for gold up in Devil's Boots, he said. Good guy? A bit strange, but you have to be strange to fossick for gold.

Did you have to be strange to live in Collingwood? Len said you had to pull your head in to live there, but he was too hilarious, too full of life, to observe any code of dourness, and there was nothing dour about Collingwood.

The last two drinkers at the tavern were young farmhands, one from Westport, the other from Ukraine. The one from Ukraine said he was related to Osama bin Laden. No, he said, I am, true. The one from Westport said, Haha! He had his mate's bush shirt on top of his pool cue and was threatening to poke it into the open door of the wood burner.

Jamie the barman dried the glasses. His marriage had gone bust. His wife had got caught up in Christ College of Trans-Himalayan Wisdom. He had an intelligent face and it also seemed to be on pretty intimate terms with suffering. He said he had moved to Collingwood after the Christchurch earthquake. He had been in the shopping mall at Shirley on February 22. He said it was like being in a matchbox. He picked up a matchbox and shook it. He said, I write poetry. He hung his head, sipped his beer; the next second, he was gone.

There was only one car parked on the main street. It was a ute, covered in mud. It wasn't parked anywhere near the kerb.


Doomsday dawned with a high tide, and big snow-white flowers twitching and trembling in the top branches of the lone pine tree on Māori Island. The flowers were actually a colony of fifteen royal spoonbills. According to local birder Chris Petyt, they arrive in Collingwood around March and winter over at Ruataniwha Inlet, returning to the Wairau River in Blenheim in September.

Len came into town at about nine for a loaf of bread. He left, and then a mud-covered ute came around the corner. How's it? said the Ukrainian. He took his gumboots off at the door of the dairy and walked in to buy a packet of Park Drive. The dairy was opposite the Collingwood volunteer library, open on Tuesdays and Saturdays.

At about ten, Briar Saunders, 49, drove her wheelchair into town to open the library door. Borrowers paid a fee. Today, she said, I might make thirteen dollars. Or it could be one dollar sixty. She had lived in Collingwood for 23 years. She arrived as a single parent and raised three kids, and had had MS for 20 years. She said, My whole left side is shot. She said, This place has adopted me. Collingwood owns me. It's put so much money into me. The community organised a sheep on a spit and a raffle, and raised funds to buy her a heat pump. She said, It's humbling.

Denny Gillooly, 73, walked in the door. He was sixth-generation Collingwood and lived in a blue stucco house on Collingwood Quay, where his wife had dozens of pots of begonias hanging up on hooks in the sunroom. Denny had an office with historic maps, photos, and documents of Collingwood and Golden Bay. His people founded Collingwood in 1853 when they came looking for lost cattle and found gold. By 1857 the population was 1,300. The boom didn't last long, Denny said. He talked about placentas buried on Māori Island, and leaving school at fourteen, and the first hippies, who arrived in the 1970s.

He walked across the road to the banks of the river. Look, he said, that's fossils in these rocks. He pointed across the river. That's the Wakamarama Range. We call it the Sleeping Lady. There's her face, her boobs, her knees. It really was a sleeping lady, gigantic and supine. She apparently ate food of the gods: on the shortest day of the year, Denny said, the sun went down in her mouth.

He talked about the December floods. The rain had fallen in sheets of water. The vital statistics were ten houses flooded, two bridges washed out, 270 lambs, 105 milking cows and 55 heifers washed away, although a hundred of the cows had been found later, safe downstream, and all but 20 of the heifers were recovered alive.

In winter, Deborah Humphries said, the wind blows its arse off, but in summer you can't fault it. Deborah and her husband Dave lived in Nelson and had whitebaited in Collingwood for years, staying with their son Callum at the camping ground. Callum's nine or ten, Dave said, and he's never had a summer here, so we bought this place in September.

Callum and a gang of mates were fishing off the wharf. They scampered along the old wooden piles, their silhouettes small and sharp in the bright sun, and they looked like a Huck Finn fantasy or characters in a classic New Zealand childhood. They *were* characters in a classic New Zealand childhood. They'd been outside all day and had caught four yellow-eyed mullet. Deborah gave them Freddo chocolate bars. Put the wrappers in your pockets when you're finished, she said, and not on the front lawn. Callum said, Yes, Mum.

Snapper in summer, whitebait August to November; Ken King left to put out his flounder net. I'm 78 tomorrow, his mother Pamela said. He's going to take me out for dinner.

They lived in a house on the corner of the main street. Ken had just moved back to Collingwood after teaching English in Japan. Ken and his Japanese wife will have one end of the house and I'll make do with this end, Pamela said. Her end was crowded with porcelain figurines. Ken calls it my build-up, she said. There was a wonderful painting of a deer in front of a waterfall. Mother bought it off a door-to-door salesman, she said.

Her mother had come to New Zealand from England as a war bride. It was her second marriage. Her father had survived Dunkirk but been killed in a hit-and-run during a blackout. It happened at Christmas, Pamela said, the 21st of December. She'd hung up her stocking but got nothing that Christmas. She was seven.

Pamela's husband Doug managed the dolomite quarry on Mount Burnett. He had been fire chief during the Great Fire of Collingwood – the fourth Great Fire of Collingwood, after the infernos of 1859, 1904 and 1930 almost razed the town to the ground. In 1967 infernos took out two shops, the pub and the movie theatre, which was playing Elvis Presley's *Flaming Star*. The siren went off at one in the morning. Pamela said, Doug turned to me and said, 'Get the kids out of the house.'

Oh the noise of it, she said, the roar of it. The wind was up, and it was that cold it felt like it was blowing in off the snow.

Her house backed on to the river. A winch in the backyard was used to haul in logs during floods. Dave Humphries had explained the law of Collingwood earlier in the day when he said, The rule here is when logs come in on the flood you rope 'em in, and there's your firewood for winter. Pamela said Doug liked only good wood. If a big rata came down he'd be highly delighted.

Collingwood's good, she said, but you get people who come here and say, 'I love Collingwood' and the first thing they do is try and change it.

There was an American who wanted to change the name of the town to Aorere. Well, she said, he didn't last five minutes. There were two museums next to each other on the main street: Collingwood Museum and Aorere Centre. Neither talked to the other or shared exhibits.

Sunday, and no one was there, nowhere on the main street, with its two museums, its pub, dairy, library, post shop, memorial hall, and café, which was for sale, asking price $155,000. Was it possible the ancient, drooling apocalyptee Howard Clamping had got it right? After the devastation of the 1967 fire, Bill Wizgell said, Collingwood is Collingwood. It will live again. But the end looked well on nigh in the deserted town on a weekend in May.

The noticeboard advised that Kent Strange had won the Collingwood playcentre raffle. Would he ever collect? Outside the playcentre, paintings were pegged on a line to dry. The school pool was empty. Collingwood looked like it did on the postcard. It was easy to find the exact spot where the photo had been taken, on the hill beneath the church. The gravel path was paved over but the cabbage tree was still there, the tide was still out – miles out, leaving a yellow, melancholic terrain. It looked vulnerable, a soft touch. But the town had recently seen off shambolic Australian mining company Greywolf, which withdrew its applications for oil exploration in Golden Bay and coal prospecting near Collingwood. Visions of some kind of economic boom collapsed, and so did fears of ecological butchery.

The spoonbills had come down from the pine tree. The day before, Department of Conservation rangers Ian Cox and Dave Homes had been out in their chopper at Farewell Spit, dealing to wilding pines – the name given to rogue stands of pinus radiata. They used the basal spraying technique. It was dangerous, intense work, pointing a hand-held wand of poison towards a tree trunk while the helicopter hovered. A dose of Grazon herbicide and oil was sprayed on to the trunk. It rolls down, Dave said, and the bark sucks it in. Ian said, It's taken to every point of the plant, and so the plant grows itself to death.

For sale: soy milk, rice milk, almond milk, hemp milk; a moveable chook run with chooks, $200; a house bus, 33 foot long, $6,000 ('Motor good. No brakes'); services, web design, holistic pulsings ('experience the magic of colour via Aura-soma'). But who was around to experience the magic?

Phyllis Goodall, 58, sat on the front porch of her rented home on Collingwood Quay and looked at the river. She was a seamstress but at the moment was on an invalid's benefit. I sit out here quite a lot, she said. Dave Humphries, two doors down, had built a good business in Nelson, recovering and selling parts from wrecked four-wheel-drives and Japanese utes. A few days before, a young boy had crashed into the bridge and gone over the side in a $2,000 Hilux. Dave said, I got a crane to pick it up and went home with it. He strips the wrecks for the gearbox, wheels, tyres and window regulators. I deal with people all week long, he said, and it drains the life out of you.

The life was drained out of Collingwood all that lovely quiet Sunday. Whitebaiting season was over. Someone had once counted 200 baiters from the mouth of the river up to the bridge. Out at Cape Farewell, black kelp twitched and trembled on top of boulders. The kelp was actually seals. Cape Farewell was the beginning of another end: it was named by Cook to mark the last sight of New Zealand before the *Endeavour* sailed back to England with news of a fertile, stunted land. In 1774 a version of Cook's map of New Zealand was produced in France. Cape Farewell was written as Adieu.

Hi! said a kid's voice. Two of Callum's mates rode past on their bicycles. The boys looked to be about six years old. One was Huck Finn and the other Tom Sawyer, probably. Were they going home? Nah, said Huck, we're gonna buy some lollies and take them back to our friends. They rode their bikes in wide happy circles on the main street of Collingwood, that golden New Zealand town built on a narrow peninsula of sand and river gravel, perfect.

# 19 WAINUIOMATA
## LOST CITY OF FITZROY

arry Martin, the former mayor of Wainuiomata, in fact the only mayor of Wainuiomata – that smoky glowing wonderland cut off from the rest of New Zealand as though it were an island – spoke of a peculiar thing. He was sitting with two other veterans of public service in a café opposite a fruit shop and a Dollar Discount Store. A sign in the Dollar Discount Store advised customers: WE DO WINZ QUOTES. 'Tomatoes are going through the roof,' said Paul Crowther, owner of Mammas Fruit & Veg, 'and apples and bananas are going out the door.'

It was a dismal winter day. Wellington Harbour looked as hard as concrete. The sky was dark. The hills were dark. The temperature fell below zero before nightfall. Wainuiomata, the most obscure suburb in Wellington's hinterland, shivered in the shade of the hills surrounding it on three sides. Every chimney smoked. Smokers queued in the Discount Tobacco store. One man queued behind himself: he had tattooed a face on the back of his shaved head.

The tobacco shop was inside the mall. The mall also had a sushi bar, Hedz for Hair, The Warehouse, McDonald's, two supermarkets, Coin Save, an optometrist, an eyebrow-shaper, a chemist, a bakery, PostShop, 4 Elements Urban Clothing, and Crackers Coffee Lounge. 'It's… it's a lot quieter than we expected,' said operations manager Dave Tomkins.

He worked in a small office opposite the public toilets and had been in the job four months. He was from England, a Liverpool fan; he talked buoyantly about the signings made by manager Kenny Dalglish, about the bags of goals Andy Carroll and Luis Suarez would score at Anfield. He came back down to earth as he said the mall had three vacant stores, which added up to 600 square metres unoccupied. But it wasn't the few vacant stores that gave the mall its loneliness. It was the fact it seemed to hardly ever have any people in it. You could have turned it into a skating rink or a firing range. Dave said, 'The way I see it, a mall should be vibrant and full of life.' He had some ways to go. 'Well,' he conceded, 'the challenges it poses are very exciting.'

College students had painted a mural at the entrance to the mall. Their art posed a challenge: they had painted the Grim Reaper standing next to urban gangsta dudes wearing hoodies and wraparound glasses. Abandon jewellery, all ye who enter. The artists were from Wainuiomata High School, which made headlines that winter when it was revealed that students held boxing matches in the school toilets, lit fires in basins, and there wasn't any soap. 'It's really unhygienic. ... They're in such a state,' said Year 13 pupil Hayden Yeats, tutting and disgusted. 'I go home if I need to go to the toilet.' Others didn't have that option: one kid defecated inside a rubbish bin rather than use the toilet.

The rest of New Zealand hears only unpleasant things about Wainuiomata. Example: the 2011 kidnapping and torture of a guy who was walking along the street one night. Two other guys drove past. Believing the man was responsible for a house burglary, they got out of their car and drove him to a house, where he was beaten up and locked in a room overnight. In the morning they drove him to another house, where he was tied to a chair and set upon with razor blades, screwdrivers, darts, a whip and a blowtorch.

Most famous example: in 2009 a Palmerston North motel owner banned the whole town. He said people from Wainuiomata were pigs. The ban came after allegedly vile behaviour from two sports teams who had stayed as guests. The motelier said he'd not visited Wainuiomata personally but had heard about it. His quote to the newspapers: 'I believe it's somewhere close to where God would put an enema.'

Trevor Mallard said the motelier was talking out of his arse. The local member of parliament was sharing a table at the café with Harry Martin and city councillor Ken Laban. The three public officials spoke of Wainuiomata as a vibrant community. Harry, a retired bookbinder, had a walking stick. Trevor, who had come off his bicycle at speed, had a pair of crutches. Ken had a moustache: he was a former cop. He was from Samoa. Harry had spent time in South Africa. Trevor lived on Planet Labour. The greying Samoan, the crippled MP and the little old one-time mayor had all long ago set down roots in Wainuiomata. Trevor and Ken grew up in the suburb, population about 16,000, which was 65,000 less than first expected when the place was settled in the 1950s and '60s.

Harry arrived in 1953. He talked about the old days. 'A peculiar thing happened,' he said. 'New Zealand decided to build two new cities. Holyoake's government. One city was to be built somewhere in the South Island and one here. Right here in Wainuiomata! It was going to be built in Moores Valley – there's a lot of land out there, acres and acres of flat land – and it was going to be called Fitzroy. I saw the plans. Hospitals, movie theatres, the whole works! I thought it was fantastic. But it never happened. It arrived out of the blue, and it died very suddenly…'

O lost city of Fitzroy – named no doubt after Captain Robert Fitzroy, New Zealand's second governor, who took charge of the new colony in 1843. Christian and liberal, he had the best of intentions but arrived in the worst of times. He had few troops to combat the rampaging Te Rauparaha or that dedicated axeman Hone Heke; more damagingly, he dared to slow the progress of laissez-faire European settlement. He was burned in effigy, mocked in bad verse, and finally sacked. The humiliation pinched the tender nerves of this gloomy depressive. He put himself out of his misery in the bathroom of his home in Crystal Palace, London, locking the door and cutting his throat while the maid prepared breakfast.

His legacy in New Zealand is here and there – Fitzroy Beach in New Plymouth, Governor Fitzroy Place in downtown Auckland, Fitzroy Bay in Wellington – but not in Wainuiomata, the city that never was, with its hospital and movie theatres and the whole works. There still are acres of vacant land in Moores Valley. From a ridge, you look over mud and fern and gorse, unpretty and good for nothing; on a cold dismal day a horse stood stock-still with a long face, and New Zealand birdlife showed itself in the raucous presence of Australian spur-winged plovers.

O folly of naming a city after a suicide. Even as a minor subplot, though, the strange episode conformed to the apparent wider theme of Wainuiomata: promise unfulfilled.

A visit to Harry Martin's house revealed a sad souvenir. He kept it in his study among other bits and pieces – an African face mask, a carving of a giraffe. The desk nameplate, about the size of a blackboard duster, read HIS WORSHIP THE MAYOR HJ MARTIN. It was only in use for a year, when Harry was the first and only mayor in Wainuiomata's history.

Harry unearthed a November 9, 1988 copy of a defunct weekly newspaper, *The Wainuiomata Advertiser*. The front page headline said WAINUIOMATA STANDS ALONE. After more than twenty years of agitating for independence from Lower Hutt, Wainuiomata had finally been granted status as a borough. The newspaper reported on a public meeting where the matter had been put to the vote. One person had voted against independence and said, 'With the attitude that is shown here tonight I will be moving away as soon as possible.' Everyone applauded. For sale in the classifieds: a piano, a wringer washing machine and a Remington rifle.

Harry unearthed a fat ring binder stuffed with green pages, the minutes of the Wainuiomata County Town Committee from 1968. It was evidence of how long Wainuioimata had fought the war for independence. Harry was quoted as saying, 'The future of Wainuiomata is going to be decided by the people of Wainuioimata.' And he'd scribbled an angry note: 'It seems incredible but the chairman stated under questioning that he agreed Wainuiomata must become a borough at some time in the future – but he would not allow this to appear in the minutes, and continues to publicly argue against Wainuiomata's claim to independence!'

Many of the green pages contained records of earnest discussions about hydatids and ragwort. The committee met at eight p.m. on Mondays. All those Monday evenings, the cold winter nights, the lovely summer twilight – and there sat the selfless servants, with Harry continually burning for the freedom of Wainuiomata. He said, 'It was the priority: we needed to take control of our own destiny. Wainuiomata grew very, very quickly. We couldn't develop the land fast enough. The population grew by a thousand, two thousand a year for many years. We actually projected a population of 81,000 by the year 2000. We were well on the way to bigger things.'

The boom years rolled on. The bust years got in on the act. Calls and petitions for independence continued to be ignored. Harry unearthed a December 20, 1982 copy of another defunct Wainuiomata newspaper, *The Weekly Courier*. Harry, then chairman of the district community council, had penned a rather lachrymose Xmas message. 'It is with some dismay that I write … It was your council's expectation that … we would by now have been a borough, or perhaps a city.'

Almost as an aside, he also wrote, 'The past has produced many strains on the lifestyle and aspirations of our residents, many more are now jobless and it is with much uneasiness that many people face 1983.' Advertisements for Farmers in Wainuiomata Mall featured cool Xmas presents such as CHiPs pedal cars for $51.50 ('blowmoulded plastic with sure-grip wheels'), and a Sanyo transistor radio with watchstrap ($17.95, or $1.80 deposit and 37 cents weekly layby).

Major industries closed down. Population growth stalled. When independence finally arrived in 1988 was it too late to do any good? 'Wainuiomata would have grown,' argued Harry. 'We'd have looked after our interests.' The following year the government intervened and forced Wainuiomata into an amalgamation with Lower Hutt. The dream ended as quickly as it began. 'Amalgamation killed Wainuiomata,' Harry said. 'It was the worst thing that ever happened. Lower Hutt wanted to be the boss. That was when it crashed completely. We lost it all. It stopped development stone dead.'

O lost city of Wainuiomata.

But there was another deeper, more enduring theme in Wainuiomata. It was there right at its very beginning, there all through the boom years, and there now, in the rising of the sun, in the whisper of the trees, in the thunder of the sea. 'Love is in the air,' sang some Romeo on the speakers playing endless love songs in the mall. He was right. Love surrounded Wainuiomata on all sides; the town was like a precious stone held in the palm of the low-lying land.

It was a strange sensation to stand at the top of the summit of Wainuiomata Hill and look across to Wellington, the harbour, the Hutt Valley, and then back to the town. Wellington looked massive, important, sophisticated. Wainuiomata looked modest, flat on its back, not up to a hell of a lot. The story goes that when the town was growing in the 1950s and '60s, homeowners could choose from only five floor plans. It seems likely they had a choice of even fewer pots of paint. Many of the houses look like each other – squat weatherboard, painted magnolia cream, and all in the same state of decay. Houses that get built together fall apart together. It can present as a depressing sight. A more direct way of putting it is that Wainuiomata can perhaps, in haste and bad light, be mistaken for a dump.

A dump built on a swamp. It was known as the Lowry Bay swamp when European settlers first made the journey up and over the hill on foot tracks, having to carry all their goods and possessions on their backs. The first person to cross on horseback was Captain John Mowlem. He was 25 years old, and master of the *Electra*, a vessel that brought to Wellington large numbers of passengers – including Agnes Sinclair. The story goes that he fell in love at first sight. He made inquiries. He found she had gone to settle in Wainuiomata. He viewed the Wainuiomata hill without wild surmise, bridled his horse, and duly rode in on it. John and Agnes had five sons and four daughters.

'Tonight I celebrate my love for you,' sang some Romeo on the speakers playing endless love songs in the mall, 'and the midnight sun is gonna come shining through.' At dawn, the surrounding hills were white with mist, big gorgeous shrouds of it rising and smoking from the deep green hills. At dusk, the lights on Wainuiomata Hill looked like fires, their gold flames trembling in the rain. The rest of New Zealand was somewhere over the hill. Wainuiomata was another Collingwood, defined by its hill, even though it took only three minutes to drive from the bottom to the top, or less in the whizzing red rocket driven by Trevor Mallard. A few hours after he shared a café table with Harry Martin and Ken Laban, he could be seen testing the hill road's skid-resistant bauxite and the sure-grip wheels of his Labour Party car as he flared through traffic.

Wainuiomata is the largest New Zealand community dependent on a single road for access. Trevor said, 'I really think it benefits from a perceived isolation. The barrier of the hill has built a community.' There were once plans to open a hilltop restaurant – only one tender was received and nothing came of it – but the biggest red herring in Wainuiomata's history is its tunnel. There was a serious effort to drill a tunnel through the hill in 1932. It was ambitious, and doomed: work closed down two years later, during the worst of the Depression. The entrance on the Wainui side has been concreted over; its exit on the fabled other side is probably covered in gorse. It lies up Tunnel Grove, a dead-end street in Gracefield, an industrial subdivision devoted to hard labour: the local massage parlour is called The Quarry Inn.

The world on one side, Wainuiomata on the other, inviolate, unto it-self, not a dump. Working-class, definitely. 'Hard working-class,' corrected Paul Crowther at the fruit shop. Terangi McGregor, 32, volunteered at Wainuiomata Community Centre and looked for work as a data processor. 'Wainuiomata's main employer,' he said, 'would have to be Work and Income.' The WINZ offices were packed that Friday afternoon. No one talked. A fat barefoot woman wearing green trackies with the legend BOSTON 34 sat with a pair of ug boots in her lap. A few jobs were advertised on the noticeboard. 'Yard worker to empty rubbish and clean drains.' There were more specialist positions. 'Picker and packer to work for a local beauty care products company. Ideal applicant will be fluent in Mandarin.'

Ken Laban said, 'There is more affluence here than people give us credit for.' Trevor Mallard said, 'There are more freehold houses here than anywhere in New Zealand.' Corey Hemingway said, 'I own my own home.' He was 21, bruised, and had Popeye arms. He was heading into McDonald's in the mall on Sunday afternoon for breakfast; he'd partied 'til six a.m. 'A few beers and good sounds.' What sounds? 'I idolise Vinnie Paul from Pantera.' Up all night with a metal drummer banging in his head; that was after he took a few blows to the head in a wrestling match. 'I'm a professional wrestler.' That was by night. By day he worked at ACC as a debt account manager. Good job, his own home, wrestling and metal, among a gang of two mates and three girls about to grease their blood at McDonald's – he was a picture of happiness. He said, 'Wainuiomata is the best place on Earth.'

In the old days no one was old. 'Everyone was young,' said Harry Martin, talking of Wainuiomata's halcyon time in the '50s and '60s. 'There were no old people here at all.' A town made up almost exclusively of newlyweds, Wainuiomata was a kind of couples' resort, Club Med without the Med, or a Club. Romantic love thrived in the brand new houses painted magnolia cream, gleaming in the sun that shone upon the town and made it glow. 'They say in heaven love comes first,' sang some Romeo on the speakers playing endless love songs in the Wainuiomata Mall. 'Oooh we'll make heaven a place on Earth.'

Heaven, set beneath the bright green ring of gorsey hills. Heaven, with Black Creek running through it. Heaven on Honey Street, Hair Street, Best Street. In the old days, the streets rang with children's laughter. 'There were 37 kids in ten houses on my street when I grew up,' Trevor Mallard said. 'When we closed the schools, there were only seven.' But the streets still rang with children's laughter. Dreadlocked Māori Rastaman Awatere, at 28, was a father of five: Tahlia, Jahkaya, Zahria, Zion and Jamaica.

He was around the corner from the mall on Queen Street, drinking a milkshake from Ziggy's Dairy. He was a man on the move. 'Got to go and dig a hāngī for a mate's fiftieth.' He'd also contribute a pig. He loved hunting, was always up in the hills with his crossbow. 'Pigs. Deer. The normal. It's all food to me. I've got a big family.' His wife Treena had another one on the way.

'If I have children,' Jason Burt said, 'they'll be brought up in Wainuiomata.' He was a 22-year-old butcher's apprentice at New World. 'My mum, brother and partner all work at New World.' He said, 'I'll always love this place. I love the hills, mate. It's the best thing about Wainuiomata. Nothing like it. They're so green! I went down south once, Blenheim and that. The hills were brown, mate. Nah, Wainuiomata's the place.'

Allison King, 43, worked two days a week in the mall's other supermarket, Countdown. 'Fourteen dollars fourteen an hour. Plus I'm on the DPB.' She was with her older sister Patsy. 'There're a lot of solo mums in Wainuiomata,' she said. 'We both are.'

Patsy worked part-time for Armourguard. 'I do the ATM machines. I'm destined to work with money and never have it.' They were big women, and laughed and joked. They had come to the mall to buy Export Dry and to get their eyebrows done by 'a lady at the back of the dairy'.

Allison lived with Patsy and their brother and mum. 'We pool our resources so we have a better life.' Patsy said, 'I always say a whānau house isn't a whānau house if it doesn't have whānau in it.' They loved Wainuiomata, had never wanted to leave. 'We know all the people,' Patsy said. 'We lead quite a sheltered life.'

Sheltered from the outside world, sheltered by the hills on three sides – at the entrance to Wainuiomata a sign reads COAST ROAD 22KM. The road shoots through the valley, past swamp and big useless clumps of cabbage trees, past sheep resting on the muddy banks of the thin Wainuiomata River. It turns off one way to the cool shaded beauty of Rimutaka National Park, with its forest canopy and its swimming holes, and ends at Turakirae Head.

Down on the beach the silvery sea collapsed in loud crashes, waves churning up the shingle shore. A seal colony carried on snizzing on rocks at the water's edge. The tide turned back out to sea; the noise it made running through the shingle sounded like the cracking of bones.

Bush and sea, and back in Wainuiomata Mall kids operated the Kiwicrane fun machine, rotating the metal arm in search of Twix chocolate bars. Children's entertainment also included a carousel of jackasses with terrifying faces, and a coin-operated police car with sure-grip wheels. 'When will our hearts be together?' sang some Romeo on the speakers playing endless love songs.

'Country music's the most popular music here, because it's a country town,' said Kevin Shaw, manager of Wainuiomata's amazing second-hand record store Wonderland. His stock contained 10,000 LPs. 'The tried and true are always going to sell,' he said, 'Kenny Rogers, John Denver.' Treasures included the complete works of Ted Nugent, and a rare copy of *The Avengers Live at Ali Baba's* in Wellington on November 19, 1968. Kevin said, 'I was there!' A tired man walked in with his frisky skipping daughter and asked, 'Do you have any Bryan Ferry on vinyl?' Kevin tested the man's selection on the shop record player. 'Slave to love,' sang the Romeo.

'Reggae and hip hop are really strong in Wainuiomata,' said Jason Fox, 30 and funky, the manager of 4 Elements Urban Clothing. He was playing them in his shop. That night he was going to see eight-piece reggae band 1814.

'It's a sell-out. That's the thing about Wainuiomata – bands know to come here because we're the only small town that consistently sells out.' Veteran R & B act Ardijah sold out; seven-piece reggae band House of Shem sold out.

Jason said he'd never leave Wainuiomata. He said he knew it was regarded as a hole 'but there's way poorer suburbs. It's just that there's always been a stigma about Wainuiomata 'cos, you know, it's separated by the hill. It sets us aside. It's kind of Wainuiomata versus the world, you know? It's always been like that.'

The republic of Wainuiomata. Town, suburb, whatever, it was a bright jewel, glowing like the emerald hills that surrounded it, a place of happiness and music. Reggae, endless love songs, country, Pantera – music swirled all around Wainuiomata, over the rooftops, in the whisper of the trees.

# 20 MAROMAKU VALLEY
## THE BALLAD OF STAN

I t looked as though long years had passed since anyone had set foot
in the abandoned shack on the side of a dusty unsealed road that
curled through a valley in the Far North. It was a little house on a
prairie, a worker's cottage in a state of picturesque disrepair, peeling and
fading, with sparrows rustling leaves in the gutters. There were three
orange kitchen chairs on the front porch. One had fallen on its side. It
felt within reason to fancy that the other two chairs invited passers-by
to stop and sit a while. I stopped and sat a while. It was early afternoon
on a Friday in spring.

The front door was nailed shut. The two front windows were dirty
but unsmashed. Inside there was a glass kerosene lamp on top of a coal
range, and the frame of a single bed in a front room on the right. Beside
the bed were two empty tuna cans, a rusted Jensen clock radio, and an
instruction manual for an electric blanket. The bed suggested a child
but the shack lacked tenderness. A woman's touch clings to a house and
so does the presence of children. No matter how long the cottage had
been abandoned, a trace or a sense would have remained of a family, but
nothing hovered above the hard bare floorboards.

A woman appeared: she had walked up the road from her nearby
house. She was dark-haired and her accent was a mystery. It gave a lovely
unfamiliar music to her voice. Her name was Jacqui Kehoe and she was

forty-eight. She said, 'I'm Chilean. I've lived here 28 years. I call myself a Chiwi.'

A stiff spring wind raked the grass. Jacqui hugged herself in her zip-up jacket. She wore a pair of dark glasses that covered her face and she didn't take them off. We stood and looked at the empty cottage. She said, 'There was a lonely old fella who lived here.' These were the first words I heard spoken about the ghost of Maromaku Valley.

'We would visit him and make sure he was all right,' Jacqui continued. 'I always feared I'd come over and find him lying on the floor, dead. And then someone did find him lying on the floor, dead.'

She couldn't remember his name. 'He had no family but a lady came to visit him. Not in that way. She was the only person he had who was anywhere close to being family.'

When had he died? Jacqui couldn't remember exactly; maybe last year, or early this year. But the cottage looked as though it had been empty for longer than a few months. There were cobwebs nearly as thick as ropes. She said it had looked even worse when the man lived there. 'The house was so filthy. A complete mess. It was full of empty cans of salmon and tuna, which he fed to feral cats. And he smelled. I don't think he ever had a bath. But he was a nice old fella. It was very sad when he died. He was lying down as though he'd tripped and fallen and hit his head. When I think of him lying on the floor, dead...'

She shivered. I turned away from the dead man's cottage, and changed the subject by asking about a house to the east, a striking example of modernist architecture. The entire front of it was glass. Jacqui said, 'Have you heard of Sid Going?' 'Yes,' I said, surprised to be asked about a legendary All Black half-back by a Chiwi on a country road. 'It's his daughter's house. And that one's his son's house.'

I thought back to photos of Going, a small, mobile, audacious player, and then remembered he was a Mormon. Jacqui said, 'That house over there – Mormon. That one – Mormon. That one – Mormon.' She continued pointing, moving her finger in an arc across Maromaku Valley. 'Mormon. Mormon. Mormon. Mormon.'

She had identified every house we could see except her own, so I pointed to it and said, 'What about that house?' She said, 'Mormon.' She was born a Catholic. 'But they have missionaries, you see, and they teach you about the church. They taught our whole family.'

Her parents had moved from Chile to Melbourne when she was a little girl. They were obviously considered ripe for an English-speaking God. 'The Jehovah's Witnesses came to our house first. They were nice people but I didn't feel anything with them.

'Then the missionaries came. They knocked on our door on a Saturday. My brothers and sisters and I, we were really angry. We wanted to go to the beach. It was just after lunch when they came. Three hours later they were still talking. We were spewing. Then, when they were leaving, they said, "We'll come back next week." We said, "Oh, great. Another wasted Saturday!" It was summertime and I was fifteen, sixteen.

'But when they came back the next week, there was a moment. There were things that touched deep.' Her hand went to her dark glasses and she trembled. A spring afternoon in the Far North, and a Chiwi Mormon in tears at the memory of a crucial moment in her life, now standing outside an abandoned house where a nameless man had maybe last year or this year tripped, hit his head, and lain on the floor, dead.

She brightened, and continued her story. Her entire family converted. She met John Kehoe of Maromaku Valley. 'He was over there on his mission.' He married her, brought her home to his dairy farm. 'It's been hard the past couple of years,' she said. 'There was so much rain last winter that the paddocks got all pugged up. Then we had a drought. But we survived it.'

I was thinking how much I liked the faraway Chilean music of her voice when she had said that flat New Zealand sentence, 'The paddocks got all pugged up.' And then she said, 'His name – it was Stan. He died in February.'

Three years of appearing at homes as strange as Lance Roberts' converted slaughterhouse loft in Hicks Bay, Jim Dennan's dusty whare in

Whakarewarewa, the igloo at Scott Base, the fales of Apia, Graeme Ingils' wretched hovel in Winton, and it had come to this, nosing around outside a dead man's abandoned shack in a valley of Mormons and kingfishers.

I drew a pencil sketch of the two feijoa trees on the property. Both trees were hunched over; their branches nearly touching the ground. I made an inventory of the cans of cat food rusting beneath the tree. Once again, as ever, I was trying to fix the scene in my memory.

Dusk falling above the desert in Waiōuru, bright sunlight on the dazzling white shell bank at Miranda. Overheard at a party in Tangi-moana: 'Remember Uncle Vic? He fell into a sawmill.' Fred Nyberg, the cheerful hermit of Notown, among the Māori hens and the black beech: 'I've had two daughters and two grandsons die. Sad. That's the way life is, isn't it?'

On a Friday at 10.30 a.m. in Morrinsville, three little girls in pyjamas and slippers walked into the Pioneer Bakery; on a Saturday morning in Cromwell, near St Bathans, nine migrant fruit pickers from Vanuatu waited for the Salvation Army op shop to open – when it did they bought sheets, pillowcases, shirts, socks, and a weed eater to send home.

Three years of itemising civilisation in the last settled country on Earth, wandering from one republic to the next. So many of the towns drew into themselves, asserted a kind of independence. It was there on the peninsula of Collingwood, a long way over Tākaka Hill; it was there in the swamp of Wainuiomata, minutes over the hill from Seaview. Distance was the point of each town's existence. In the spaces in between, in the regional qualities of silence, something was missing. Even in the age of infill housing and noise control officers, much of New Zealand seemed to be on close terms with abstraction. Was this where country music stepped in and gave it shape?

The novelist David Foster Wallace once shared an epiphany about country music: 'What if you imagined that this absent lover they're singing to is just a metaphor? And what they're really singing is to themselves, or to God? "Since you left I'm so empty, my life has no meaning." That … they're incredibly existential songs. All the pathos and heart that comes out of them is they're singing about something much more elemental being missing, and their being incomplete without it.'

New Zealand, the lonely country, gothic and troubled, but that wasn't the half of it. Much more than half of it was cheerful and inventive, waiting for the tide, filling its face with fresh food, knocking about on the porch with a beer and a burnt sausage. Tremendous friendliness shimmered in the air. Great fun was to be had in the pub in Waiōuru on Friday night, in the pub in Greymouth on Saturday night, in the pub in Mosgiel on Sunday afternoon. There was even fun to be had without alcohol. Every town was welcoming, hospitable.

Three years of reading the local paper in the tearooms and the Subways. The headlines were enough: you could read them for directions. They mapped things out. FARMER CRUSHED BY COW. PITBULL STRANGLED IN DOMESTIC ROW. ACCUSED DRUNK IN DOCK. DESERT ROAD CLOSED. TRAMPER LOST. APPLICANTS QUEUE FOR 20 JOBS AT NEW KFC. MĀORI LEADER WANTS TO TAKE TROUT 'AS A RIGHT'. WOMAN TASERED IN MOSGIEL. Three years of writing my own hieroglyphics in the Warwick 3B1 notebooks I took from town to town.

There had been the pleasure and privilege of entering the lives of strangers. I was constantly reminded of the ringing endorsement that the historian Michael King gave New Zealanders in his famous closing passage of *The Penguin History of New Zealand*. It was one of the last things he ever wrote. King, lively, eminently sane, died in a freak road accident only a few months after the book was published in 2003. It was an instant best-seller.

It has a happy ending. 'Most New Zealanders, whatever their cultural backgrounds,' King wrote, 'are good-hearted, practical, commonsensical and tolerant. … They are as sound a basis as any for optimism about the country's future.'

So long as New Zealand actually had New Zealanders in it, but about a thousand were jumping across the Tasman every week. The great migration to Australia sometimes made it feel you belonged to a minority – the people left behind, the last remaining Māori and Pākehā, hemmed in by tides of Pacific Islanders and Asians and refugees from Africa, the Middle East and Hollywood. Look, there's James Cameron! The director of *Titanic* and *Avatar* has New Zealand residency. He visits Mondays and Thursdays.

I never came across anyone remotely famous. The farmers and shearers, the carpenters and carpet-layers, the birders and alcoholics, the New Zealanders, went about their business in a land of Lotto and kapa haka, Harvey Norman and Dick Smith, Sky Sports and the widening gap between rich and poor.

Three years of motels. There was an afternoon in the Gibson Court Motel in Rotorua when I did nothing more than watch motes of dust in the sunlight. Unable to sleep in the Sunset Motel in Greymouth, I got up at two a.m. and walked across the Cobden Bridge, my face as cold as the fast, black Grey River that rushed to the sea.

I wanted to see where other people lived, but every chapter is an unwritten record of loneliness. I was homesick for the house where I lived with my girlfriend and our daughter, who turned two, then three, then four years old. They came to the airport to pick me up after I got back from Antarctica. After those white days and white nights, seeing the two of them was like coming back to life in full colour.

My daughter laughed to hear the names of places I visited. Greymouth. Mosgiel.

'What was it like, dad?' she always asked.

I always told her, 'You'd love it.'

Maromaku Valley veers off the State Highway just past Towai Tavern. The road leads north, winding through farmland, forest, bush, scrub and wetland, and 30 or 40 minutes later joins the highway again at the hard-case, hard-done-by town of Moerewa. It just about passes as a scenic detour. It's dense and damp. There are rushes and flax and manuka, and heavily bearded cabbage trees. Azolla rubra, New Zealand's native floating fern, covers swamps in blankets of scarlet. The water attracts a tremendous population of kingfishers, which you would expect, although I also made seventeen sightings of that bright Australian parrot, the eastern rosella.

But its strangest feature is the Maromaku Church of Jesus Christ of Latter-day Saints. It may be the loveliest, most bucolic setting for a Mormon temple anywhere in the world. White and gleaming on an immaculate lawn and beside four magnificent California palm trees, the building presented itself as a tribute to the two great forces in the valley: God and the Goings. Percy Going built the first Mormon chapel in Maromaku. His son Cyril had six children with his first wife, but she got breast cancer. A young Māori woman, Mary, nursed her. After his wife died, Cyril married Mary and had another six children, including Sid. Mary is now 103. She doesn't need glasses to read.

The condensed family history lesson was courtesy of Karen Horsford. Karen and her friend Pauline Pokoina were at the church on Friday afternoon, making props for a music festival that night at the 'stake' – Mormon vernacular for church – in nearby Kaikohe.

'Most of us are related to each other in the valley,' Pauline said. 'Karen's husband is my second cousin. Did you say you met Jacqui? I'm her husband John's sister.'

'Then you have situations where two Tucker boys married two Going sisters, and two Rouse brothers married two other Going girls,' Karen said. 'A lot of that goes on. I suppose it's because you always go everywhere with your brothers and sisters when you're young.'

They talked about their own families. 'My sweetheart is the stake president,' Karen said about her husband. 'His name's Maxwell but everyone calls him Butch.'

Pauline and her family moved back to Maromaku from Auckland three years ago. 'My eldest son Quincy, who's eighteen, was seeing a girl in Auckland whom I wasn't too happy about. When my brother asked if we'd like to come and work on the farm, I snapped at it. But actually she would've been a better influence than the girlfriend he's got here. That's the irony of it.'

She sighed. He'd left the church, she said. 'He's bucking the system. He says he believes in the church and one day he'll be back, but right now he's not comfortable with it.' She said, 'It's very disruptive.' Then she said, 'It hurts.'

I changed the subject. Yes, Pauline and Karen said, of course they were both related to the Going family. They merrily explained which cousin was whose sister who had an aunt who married which Going. They could account for everyone in the valley that way, but there was an odd man out: the ghost of Maromaku, who had lived by himself in the valley for about 25 years. 'His name was Stan Stuart,' Karen said, 'and he died in March.'

Pauline said, 'His cottage was – bizarre's a good word. He had piles of chocolate biscuit wrappers, margarine containers, Weet-Bix packets, ginger kisses wrappers, boxes of empty beer cans. He'd made tracks between the piles. It was very orderly rubbish. He'd cleared room on his one table for a stack of library receipts going back to the first book he'd ever taken out.'

'He went to the library in Kawakawa faithfully every Tuesday,' Karen said. 'His bed was to the right of the door,' Pauline said. 'It was more like a cot than a bed. He'd sit there to do his reading, because that room got the sun. He had a rough old mattress and army blankets.'

'He kept his lawnmower inside,' Karen said. 'It was the best, most modernest thing he owned.'

Underneath one of the two feijoa trees on either side of Stan's cottage there was an old Masport mower. 'It wasn't that one,' Karen said.

Both of the women were standing up. They had been on their knees, rolling up a backdrop painted with the moon and stars. They used bamboo poles that Pauline had cut down on her brother's farm. They were the only people in the church that afternoon. Sunday's congregation would probably number about ninety. An email from Sid Going was printed out and stapled to a noticeboard; with his wife Colleen he was performing missionary work in Sydney. Down the hallway, a door to an office was marked with the number 12 and the word BISHOP.

'Stan would go to the pub every night for his dinner,' said Pauline. 'He wasn't a hermit. Not really,' said Karen. 'He said, "I don't do the social thing." But he appreciated everything people did for him. We found a bag in his cottage after he died. We were looking for some form of ID. No one knew anything about him, where he was from, whether he had family somewhere. And we found a bag – you know, like a bowling bag that people keep bowling balls in – and that's where he kept his treasures. He had kept every Christmas card that people in the valley had given him. The whole lot. And there was a piece of paper with a lady's name and a telephone number. Beside it, he'd written the word SISTER.'

Moerewa, pop. 1500, almost entirely Māori, is a kind of usual suspect: it's constantly mentioned whenever the media wish to discuss poverty, unemployment, feral behaviour and 'Māori initiatives' in the Far North. But on that Friday afternoon in spring it had the carnival atmosphere that invigorates all small towns when school is over and done with for the week. Teenagers stood on the pavement and leaned against the Food Market scoffing iceblocks and gossiping. There was also a burger bar, a bakery, a butcher: 'PORK HEADS. MUTTONBIRDS.'

Moerewa's famous Tuna Café – tuna as in Māori for eel, famous as in many glowing reviews for its coffee and its kai – had closed down that day. The next-door hair salon was for sale.

A man parked his van to get a box of Lion Red at the Four Square. His trailer was full of kiwifruit, which he'd bought for $30. A kid with an eager face said, 'Can I've one please mister?' Another kid rode past on his bike and said, 'Did you see that bunny hop I done?'

I sat a while outside the bakery. I was happy. I liked Moerewa. But I wondered how long it had been since a tourist or any kind of visitor had lingered in plain view there. It wasn't that the place was dangerous. There are streets, neighbourhoods, whole towns, entire cities that radiate a distinctive New Zealand nastiness. Moerewa lacked that edge. But the town centre was only just hanging on. Moerewa was at the gateway to the Bay of Islands' pleasure resorts of Paihia and Russell, but it seemed unlikely that any of the German or American drivers of the passing fleets of campervans would ever stop on Main Street, look around, and buy a box of Lion Red or a pork head.

The campervans took their loot and their bladders five minutes away to Kawakawa, the town that has marketed itself as a urinal, thanks to colourful public toilets designed by Austrian fanatic Friedensreich Hundertwasser. I went to Kawakawa on another pilgrimage. I was on the trail of Stan Stuart.

I liked everything I'd heard about Stan. People we celebrate as larger than life are usually enormous bores, bereft of subtlety or grace; Stan was smaller than life, private and intricate, a loner surrounded by Mormons and biscuit wrappers, a reader.

At the library in Kawakawa, librarian Shakira Pia ('I think it's French') said, 'He came in every Friday. He liked cowboy books mostly. He was very brief. "Hello, Shakira," he'd say, and that was it. But he used to give me a gift every Christmas. A bottle of wine once. A box of chocolates last Christmas.

'He used to park around the back of the shops and he'd take forever to cross the street. I kept thinking he'd be knocked over. He was so creaky. The last time I saw him he was really struggling to walk. His face was all sweaty. I was worried for him. I rang the district nurse the next Friday when he didn't come in. I knew something must be wrong. Poor old Stan.'

The library was empty. Shakira was about to close it for the weekend. She was in a wistful mood. She was thinking back to the shy customer who came in every Friday to rustle up another cowboy book. 'He was a nice man,' she said. 'He was humble.'

Friday afternoon on the main street of Moerewa was happy with the freedom from school. Friday night at the low, roomy Klondike Tavern was happy with the freedom from work. There were maybe 60 or 70 drinkers, most in their twenties, the girls in ponytails and the guys in laceless slippers, laughing and playing pool and knocking back cans of bourbon and coke.

I spoke with Frankie Owen. 'You've heard of Rena Owen, the actress? She's my auntie.' Like the Goings, the Owens were one of the great local dynasties, and unlike the wholesome Goings in pretty much every other respect – drinking, all the rest of it – except that at 23 Frankie was just as much a solid citizen as any Mormon. In fact, he'd settled down with a Mormon when he was sixteen.

They were parents of two girls, newborn Paskelle and seven-year-old Sativa. I said, 'As in cannabis sativa?' 'Pretty much,' Frankie said.

He had left school and got a job at the Affco freezing works in Moerewa when Sativa was born. He'd held down the job, and lived with the girls' mother, Charis, in a rented house on Main Street. They were preparing to make an offer to the landlord. Frankie thought they could buy it for maybe $180,000.

I saw the Owens taking an afternoon stroll on Saturday. The young parents, the sleeping baby tucked up in a pram, Sativa racing ahead on a child's motorbike: it was a cameo of ordinary happiness and the New Zealand way of life. And it set the theme for everywhere I went that day. The theme was family.

Family, on the bare front porch of a house on the main street, where young mum Aroha Cooper had come outside to cuddle her baby son Paepae. They had recently moved from Porirua. She had come to visit her grandfather, who was sick, and then her partner found a job. She said, 'We don't know much people.' A paddock separated her house from the freezing works. 'It's good having cows next to you knowing you're gonna eat them one day.'

Family, on the crowded front porch of a house around the corner, where Ginger Harris, large and puffing and 75, peeled oranges with a knife. The fruit had fallen from the two trees in his garden. 'I'm bloody smothered with the things. I pick up three bucketfuls every day. The wind blows them all left, right and sideways. I cut 'em up, juice 'em and stick 'em in the fridge for the grandchildren.'

He'd lived in Moerewa for 46 years. 'Said I'd never live here. The freezing works bloody stank the whole town. Well, I got a job there and the money never stank. When I got my first pay cheque I'd never seen so much money in my life.'

He opened a dairy, drove a taxi. He also possessed the wit to set up a mobile hāngī food cart. A souvenir from that adventure was among the clutter on the porch: a massive stainless steel chamber. 'I'd cook 400 meals at a time in it, all done in heavy duty tinfoil, and the food would taste exactly like a hāngī.'

Family on horseback on Main Street, when brothers Gavin and Harley (Like the motorbike? 'Pretty much') Brown, saddled up with rifles, were heading south. 'We're going hunting,' Gavin said. Pig hunting? 'Nah, beef hunting,' Harley said. 'Wild cows up in the bush.'

Family at the Moerewa Tigers rugby league clubrooms in Simpson Park, where Harrison Williams and his wife Meri, both 71, sat sipping beer as Dave Bristoe took the microphone and announced the prize-giving after the day's round robin seniors' tournament between teams from Moerewa, the Far North, and the Ngāwhā Corrections Department.

'We're not doing player of the day or any of that Pākehā bullshit,' Bristoe said. Everyone who had played that day was given a ticket. The winning ticket would be taken out of a hat. First prize was a water blaster. 'We've also got prizes of $20 meatpacks from G & H Meats in Kawakawa,' Bristoe said.

He started raving. He'd had a skinful. 'There's some good shit in those packs. We're not gonna say, "Here's your prize, cunt, now fuck off." We're gonna say, "Good one, cunt." Yeah.'

Family, wholesomely, on the Maromaku Valley farm of Jared and Kaelin Going, and their daughter, Lijana, eighteen months. I visited Jared because he had been the landlord to the man without family: Stan Stuart, the tenant in a shack on Mormon land.

'He only ever paid the rent in cash,' Jared said. 'He was reliable as. I'd forget when it was due but he'd always show up, almost to the minute. We'd have a little chat and then he was off. You'd say, "What're you doing today, then, Stan?" He'd say, "I'm going home to read a book." And then he'd leave to do just that.'

Jared's father Sid Going had performed the funeral service. 'Stan was the first person to be buried at Towai Cemetery for 50 years. It was a real big funeral, would have been a hundred people, easy.' I imagined the bowed heads, a Bible passage read out loud by an All Black legend. I tried to imagine the meaning that people took from the outsider and misfit in Maromaku Valley. 'Everyone liked him,' Jared said, 'but no one knew him.'

But someone did know him: the woman whose name and number he had written down on a piece of paper next to the word SISTER. I asked Jared Going for her details. On Sunday morning, at a large lovely home in the suburb of Kensington Heights in Whāngārei, I called on Shona Nash.

Her husband Neville boiled the jug. Their children were visiting for the weekend – Matt, a fashion design student, and Rachel, who had been up most of the night with her restless baby. They moved around each other with the easy, casual affection of a typical New Zealand family; the ghost of Stan hovered at their side.

Shona brought out a folder. It was marked STAN'S AFFAIRS. It included his birth certificate (November 1, 1928), an ancient reference from an employer ('I have always found him to be an honest and obliging boy'), and a winning Lotto ticket from 2004, when Stan pocketed $5,885. 'Stan's girlie magazines,' winked Neville, when he showed me two 1974 copies of *Australasian Post*, kept in a box with encyclopaedias, and cowboy magazines that included a 1973 copy of *Old West*. 'No fiction,' boasted the cover.

Stan, propped up on top of his small bed with the bright light of the Far North falling through his bedroom window, happily reading true stories about prospecting in El Paso, a ghost town in the Ozark Mountains, running whiskey, lassoing a bear… What would he have made of the story about Russian exiles in British Columbia who formed a religious cult, lived on fresh or sun-dried fruits and vegetables, and staged acts of public nudity to protest the government's demand that their children attend school? The lonely reader, dreaming of sagebrush and six-guns, angry bears and naked Russians – and playing a minor role when violent New Zealand reality came to his door one night in November 2006.

Two young Dutch honeymooners had parked their campervan in a car park at Haruru Falls near Paihia when they were seized by two men armed with a shotgun. The couple were handcuffed and driven around Northland; $900 was taken from their ATM card; the woman was forced to swallow sedatives, and raped. 'Despicable in the extreme,' said the judge, sentencing the main offender to preventive detention.

The couple were dumped on the roadside by Towai Cemetery. From there, they called on the closest house: Stan's. 'The couple knocked on his door, but he slept through it,' Tony Wall wrote in *The Sunday Star-Times*, 'which is possibly just as well as he is not set up to cater for visitors.'

Tony had gone inside Stan's shack. I was still outside on the porch, peering through the windows, even as I visited Shona Nash at her nice house in Whāngārei. The girlie magazines, the winning Lotto ticket – the cardboard box contained the few remnants of his life. The rest belonged to Shona's memory.

When her parents lived in Ōamaru, they had taken Stan in as a boarder. He was eighteen. He got a job on the railways. This was before Shona was born; she was the youngest child in the family. When she was three, the family moved to Whananaki, a seaside town in Northland. The amazing thing – Shona couldn't explain it, it was just something that happened – was that Stan came too, and continued to live with the family. He took a job as a rural delivery mailman. His folder included a Kodak snapshot of a baby-blue mail van, dazzling in the sunlight of a Northland summer day. Shona grew up and moved to Whāngārei; Stan moved to nearby Maromaku Valley and worked at the freezing works until he retired. He never married.

'He was a very clever, very intelligent person,' Shona said. 'He could tell you anything about anything in the world. He was like an encyclopaedia. That's what he'd read, encyclopaedias, things like that, as well as his cowboy books.

'But he was so simple. No, not simple, simplistic. No fridge, no stove. I suppose he was eccentric. He was very shy. A little bit socially awkward. He was also the most trustworthy person, and so punctual! You could set your clock by him. He was so methodical. He would spend hours doing the dishes.

'He had this ritual when he came to town. He had a track he'd stick to – meal at McDonald's and then groceries at Countdown. You'd see him on the odd occasion but he wouldn't stop; he'd just say hi, and keep going. He had a path and that was it.

'He'd come here twice a year to get a haircut. It'd be down over his face. It really got away from him. He'd sit here, get his haircut, and then he'd be out of here like a scalded cat. It wasn't him being rude; he was never like that. But that was Stan for you. He wouldn't hang around. He was always in the background.

'He didn't leave much behind. He had only about two sets of clothes, and a suit in the wardrobe – I'm sure it was the suit he wore to our wedding 35 years ago. His possessions were in a suitcase that was at least 50 years old, and some in a box.'

Yes, she said, there were a few Christmas cards he'd kept in a leather zip-up bag. Shona found a card marked 'From Nolan and Darlene Going and the kids'. A child's hand had written, 'Hope you never change 'cos you are special.'

'When he died,' Shona said, 'Sid and Colleen – yes, the Goings – said, "We've organised the funeral." It was a real sign of respect. I was blown away by how many people came. To see such a humble person loved by so many people. The funeral was at six on a beautiful evening in March.' I imagined the golden light at the end of a summer's day in Northland. And then Shona said, 'Sid filled in the grave with a front-end loader.'

I'd visited the grave earlier that morning. A pair of eastern rosella parrots yelled in the trees. The stiff spring wind that blew all weekend continued to blunder its way around. This was the end of the Stan Stuart story but it was still only in outline; there was something else to it, something that really mattered.

Shona's husband remarked on Stan's visits to the house over the years. He said, 'He adored you.' Their son Matt remarked on the family snaps that Stan had kept in his suitcase. 'They were all of Mum. All of them, from when she was a kid to when she was an adult.'

Shona remarked, 'Stan looked after me when I was little.' Like a playmate? No, not really, she said. More like someone who made sure she was all right, who protected her.

Stan, the old man who read cowboy stories ('no fiction') in a single bed in a shack, who rode out one day from the South Island to live in a valley at the top of the North Island; Stan, who followed his heart when he followed Shona. He wrote his own story with that one word on a piece of paper: SISTER. The ghost of Maromaku Valley had left behind a love story.

# ACKNOWLEDGEMENTS

Many thanks to the benevolence and generosity of the CLNZ Writer's Award for making this book possible; to *North & South* editor Virginia Larson and former publisher Sally Duggan, who were the perfect employers; to Mary Varnham and Sarah Bennett at Awa Press, for their honesty and kindness, respectively; to Finlay Macdonald, for his intelligent advice and black humour; to Matt Vance at Antarctica New Zealand, for the passport to hell; to Southland Tourism, for the trip to beautiful Winton; to Martin Unwin, Caroline Harker and Beth McArthur, for permission to publish their stories from the Upper Clutha Arts Council Autumn Art School writing workshop in Wānaka; to Brian and Diane Miller, for the extract from *Macandrew Bay: A history of a community on the Otago Peninsula*; and to everyone who welcomed me into their homes and enriched my life during these travels, especially Lance Roberts (Hicks Bay), Heriata Porter, Nathan Rayner, and Jim Dennan (Ōhinemutu), Jean Smith (Te Aroha), Tanielu Pololua and Fesouaina Matalavea (Samoa), Ross Mitchell-Anyon (Wanganui), Des Thomas, Jeanette Thomas, and Bill Thomas (Mercer), Graeme Ingils (Winton), Ken Reeves (Mosgiel), Tracey Thomsen, Marcus Thomsen, and Kieran Grice (Tangimoana), Fred Nyberg (Notown), Harry Martin (Wainuiomata), and the ghost of Stan Stuart (Maromaku Valley). The deepest thanks are to Jane Ussher, who was there every step of the way, suffered for it, but never once wavered in her friendship.

## How to Watch a Bird
### Steve Braunias
978-0-9582629-6-5

'Braunias's wit and charm are put to work to explain in
easy non-scientific ways why looking at the commonest
birds can be such a pleasure'
*The Dominion Post*: Best Non-Fiction of 2007

Prize-winning journalist Steve Braunias is standing on the balcony
of an inner-city apartment on a sultry summer evening when a
black-backed gull flies so close he is instantaneously bowled over
with happiness. 'I thought: Birds, everywhere. I want to know more
about them.' This highly engaging book is the result – a personal
journey into an amazing world. It's also a New Zealand history, a
geographical wandering, and an affectionate look at the tribe of
people ensnared, captivated and entranced by birds.

'Braunias has touchingly brought love and bird-watching together in a book
that stalks sewage ponds and grey warblers with curiosity and affection,
and ends with contentment, bliss and a baby born. A lovely book'
*New Zealand Listener*: Best Books of 2007

'A small and perfectly formed jewel'
*The Sunday Star-Times*

'Awa Press plus Braunias plus birds makes for a tantalising
literary marriage'
*New Zealand Life & Leisure*

*Available from all good bookstores and online at*
**www.awapress.com**

*Smoking in Antarctica*
## Steve Braunias

978-1-877551-11-6

'This comedic book is the fourth by Kiwi writer and columnist
Steve Braunias – and it's without a doubt his best. …
Cheeky, engaging and downright funny'
*New Idea*

Whether gently but firmly lambasting airhead politicians,
unrepentant murderers, apostrophe vigilantes, literary poseurs, or
the purveyors of awful food, Steve Braunias shows his exceptional
mastery of the art of column writing. But this winner of over 20
writing awards is also a passionate New Zealander, who has become
famous for his tender evocations of the country's heart-tugging
landscapes, chequered history, and spirited population.

'Typically quirky, honest and a pleasure to read. …There is not much
writing like Braunias's in New Zealand. *Smoking in Antarctica* is a wonderful
collection to keep around – in the car for brief moments while waiting, in
the beach bag to dip into between swims. Or by the bed, on top of Braunias's
other books, all of which have proved as timeless as this one will'
*Nelson Mail*

'This book works on many levels. It's funny, personal, and often deeply
evocative – just a few reasons why it will endure
*Kiwiboomers*

'By the funniest and most thoughtful columnist in New Zealand'
*Greymouth Evening Star*

*Fish of the Week*
## Steve Braunias
978-0-9582750-6-4

'If you are ever feeling blue, read one of these delicious essays.
The sun will soon shine again ... Every one is a gem'
Graham Beattie, *Beattie's Book Blog*

Steve Braunias's satirical and closely observed writings have
driven readers to drink, God, lawyers, and sometimes to the shops
to shower him with gifts. In this lascivious selection he addresses the
state of New Zealand steak, the beauty of mangroves, the lunacy of
film festivals, the attractions of small towns ('There is no statistic that
says a village can accommodate only one village idiot'), the charms
of Cambridge University and the strange habits of the English,
and more – as well as his own intimate, seesawing, surprisingly
vulnerable life as a writer and lovestruck father.

'Diverse, whimsical, clever ... absolutely recommended'
Sonja de Friez, *Radio New Zealand Nine to Noon*

'Braunias has intelligently wormed his way into my heart, stirred me with his
gentle eloquence, bowled me with his wit ... damn funny and insightful'
Matt Rilkoff, *Taranaki Daily News*

'A brilliant and eccentric collection'
Philip Matthews, *Your Weekend*